OXFORD STUDIES IN AFRICAN AFFAIRS

General Editors
JOHN D. HARGREAVES *and* GEORGE SHEPPERSON

THE NORTHERN GABON
COAST TO 1875

PATTERSON, K. David. The northern Gabon coast to 1875. Oxford, 1975. 167p map tab bibl. 13.25. ISBN 0-19-821696-3

CHOICE   JAN. '76

History, Geography &

Travel

Africa

The area covered in this brief but expensive monograph is not comparable in historical importance to those on the Guinea Coast or nearer the Congo, but it deserves the attention the author gives it. From an investigation of an impressive variety of sources (though few oral records), Patterson provides a welcome survey of political and economic developments of the region around the Gabon estuary and the lower Ogowe during the late 18th and most of the 19th centuries. This includes sketches of the Mopongwe and Orungu chieftaincies, their trading activities, especially involvement in the slave trade, and relations with various European groups up to the imposition of French control. Patterns emerge in this story that resemble those elsewhere in the history of African-European contact, i.e., the Niger Delta, but, as Patterson points out, "Gabon was one of the first places on the western coast where the indigenous trading system was challenged and smashed." For this reason alone the book merits a place in Africana collections. The nature of the sources used determined that this study would emphasize the European impact on the area, yet enough is said about the in-

digenous peoples to qualify it as a contribution to African studies, albeit a minor one. Libraries supporting work in African history should acquire it.

THE NORTHERN GABON COAST TO 1875

by

K. DAVID PATTERSON

CLARENDON PRESS · OXFORD
1975

Oxford University Press, Ely House, London, W.1

GLASGOW NEW YORK TORONTO MELBOURNE WELLINGTON
CAPE TOWN IBADAN NAIROBI DAR ES SALAAM LUSAKA ADDIS ABABA
DELHI BOMBAY CALCUTTA MADRAS KARACHI LAHORE DACCA
KUALA LUMPUR SINGAPORE HONG KONG TOKYO

ISBN 0 19 821696 3

© *Oxford University Press 1975*

*Printed in Great Britain by
William Clowes & Sons, Limited
London, Beccles and Colchester*

To
CLDP

Preface

THE early history of Gabon has received almost no attention from scholars. Indeed, despite recent contributions such as Phyllis Martin's study of Loango,[1] the whole region of Western Equatorial Africa remains something of a historiographical void. A study centring on two coastal groups, the Mpongwe of the Gabon Estuary and the Orungu of the Cape Lopez area, is an obvious starting point for two reasons. The first is methodological; no other peoples between the Cameroun River and Loango are even remotely as well documented for the pre-colonial period. Records for other places on the coast, even Mayumba, are much scantier. With the singular exception of Andrew Battell's early seventeenth-century wanderings, European observers did not go inland until well into the nineteenth century. The absence of contemporary European writings, together with the paucity of modern studies of oral tradition and anthropology, means that the early history of interior peoples is very obscure. In addition to the relative accessibility of their past, the Mpongwe and Orungu are especially worthy of attention because of their vital role in the history of northern Gabon. They became highly specialized and successful commercial middlemen who, because of their monopoly on trade with Europeans, had a major impact on the peoples of the hinterland.

All historical studies are shaped to some extent by the nature of the source materials available, and this is especially true for sparsely documented places and periods. The sources for early Gabonese history are scanty, largely external, widely scattered, and often not very detailed. Unlike the Gold Coast, northern Gabon was not a constant centre of activity for record-keeping Europeans. As important as maritime commerce was for the Mpongwe and Orungu, the value of their trade was small compared to that of the Niger Delta or the Congo River-Angola region. Consequently, descriptions of the Gabon Estuary and Cape Lopez are generally found as short

---

[1] Phyllis M. Martin, *The External Trade of the Loango Coast 1576–1870: The Effects of Changing Commercial Relations on the Vili Kingdom of Loango* (Oxford, 1972).

addenda to accounts of more profitable and populous regions. The inhabitants of nearby São Tomé and Principe were probably in fairly continuous, if not always intensive, contact with Gabon from the early sixteenth century, but unfortunately the islanders were not literarily inclined.

Many short but useful descriptions of Gabon were written in the seventeenth century, especially by Dutch merchants. For the eighteenth century, except for a very brief account of Cape Lopez in 1722, the only European materials consist of brief notices of commercial transactions and possibilities. Internal developments in the eighteenth century are extremely hazy; many changes can only be surmised from the observations of nineteenth-century travellers. With the establishment of an American mission station in the Gabon in 1842, a French naval base in 1843, and a Roman Catholic mission a year later, information becomes more abundant and some flesh can be added to the shadowy outlines of changing African societies.

Oral traditions, which would not only provide more data, but also a much-needed internal viewpoint, are unfortunately not very abundant. Abbé Walker, Père Gautier, and Governor Deschamps have published some valuable material[1] which will be frequently cited, partly because the enforced brevity of my stay in Gabon precluded the collection of anything new. However, it may well be that there is relatively little pre-1900 oral evidence left to collect. An Orungu scholar, J. Ambouroué Avaro, abandoned a projected study of the estuary region because of the paucity of both written and oral sources, and, although he has collected some new testimonies, he often has to cite oral data on the Orungu gathered by Walker and Deschamps.[2] Published traditional evidence, while not very extensive, is of value for understanding internal developments and, especially in the case of Orungu, for establishing a chronology.

Thus, the scattered and limited sources force us to view the Mpongwe and Orungu largely through the eyes of foreigners, most of whom were merchants. And, as was discussed above, these foreigners were sometimes infrequent visitors. Not enough African sources are available to present an inside view; the most detailed

[1] Abbé André Raponda Walker, *Notes d'histoire du Gabon* (Brazzaville, 1960); Gautier, *Étude historique sur les Mpongoués et tribus avoisinantes* (Brazzaville, 1950); Hubert Deschamps, *Traditions orales et archives au Gabon: Contribution à l'ethnohistoire* (Paris, 1962).

[2] J. Ambouroué Avaro, 'Le Bas-Ogowe au dix-neuvième siècle', unpublished doctoral dissertation (Sorbonne, 1969), p. 5 and *passim*.

information on internal African events comes from the writings of a few of the more sensitive missionaries. The Mpongwe and Orungu emerge as people almost entirely concerned with trade and the preservation of their commercial prosperity. This 'trade and politics' image is obviously inadequate and incomplete, but it is difficult to modify because almost all literate observers saw the coastmen only as people seeking to buy cheap and sell dear.

I am grateful to a number of persons and institutions who have aided my research. I am particularly indebted to Dr. Robert G. Gregory of Syracuse University, who introduced me to the study of African history, and to my dissertation adviser at Stanford, Dr. G. Wesley Johnson, who helped direct me into the important post-1845 period. The staffs of the archives visited were uniformly helpful; special thanks are due to R. P. Bernard Noël, archivist of the Congrégation des Pères du Saint-Esprit. Much work was done in the outstanding African collections of Stanford University and the Hoover Institution, where Dr. Peter Duignan, and Miss Karen Fung were of great assistance. Mrs. Florence Chu, an invaluable ally of researchers at Stanford, obtained unusual items on inter-library loan with amazing efficiency. The latter stages of research have been facilitated by Mrs. Lorraine Penninger and Miss Virginia Kerr of the library of the University of North Carolina at Charlotte. Dr. Phyllis Martin of Bloomington, Indiana, Dr. Joseph C. Miller of the University of Virginia, and Mr. Henry Bucher of the University of Wisconsin have all made useful comments on various phases of my work. I am especially grateful to Dr. David E. Gardinier of Marquette University for his counsel, encouragement, and friendship. Research for this book would have been impossible without the financial assistance of the International Studies Committee of Stanford University and the Foundation of the University of North Carolina at Charlotte. My greatest debt is to my wife Carolyn, who stayed home while I travelled, and typed when I returned.

KDP

Charlotte, North Carolina, 1974

Contents

List of Maps

CHAPTER I

The Coast to 1700: The Rise of Mpongwe Trading Polities

THE northern Gabon coast, the area between the Bay of Rio Muni and the Fernan Vaz Lagoon, has been dominated for most of its history by two peoples, the Mpongwe in the north and the Orungu in the south. These peoples played a classical middleman's role, selling the products of the interior for European manufactured goods. The trading activities of the Mpongwe and Orungu and the effects of their struggles for commercial supremacy on their own societies are the major themes of this study.

The Mpongwe people were centred around the shores of a narrow inlet of the sea, invariably but erroneously called the Gabon 'river' or 'estuary'.[1] The Gabon inlet extends about sixty miles inland and forms one of the best natural harbours on the coast of West Africa. Several streams enter it on both the north and south banks, while the larger Como River flows into the eastern end. In the middle of the estuary are two hilly islands, Dambe (Koniquet, Konig, King's Island) and Mbini (Isle of Parrokeets, Prince's Island). The northern bank of the Gabon is higher and seems generally to have been more densely populated than the mangrove-fringed southern shore. Both banks, as well as the surrounding hinterland, are covered with dense tropical forest.

North of the Gabon is another large inlet called the Moondah 'river'. Its marshy shores were a source of redwood to the Mpongwe, who also ventured north to the island of Corisco and the Rio Muni.

South of the Mpongwe in the nineteenth century were the Orungu settlements of the Cape Lopez region.[2] The Orungu lived on the eastern side of the Bay of Nazareth[3] and along the rivers of its southern shore. Cape Lopez itself, often called Mandji Island, was

[1] Known to the Portuguese as the Rio do Gabão and to the English as the Gaboon.
[2] Originally called Cabo do Lope Gonçalves after its Portuguese discoverer.
[3] Or Bay of Cape Lopez.

usually not permanently settled, but was used as a fishing camp and a place to trade with European vessels.

Cape Lopez had been a prominent nautical landmark from the sixteenth century. Vessels which had traded on the Gold or Slave Coasts often followed the prevailing winds and currents eastward into the Bight of Biafra and then sailed south to the latitude of Cape Lopez to pick up the trade winds which would carry them to the Americas. Ships often called at Gabon, Cape Lopez, or the Portuguese islands of São Tomé or Principe for wood, water, provisions, or to make repairs before heading westward.

Europeans did not realize until well into the nineteenth century that the maze of waterways around Cape Lopez, from the Nazareth River in the north to the Fernan Vaz lagoon system in the south, was, like the 'Oil Rivers', the outlet of a major river. The Ogowe, together with its southern tributary the Ngounie, drains most of the densely forested Gabonese interior. The Ogowe system, which can be easily reached by a short portage from the creeks flowing into the Gabon, has long been a route for people and goods going between the coast and the interior.

The coast of Gabon south of Cape Saint Catherine, including the trade centres of Sette-Cama and Mayumba, was within the political and economic sphere of the Loango kingdom. For European sailors this coast was part of 'Angola', and its commerce was handled by ships venturing north from the Congo region rather than, as for the northern coast, by Guineamen sailing south from their usual trading grounds.

Since the equator bisects the area under discussion, the climate is very hot and humid. Rainfall is heavy, except in the short dry season between June and September. The many rivers which cut through the thick forests have served as the major transportation arteries; seasonal variations in river depths did not seriously affect the small local boats.

Except for the Fang, very little anthropological work has been done on the peoples of Gabon. Hauser's 1954 survey conveniently summarizes available data on the Mpongwe and the Orungu.[1] The Mpongwe are presently divided into sixteen exogamous patrilineal clans, several other clans being extinct. Each clan had a head (*oga*), but political life revolved around a few powerful men, generally also

[1] André Hauser, 'Notes sur les Omyene du Bas-Gabon', *Bulletin de l'Institut français d'Afrique noire*, B, xvi, No. 3/4 (1954), pp. 408–10.

clan heads, who exerted varying degrees of influence over a geographical region and its inhabitants, regardless of clan affiliation. In the nineteenth century there were four such 'kingdoms' and many of the clans had members in two or more of these political units. Tribal unity was fostered by constant communication between the various settlements, by an annual August meeting of clan heads on Mbini Island, and by a rigid social distinction between Mpongwe and the neighbouring 'bush' tribes.

The Orungu were divided into twenty-four clans, but, in contrast to the Mpongwe, were a matrilineal group. Exogamy was subclannic. Clan and sub-clan heads were recognized, the latter often acted as a village chief. The head of the Aboulia clan was the king over all the people and by the nineteenth century he enjoyed great power. His title, *Agambwinbeni*, meant 'judge of the sea', signifying royal control over trade with the Europeans.

The Mpongwe and the Orungu belong to a cluster of six tribes called Omyene, from the common Mpongwe expression *myene*— 'I say that'. One of these groups, the Adyumba, were an Mpongwe clan driven inland to Lake Azingo about 1700. They retain the Mpongwe language and patrilineal descent system.[1] The Galoa and Enenga are riverine peoples, living along the lower Ogowe in the general area of modern Lambarene. They are usually described as offshoots of interior groups, the Eshira[2] or Okande,[3] who had adopted the Mpongwe language by 1815, probably as a result of trade contacts. The Nkomi and Orungu also were probably 'Omyene-ized' on the lower Ogowe, prior to their arrival on the coast at Fernan Vaz and Cape Lopez respectively.[4] Unlike the Mpongwe whose language they perhaps adopted, the Nkomi, Galoa, Enenga, and Orungu retain the matrilineal inheritance systems prevalent in southern Gabon and among the peoples southward to and beyond the mouth of the Congo.

It is possible, however, that all of the Omyene peoples share a common origin. The Gabonese scholar Avaro believes that the group

---

[1] Ibid., p. 407.

[2] Abbé André Raponda Walker, 'Les Tribus du Gabon', *Bulletin de la Société des recherches congolaises*, No. 4 (1924), p. 76, n. 1.

[3] Marcel Soret, 'Introduction', in Abbé André Raponda Walker, *Notes d'histoire du Gabon* (Brazzaville, 1960), pp. 7–8; Gilles Sautter, *De l'Atlantique au fleuve Congo: une géographie du sous-population* (Paris and The Hague, 1966), ii, pp. 741–2.

[4] Abbé Walker, *Notes*, pp. 71, 83.

comes from an Okande–Mitsogo–Apindji stock, with the Mpongwe being the first to split off and migrate towards the sea. In his opinion, the Omyene peoples speak a common language because of a common heritage, and not because they all adopted the language of the prestigious and commercially dominant Mpongwe.[1] Although this theory is a minority view, it is not inherently implausible. Further study of clan histories may clarify the situation.

Several other ethnic groups should be mentioned. The small Benga tribe inhabited Cape Esterias, Corisco Island, and part of the southern coast of modern Equatorial Guinea. They were excellent sailors and by c. 1800 were important middlemen in the redwood and ivory trade north of the Gabon estuary. The nineteenth-century Mpongwe were surrounded by three concentric layers of 'bush' people. The Seki or Shekiani lived along the Moondah and in the immediate hinterland of the Gabon river, and, like the warlike Bakalai still further inland, acted as suppliers of raw materials for the Mpongwe middlemen. By the early nineteenth century, the large Fang tribe was settling near the Bakalai and beginning to push closer to the sea. Peoples of the Upper Ogowe and the region south of the river, such as the Adouma, Apindji, Eshira, Okande, and Mitsogo, supplied many of the slaves sold on the coast.

Gabon is a very sparsely populated country[2] and none of the groups mentioned above are or were very large. Early observers gave conflicting estimates, and, even in the colonial period, population data are scanty and probably not very accurate. However, by the mid-nineteenth century the Mpongwe apparently numbered about 5,000 and the Orungu about the same. The other Omyene peoples perhaps totalled fifteen or twenty thousand. The Benga, Shekiani, and Bakalai perhaps numbered several thousand each. The entire northern Gabon trading area, including the 'slave reservoir' peoples of the interior, included something in the order of 100,000 people.[3]

---

[1] J. Ambouroué Avaro, 'Le Bas-Ogowé au dix-neuvième siècle', unpublished doctoral dissertation (University of Paris, Sorbonne, 1969), pp. 69–72, 81–3. Avaro is not certain about the position of the Nkomi.

[2] In 1958 the population of the whole country was only about 400,000, or 1·5 persons per square kilometre. Guy Lasserre, Libreville: la ville et sa région (Paris, 1958), p. 96.

[3] These figures should be treated as very rough approximations only. They are based on data in Lasserre, Libreville, p. 105; Ernest Haug, 'Le Bas-Ogooué', Annales de géographie, xii (1903), pp. 169–70; J. L. Wilson, 'Mr. Wilson's Description of the Gaboon', The Missionary Herald, xxxix (1843), p. 231; and Lt. R. Avelot, 'Recherches sur l'histoire des migrations dans le bassin de l'Ogooué

The history of Gabon in pre-European times is almost completely unknown. Traditional histories collected by Deschamps in 1961 suggest that the area was only very recently penetrated by Negro peoples, who either found the country empty or else encountered just a few bands of pygmies.[1] However, the large extent of secondary forest suggests a long period of slash-and-burn agriculture,[2] and a few stone implements have been found.[3] Future archeological work may clarify the situation.

Gabon's geographical position, just south of the presumed homeland of the early Bantu peoples and between the state-clusters on the Guinea coast and the lower Congo, suggests that the area may be of some importance in the early history of Africa. Comparative studies of political systems in the Nigeria–Cameroun area, Gabon, and the lower Congo may reveal important connections between these regions. Or, conversely, Gabon may have derived different ideas from both north and south; the patrilineal Mpongwe and Fang may have 'Cameroun' systems while the matrilineal peoples of southern Gabon may reflect 'Congo' influence. In this view, the Gabon region becomes an isolated backwater where outlying fringes of two great culture areas overlap, rather than a vital corridor connecting the two. Another possibility is that the Gabonese peoples developed pretty much on their own, with a minimum of outside contacts. While such larger issues are beyond the scope of this study, and the problem can hardly be attacked in the absence of anthropological data and a reliable sub-classification of the Bantu languages, some relevant evidence will be mentioned in the following chapters.

Seventeen leagues south of Corisco Island, wrote Duarte Pacheco Pereira, 'is a fairly large river having nine fathoms of water at its mouth and in its channel. It is called Rio de Guabam. Its territory is densely populated, but we have no knowledge of any trade with the

---

et la région du littoral adjacente', *Bulletin de géographie historique et descriptive*, xx (1905), p. 398. Changes over time are even more nebulous. Contemporary observers in the nineteenth and early twentieth centuries were convinced that the coastal and riverine peoples in close contact with Europeans lost strength due to alcoholism, new diseases, competition with vigorous new groups from the interior like the Fang, and general demoralization. There may have been some truth in these observations, but prophecies of mass tribal extinction have proven premature.

[1] Hubert Deschamps, *Traditions orales et archives au Gabon* (Paris, 1962).

[2] Lasserre, *Libreville*, p. 97.

[3] Deschamps, *Traditions orales*, pp. 168–70. Only surface collections have been made and no dating has been possible.

negroes of this or in the preceding countries.' Further south, the
Cabo de Lopo Gonçalvez was also 'densely populated by negroes, as
densely as in any part of the world'.[1] This description, written in the
first decade of the sixteenth century by the Portuguese navigator, is
the first known account of the northern coast of modern Gabon. The
ancestors of one of the dominant groups in the history of the region,
the Mpongwe, were already living along the coast.

All observers of the Mpongwe agree that the tribe originally came
from the interior. American missionaries, the first recorders of
Mpongwe traditions, were told that they had migrated down along
the river from the interior.[2] Other nineteenth-century visitors were
told the same story. The most detailed account of the Mpongwe
migration to the coast was published in 1950 by the French priest
Gautier.[3] Following the dubious authority of Avelot,[4] he located the
ancestral Mpongwe clans in the tenth century on the upper Ivindo
River about 200 miles east of the Gabon estuary. Under pressure
from the Bakalai and Fang, they moved in the twelfth century about
140 miles westward to the upper reaches of the Como River. Here there
was a dispute and the tribe split into two groups of clans. One, led
by the Ndiwa clan, proceeded down the left bank of the Como and
settled along the south shore of the Gabon estuary as far as Point
Pongara. The other clans eventually went along the right bank of the
Como, settled the north shore and displaced the aboriginal pygmy
population, although this was not until after the Ndiwa had been
there for some time.[5]

This narrative is basically confirmed by other, earlier, versions of
Mpongwe traditions,[6] although there is no evidence to support
Avelot's theory of a starting point on the Upper Ivindo. The idea of
Bakalai and Fang pressure, while true enough in the nineteenth
century, is certainly anachronistic for the twelfth. Winwood Reade
heard a legend that all people originated on the Como River and
that the pygmies were the first people on the coast;[7] Touchard was

[1] Duarte Pacheco Pereira, *Esmeraldo de situ orbis*, ed. G. H. T. Kimble
(London, 1937), pp. 135–7.   [2] *The Missionary Herald*, xlv (1849), p. 120.
[3] Père Gautier, *Étude historique sur les Mpongoués et tribus avoisinantes*
(Brazzaville, 1950), pp. 9–16.
[4] Lt. R. Avelot, 'Recherches', p. 370.   [5] Gautier, *Étude*, pp. 9–16.
[6] 'Travail du R. P. Neu sur le Gabon', MS. *c.* 1885, Archives du Cong. St.
Esp., Boîte 148, I, fos. 82–90.
[7] Winwood W. Reade, *Savage Africa, Being the Narrative of a Tour in Equatorial, Southwestern, and Northwestern Africa* (New York, 1864), p. 415.

told that the pygmies were virtually annihilated by the Mpongwe after their arrival from the interior.[1]

The first non-pygmy peoples to live on the Gabon estuary were, by all accounts, the Ndiwa. Gautier and Walker both consider the Ndiwa to be an Mpongwe clan,[2] although there are accounts of their rising up from the earth or from the depths of the estuary,[3] which suggests that some of the later arriving clans thought they were autochthonous.

The Ndiwa clan arrived well in advance of the others. After reaching the south bank, their leader, Rogombe, built a raft of mats and went to settle on Dambe (Koniquet) Island. Other Ndiwa lived on the south bank at Nengue Awoga Island and at Ovendo on the north side. All of this took place before the arrival of the other clans.[4] Rogombe, described in 1843 as an African Confucius, is remembered as the creator of the Mpongwe language and laws.[5]

Other clans gradually arrived on the coast, with the Adyumba moving south to Cape Lopez, although the timing of the arrival of these post-Ndiwa migrants is not clear. As will be described later, some of the historically important groups seem to have remained inland until the end of the seventeenth century, but other Mpongwe speakers had already occupied the littoral of the Gabon estuary and the coast as far south as Cape Lopez when the first Europeans arrived.

The Portuguese first reached the Gabon River-Cape Lopez area about 1471 or 1473.[6] Cape Lopo Gonçalvez was named after its discoverer, while the 'Rio do Gabam' was named for its supposed resemblance to a seaman's cloak.[7] Both places are shown and named on Christoforo Soligo's map of c. 1485;[8] the whole region was

---

[1] F. Touchard, 'Notice sur le Gabon', *Revue maritime et coloniale* (Oct. 1861), p. 9.

[2] Gautier, *Étude*, p. 9; Abbé Walker, *Notes*, p. 52.

[3] Abbé Walker, *Notes*, p. 58.　　　[4] Ibid.; Gautier, *Étude*, pp. 15–16.

[5] William Walker to Prudential Committee, 28 Dec. 1843, American Board of Commissioners for Foreign Missions Letterbooks, A. B. C. 15.1, vol. ii, No. 28.

[6] Père J. Bouchaud, *La Côte du Cameroun dans l'histoire et la cartographie, des origines à l'annexion allemand (1884)* (Yaounde, 1952), p. 218; Robert Reynard, 'Recherches sur la présence des Portugais au Gabon', *Bulletin de l'Institut des études centrafricaines*, N. S., No. 9 (1955), p. 18.

[7] Filippo Pigafetta and Duarte Lopes, *Description du royaume de Congo et des contrées environnantes*, ed. Willy Bal (Louvain and Paris, 1965; original eds. 1591), p. 16.

[8] Bouchaud, *La Côte du Cameroun*, p. 183.

charted in some detail by the mid-sixteenth century.[1] However, very little is known of the people of the Gabon coast or their relations with Europeans until the Dutch voyages at the turn of the seventeenth century.

Portuguese merchants, mostly from São Tomé and Principe, traded along the Gabon coast during the sixteenth century, but almost nothing is known of their activities. Pacheco Pereira's account shows that commerce had not yet developed by c. 1508,[2] but seventy years later Duarte Lopes noted that island traders were active along the coast from Cameroun to Corisco and in the Gabon River. From the Gabon the Portuguese obtained 'ivory, wax and honey, palm oil and black slaves'.[3] A Vatican document probably compiled in the 1590s described the people on the continent opposite Principe as cannibals who sold ivory and hippopotamus teeth for cloth and old iron, 'which they esteem more than monnies of gold'.[4]

Cape Lopez was a prominent landmark for Portuguese shipping heading southward. In 1584 a vessel bound to Angola from Lisbon stopped there for supplies and a passenger, Brother Diogo da Encarnação, recorded his observations.

Many negroes came to meet us, bringing many good provisions, among them honey and wild cows [buffaloes] they call *Epacaça*. They came to buy fabrics and multicoloured cloths. We asked them if they would like to become Christians. They said yes, if their King agreed and if the Portuguese gave them some help against other negroes with whom they were waging war. They were very kind to us, and gave us gifts, fish and *Epacaça*, because we were *Gangas* (which is what they call their witch doctors or priests). For all that they brought, they [the Portuguese] gave in exchange old nails, and they did not want to take anything else.[5]

This passage shows that Cape Lopez was already beginning to be used as a supply point by European sailors and that the inhabitants

---

[1] A. Cortesão and A. Teixeira da Mota, *Portugaliae Monumenta Cartographica* (Lisbon, 1960). Anonymous maps of Guinea, 1502 and 1506, vol. i; maps of Diogo Homem (1558) and Lazaro Luis (1563), vol. ii. A. Teixeira da Mota gives data on several place names in Gabon in *Topónimos de Origem Portuguesa na Costa Ocidental de Africa desde o Cabo Bojador ao Cabo de Santa Caterina* (Bissau, 1950).

[2] Pacheco Pereira, *Esmeraldo*, p. 136.

[3] Pigafetta and Lopes, *Description*, pp. 16–18.

[4] Mgr. J. Cuvelier and Abbé L. Jadin, *L'Ancien Congo d'après les archives romaines (1518–1640)* (Brussels, 1954), p. 114.

[5] 'Carta de Frei Diogo da Encarnação, 27 September 1584', in Brasio, *Monumenta*, vol. iii, p. 277.

were eager for trade. European cloth was appreciated and the demand for 'old nails' suggests a shortage of iron.

The Portuguese lost their trade monopoly on the central African Coast to the Dutch about the turn of the century. Barent Erikszoon bought ivory in Gabon and visited Cape Lopez in 1594,[1] and he was followed by a host of other Dutchmen. Portuguese merchants, unable to compete with the newcomers either economically or militarily, were soon almost completely displaced.[2] An anonymous Portuguese writer in 1607 gave an estimate of the value of the Gabon trade now lost to the Dutch.

The *resgates*[3] of the Gabon river, the Sambasis River,[4] and Cape Lopo Gonçalvez would be able to yield 500 milreis. However, all of these *resgates* are entirely lost, having been occupied by Dutch corsairs and others. And neither Your Majesty nor your vassals receive the profits, which would be considerable.[5]

The author estimated the value of the Ardra trade at 800 milreis per annum, Benin and Popo at 400 milreis each and Warri at 200 milreis.[6] It would thus appear that the Portuguese trade in Gabon had grown to considerable proportions by 1600.

Dutch navigators, unlike their Portuguese counterparts, have left useful descriptions of the peoples of the northern Gabon coast. The period of Dutch commercial ascendancy in the region, the seventeenth century, is much better documented than the sixteenth or even most of the eighteenth centuries. However, the sources are still scanty and leave much to be desired. Data from Barent Erikszoon's 1594 voyage were written up by a Dutch scholar and incorporated into Linschoten's book; 'D. R.' published an account of Cape Lopez and Gabon as an annexe to de Marees's work on Guinea. Van den Broecke (1608), Ruiters (before 1611), and Brun (1611–14) provide some information in their sparse trading journals. Later authors, such as the geographer Dapper and the merchants Barbot and Bosman, mix contemporary and even eyewitness information with material

---

[1] Robert Reynard, 'Note sur l'activité économique des côtes du Gabon au début du XVIIe siècle', *Bulletin de l'Institut des études centrafricaines*, N. S., Nos. 13–14 (1957), p. 51.

[2] Reynard, 'Note', p. 53; 'Relation of Garcia Mendes Castelo Branco, 1620', in Brasio, *Monumenta*, vol. vi, p. 472.

[3] Trading sites.

[4] The San Mexias, one of the mouths of the Ogowe, south of Cape Lopez.

[5] 'Relation of the Coast of Guinea, 1607', in Brasio, *Monumenta*, vol. v, p. 382.

[6] Ibid., p. 381.

lifted from earlier sources. The dangers of anachronism are obvious. Modern critical translations of early Dutch works would be of great value to students of West African coastal history.

Early Dutch visitors were much taken with the physical appearance of their new trading partners, the Mpongwe clans which then inhabited the Cape Lopez region as well as the estuary.

The Negroes of this coast file their teeth as sharp as awls and appear quite horrible whenever they laugh or grin: Besides that they have a broad flat nose with very wide nostrils and a large hole in the lower lip, where they stick in teeth from such animals as they know how to catch, some of which are six inches long. . . . and their hair is braided like horns on their heads, so that they resemble more a picture of evil than men.[1]

The Mpongwe used a red dye to colour their bodies, and often painted the area around one eye white or yellow.[2] They wore clothes 'made from the bark of trees, as fine as silk',[3] and from animal skins. Women wore heavy rings made of iron, copper, or tin around their arms and legs. At Cape Lopez there was apparently no filing of teeth,[4] but other details of dress and adornment were similar.[5]

The Mpongwe lived in houses made of 'reeds covered with banana leaves'.[6] They enjoyed a diet of several varieties of yams, beans, plantains, oranges and other fruits, sugar cane, elephant, buffalo

[1] Dierick Ruiters, *Toortse der Zee-Vaert* (Flushing, Holland, 1623, new ed. The Hague, 1913), p. 86.

[2] Jan Huygen van Linschoten, *Beschryvinghe van de Gantsche Cust van Guinea, Manicongo, etc.*, ed. C. P. Burger and F. Hunger (The Hague, 1934), p. 7, and Olfert Dapper, *Description de l'Afrique* (Amsterdam, 1686), p. 319.

[3] Ruiters, *Toortse*, p. 86. Bark cloth was a major product of Loango and was exported as money to Angola. Phyllis Martin, 'The Trade of Loango in the Seventeenth and Eighteenth Centuries', in Richard Gray and David Birmingham, eds., *Pre-Colonial African Trade: Essays on Trade in Central and Eastern Africa Before 1900* (London, 1970), pp. 141–3.

[4] This custom seems to have died out by the end of the century in the Gabon.

[5] Linschoten, *Beschryvinghe*, pp. 6–7; D.R., 'The Passage from the Gold Coast to the Kingdome of Benni, or Rio de Benni, and Rio Floreado: The Citie, Court, Gentry, Apparell: Also Other Places Adjoyning, Described', in Samuel Purchas, ed., *Hakluytus Posthumus or Purchas His Pilgrimes* (Glasgow, 1905–7; original English ed. 1625, Dutch ed. 1602), vol. vi, p. 363; John Barbot, *A Description of the Coasts of North and South Guinea and of Ethiopia Inferior, Vulgarly Angola*, in Awnsham and John Churchill, *Collection of Voyages and Travels* (8 vols., London, 1732), vol. v, p. 392.

[6] D.R., p. 365. 'D.R.' has been identified as Dierick Ruiters (Alan F. C. Ryder, *Benin and the Europeans, 1485–1897* (London, 1969), p. 55, n. 1; G. Thilmans and J. P. Rossie, 'Le "Flambeau de la navigation" de Dierick Ruiters', *Bulletin de l'Institut fondamental d'Afrique noire*, B, xxxi (1969), pp. 106–7), but his 1623 book shows little relation to D.R.'s text.

and monkey meat, and dried fish. Beverages included palm wine and a fermented honey drink.[1]

Early relations between the Dutch and the Mpongwe clans of the Gabon River were marked by hostility and mutual suspicion. Problems began in 1600, when one Balthasar de Moucheron erected a fort on an island (probably Elobey) in the mouth of the Rio d'Angra,[2] about sixty miles north of the Gabon. Captain Edward Hessius was left in charge and he began to trade along the coast for ivory. The people of the Gabon reacted promptly to what they probably saw as a threat to their trade by sacking the fort and wiping out the garrison. This led to wars with the Rio d'Angra people.[3]

The booty from this raid seems to have convinced the Mpongwe that it was easier to get European luxuries by robbery than by trade. In 1601 they sacked a Spanish[4] and two Dutch ships, murdering and allegedly eating the crews. Since there were 'divers others such trickes more by them done',[5] the Gabon people quickly gained an unsavoury reputation. Ruiters warned his colleagues not to let too many Africans on board at one time, or they would kill the crews, steal the goods, and run the ships aground to get at the iron nails. Captains must not hesitate to flog offending blacks soundly, because their skin was so thick that a mild beating made no impression.[6]

A few years later, Samuel Brun told of the fate of some Dutch sailors who had accepted an invitation to visit the shore. After the men became drunk on palm wine, they were killed and the few crewmen who had remained on board were unable to resist an Mpongwe attack. The Africans beached the ship, landed the eight cannons, and began to celebrate the victory by firing them off. Brun happily reported that an overloaded gun had burst, killing or wounding thirty people. The Mpongwe excused their conduct by claiming that they thought it was a Spanish ship, and offered Brun 200

[1] Linschoten, *Beschryvinghe*, pp. 7–8; D.R., pp. 362, 365; Barbot, *Coasts of North and South Guinea*, p. 392. Oranges were probably introduced by the Portuguese.

[2] The Rio Muni. Originally called Rio d'Angra or 'River of the Bay' by the Portuguese, it was later transformed to the 'River Danger' by English sailors.

[3] D.R., p. 360.

[4] The ship may well have been Portuguese as the Dutch considered Spain and Portugal a hostile unit after the Iberian dynastic union of 1580.

[5] D.R., p. 366. These and other accusations of cannibalism probably should not be taken at face value.

[6] Ruiters, *Toortse*, p. 85.

tusks, weighing 20,000 pounds for balls, powder, and a gunnery instructor. Brun prudently declined the offer.[1]

The Mpongwe of Cape Lopez had a much better reputation, and the Dutch seem to have had no fears about landing there,[2] at least after having given out a few presents.[3] Theft was a problem, as it was in the Gabon, but the population of the Cape was considered much more peaceful and trustworthy.[4] Cape Lopez was much more frequently visited than Gabon; the people there were more accustomed to dealing with Europeans and enough ships called so that their new needs could be met by peaceful trade. On the other hand, the Mpongwe further north had scared off all but the boldest captains and apparently were determined to get as much as possible from the few ships which visited them.

Despite these obstacles, trade continued, and, although the early hostilities were remembered in later years, the northern Mpongwe increasingly realized the value of peaceful commerce. Some decades later Barbot wrote that 'these people are not now altogether as savage as formerly, by reason of the frequent resort of European nations to the river Gabon, though they still preserve some of their antient [sic] rudeness'.[5]

Another source of danger for the sailors, at least in the eyes of their officers, was the female population. The Dutch captains universally condemned the aggressive sexual behaviour of the Mpongwe women. D. R. complained that they were 'much addicted to Leacherie and Uncleannesse'.[6] Men offered their wives and daughters to the sailors for what the Europeans considered mere trinkets. Samuel Brun, a ship's surgeon, complained that women were actually chasing the crewmen, and noted that six men had died after intercourse with the apparently poisonous ladies of Cape Lopez.[7] But, as Bosman grudgingly conceded, the sailors were much less concerned about moral uprightness than were their officers. He described the Mpongwe women and his own men in scathing terms.

---

[1] Samuel Brun, *Samuel Brun, des Wundartzet und Bergers zu Basel, Schiffarten* (Basle, 1624; new ed., The Hague, 1913), p. 33.

[2] Brun, *Schiffarten*, p. 34; D.R., p. 362.   [3] Ruiters, *Toortse*, p. 87.

[4] Willem Bosman, *A New and Accurate Description of the Coast of Guinea* (ed. J. Pinkerton, London, 1814; 1st. ed. 1705), p. 513.

[5] Barbot, *Coasts of North and South Guinea*, p. 390.   [6] D.R., p. 362.

[7] Brun, *Schiffarten*, p. 35. Van den Broecke also encountered problems with the ladies of Cape Lopez. *Reisen naar West Afrika (1605–1614)* (The Hague, 1950), p. 26.

They besmear their Bodies with Elephants' and Buffel's Fat and a certain sort of Red Colour, which makes them stink abominably; especially the Women, which one can hardly come near without turning Sick. And yet they venture to drive a publick Trade with their Bodies, exposing their Favours to Sale at a very cheap Rate: And where they fear no Danger, they will readily relieve the languishing Lover for a Knife or a Trifle of that value. But those who engage with these Ladies, must be very fond of New Faces, for if a Man happen to be the least Nice or Squeamish, he will sufficiently wind them at Twelve-score Yards, to deter him from any nearer Approaches.

But the Case is different with a common sailor, who is content with every thing that is but Woman.[1]

Even allowing for the exaggerations of Calvinistic captains, it would appear that prostitution was a lucrative supplement to the ivory trade.[2]

Ivory was the most important commodity sought by the Dutch. Large herds of elephants still inhabited the south shore of the Gabon at the end of the seventeenth century,[3] and ivory always was available in good supply there and at Cape Lopez.[4] Bees-wax and honey were important secondary products.[5] Miscellaneous items included parrots' feathers and elephants' tails,[6] the hairs of which were sold on the Gold Coast and Angola as amulets.[7] Some dyewood was bought at Cape Lopez.[8]

A notable omission from this list is slaves. Until their conquests in Brazil beginning about 1630, the Dutch were not especially interested in the slave trade. After that date, they began seeking slaves in Loango and Angola,[9] but Gabon never seems to have been a significant source of supply. Barbot does mention the sale of a few

[1] Bosman, *New Description*, p. 510.

[2] Offering feminine companionship to guests is still considered an act of hospitality in parts of Gabon. Perhaps the Dutch mistook common courtesy for organized vice. But, given the sudden arrival of large numbers of wealthy strangers, the line might have been easily crossed.

[3] Bosman, *New Description*, p. 511.

[4] Linschoten, *Beschryvinghe*, p. 11; Pieter van den Broecke, *Reisen*, p. 26; Brun, *Schiffarten*, pp. 32–3; Bosman, *New Description*, p. 513.

[5] Bosman, *New Description*, p. 508; Ruiters, *Toortse*, p. 84.

[6] Brun, *Schiffarten*, p. 34.

[7] For Angola, see Barbot, *Coasts of North and South Guinea*, p. 473; for Gold Coast, see Dapper, *Description*, p. 319.

[8] Barbot, *Coasts of North and South Guinea*, p. 395.

[9] Phyllis M. Martin, *The External Trade of the Loango Coast, 1576–1870: The Effects of Changing Commercial Relations on the Vili Kingdom of Loango* (Oxford, 1972), pp. 53–9.

war prisoners at Cape Lopez,[1] but this seems to have been uncommon. Indeed, in the seventeenth century the Mpongwe were buying slaves from the Dutch. About 1611 Brun found that the people of the Rio de Gabon 'desire no other goods than black slaves'.[2] At Cape Lopez, he was offered ivory, 'for which they desired no other goods than men and iron. They needed the men for their wars and iron for weapons.'[3] At mid-century, the Dutch were selling Camerounian slaves in the Gabon at a rate of one adult male for 150–200 pounds of ivory in tusks of 30–40 pounds each.[4]

Slaves were probably a relatively minor item sold to the Mpongwe, although the Dutch writers were not very specific on their exports. Erikszoon bought ivory for iron, while Ruiters used beads, brandy, copper bowls, copper armbands, and bracelets,[5] and Brun used small knives and Benin cloth.[6] The crewmen often traded old hats and clothes for parrots and monkeys.[7] Guns[8] and tin dishes[9] were also traded. In Barbot's time, the people of Cape Lopez were exchanging dyewood, bees-wax, honey, and ivory for knives, beads, iron bars, old sheets, brandy, malt spirits, rum, axes, cowries, annabas,[1] copper bars, brass basins, muskets, powder, ball, small shot, and flints.[2] Similar items were presumably sold at Gabon.

Following Rodney's classification, the goods imported by the Mpongwe (except for the slaves) can be divided into five classes; weapons, cloth, metal, alcohol, and trinkets.[3] Firearms had an obvious use in warfare, as well as in hunting for food and for the ivory to finance more imports. The extent of cloth and ready-made clothing imports was apparently sufficient to drive out indigenous bark cloth production by the end of the century.[4] As was true elsewhere on the African coast, metals and metal goods were in great demand as even old nails were highly valued and captured vessels were stripped

---

[1] Barbot, *Coasts of North and South Guinea*, p. 398.
[2] Brun, *Schiffarten*, p. 32.   [3] Ibid., p. 34.
[4] Barbot, *Coasts of North and South Guinea*, p. 391.
[5] Linschoten, *Beschryvinghe*, pp. 11–12; Ruiters, *Toortse*, p. 84.
[6] Brun, *Schiffarten*, p. 33. As the name implies, Benin cloth was made in Benin and bought there by European captains, who used it to trade for slaves and ivory on the Guinea coast as well as in Gabon and Angola. Ryder, *Benin*, pp. 93–5.
[7] Bosman, *New Description*, p. 509.
[8] Ibid., p. 512.   [9] Dapper, *Description*, p. 318.
[1] A type of Benin cloth. Ryder, *Benin*, p. 94, n. 5.
[2] Barbot, *Coasts of North and South Guinea*, p. 395.
[3] Walter Rodney, *A History of the Upper Guinea Coast, 1545–1800* (Oxford, 1970), pp. 171–2.   [4] Bosman does not mention bark cloth.

of all iron.[1] Knives, axes, and basins were of obvious use; bars of iron could be made into spears, knives, and tools, while the copper was probably used to make arm and leg rings. The last two categories, alcohol, and decorative items like beads and cowries,[2] may be considered luxury goods of no productive use; but, as elsewhere in Africa, they were in great demand. Bosman scornfully observed that the Mpongwe were such lovers of European spirits that they eagerly consumed brandy diluted by one half with soapy water.[3]

Little can be said about the mechanics of trade. In the early days, when the Dutch still feared to land at Gabon, small parties of Mpongwe presumably came on board ship to trade. Trade was apparently always conducted on shore at Cape Lopez. A pidgin Portuguese was employed at both places.[4] No currency was used; tusks and other local products were probably sold for a bundle of assorted goods, as was the contemporary practice elsewhere on the coast.[5] Bosman has described the negotiating procedure for ivory at the end of the century. African traders came aboard for small presents, which had to be given before they would drink some of the ship's brandy. This ritual completed, a long bargaining process would begin over the individual tusks. Bosman, accustomed as he was to dealing 'with such civil Negroes at Fida [Whydah] for a hundred times more than the commerce of this place', took a strong dislike to the Mpongwe and was glad to turn over the trading to another captain,[6] because, 'to sell one tooth, they would sometimes haggle a whole day; go five or six times away and come again; ask and bid as if they were on a fish-market, and come to no resolution. Thus the merchant which would trade here, ought to be well supplied with Job's weapon, without which nothing is to be done.'[7]

The usual trading site for the southern Mpongwe was the tip of Cape Lopez. Most of the people lived across the bay near the mouth of the Nazareth branch of the Ogowe. Ships arriving at the Cape would fire cannons to attract the people, who generally took a day

---

[1] Brasio, *Monumenta*, vol. iii, p. 277; Ruiters, *Toortse*, p. 85.

[2] Cowries were used in this area as ornaments, not as currency.

[3] Bosman, *New Description*, p. 509.

[4] Barbot, *Coasts of North and South Guinea*, p. 398; Dapper, *Description*, p. 319.

[5] The assorted bundle was used to buy Gabonese products by the nineteenth century and probably much earlier.

[6] Bosman and his colleague were agents of the Dutch West India Company.

[7] Bosman, *New Description*, p. 509.

to get there. They brought their whole families and erected temporary houses to use while the ship was there to trade.[1] A small present, such as a few knives or a bottle of 'malt spirits', was given to the king for permission to get water.[2] Some vessels visited the village of Olibatta, on the Nazareth, for ivory[3] and dyewood. The king personally controlled the wood trade. Ships loaned him axes and saws and he sent his men far up the Nazareth (or Olibatta) River to cut wood. He delivered the dyewood on the coast at the agreed date in forty or fifty ton lots. Captains paid twenty to thirty shillings worth of goods for a ton, or one iron bar for a ship's boat full of two-foot sticks.[4]

Gabon and Cape Lopez had developed into busy trade places, and many other ships called for food, water, and repairs. As early as c. 1602, D. R. recommended Gabon, despite the hostility of the people, as a place for careening and caulking ships.[5] Mbini or Parrokeet Island was the favourite site for this. Ships would unload heavy guns, anchors, and water casks on the shore and then beach themselves at high tide. The exposed ship could be careened, caulked, and repaired at low tide and then floated off again at a high tide. Wood, water, and foodstuffs were all readily available at Gabon.[6] Cape Lopez was an even more popular refreshment point. Ships could get fowls, hogs, buffalo meat, bananas, potatoes, yams, fish, pepper, and oysters, as well as water and wood for cooking and repairs.[7] Many slaving vessels, after loading on the Guinea coast, stopped at Cape Lopez to get provisions for their cargoes.[8]

The volume of European shipping on the northern Gabon coast was quite large. Even by c. 1611, Brun noted that many Dutch, French, English, Spanish, and Portuguese ships visited Cape Lopez each year. A large tree served as a European community billboard where captains could nail up messages for their colleagues.[9] When D. R. visited Cape Lopez (c. 1601) he found three other Dutch vessels there.[1] Barbot wrote that it was a rare day when no ship was

[1] Ruiters, *Toortse*, p. 86; Brun, *Schiffarten*, p. 34; Barbot, *Coasts of North and South Guinea*, p. 395.

[2] Bosman, *New Description*, p. 512.   [3] D.R., p. 366.

[4] Barbot, *Coasts of North and South Guinea*, p. 396.   [5] D.R., p. 366.

[6] Bosman, *New Description*, p. 508.

[7] Barbot, *Coasts of North and South Guinea*, p. 395; Brun, *Schiffarten*, p. 34.

[8] Elizabeth Donnan, *Documents Illustrative of the History of the Slave Trade to America* (4 vols., Washington, D.C., 1930–5), vol. i, p. 142, 'Journal of the Slaver *St. Jan*' (1659); and p. 231, 'Journal of the *Arthur*' (1678).

[9] Brun, *Schiffarten*, pp. 34–5.   [1] D.R., p. 362.

anchored at Cape Lopez, and that Gabon was also visited by 'many' ships.[1] In Bosman's time, Cape Lopez was more popular than Gabon, although 'Zeeland interlopers' interfered with the company's trade at both places. At Cape Lopez, 'multitudes' of ships called 'daily'.[2] Although Dutch vessels were most common, English, French, and Portuguese ships also visited the coast during the seventeenth century.

Cape Lopez also attracted clerical visitors. Father Colombino, a French Capuchin, talked to some magicians and sorcerers during his brief 1634 visit to Cape Lopez.[3] Barbot was told that Portuguese priests had been active on Cape Lopez, but that they had all died of disease or gone away. Priests from the islands continued to visit from time to time and were treated with great respect. Some people were baptized, including 'prince' Thomas, his wife Antonia, and their son.[4] The dating of these abortive missionary attempts is unclear. Barbot wrote from personal knowledge; his last voyage to Africa was in 1682. Colombino made no mention of other missionaries. According to a nineteenth-century Portuguese writer, Italian Capuchins came to São Tomé in 1684 and sent missions to Benin, Calabar, and Gabon for the next two or three decades.[5] At any rate, there were no permanent results from seventeenth-century efforts to convert the Mpongwe.

At the beginning of the seventeenth century the Mpongwe of the Gabon river were divided into three political communities. D. R. gives the following description.

This River hath three mightie Kings in it, which raigne therein, as one King on the North point, called Caiombo, and one upon the South point, called Gabom, and one in the Iland, called Pongo, which hath a monstrous high hill; he of Pongo is strongest of men, and oftentimes makes warre upon him of Gabom, he of Caiombo is a great friend to him of Pongo, and the Inhabitants of the South point of the River, are great friends with those of Cape De Lopo Gonsalves.[6]

It is clear from this account that the original Ndiwa stronghold of

---

[1] Barbot, *Coasts of North and South Guinea*, pp. 395, 391.

[2] Bosman, *New Description*, pp. 508, 512–13.

[3] 'Letter of Colombino of Nantes to Peirsec, 30 June 1634', in Brasio, *Monumenta*, vol. viii, p. 284.

[4] Barbot, *Coasts of North and South Guinea*, p. 399. See also Montauban, *Relation du Voyage de Sieur de Montauban, Capitaine des Flibustiers, en Guinée, en année 1695* (Amsterdam, 1698; microfiche ed. Paris, 1972), pp. 383–95.

[5] José Joaquim Lopes de Lima, *Ensaios sobre a Statistica das Possessões Portuguezas na Africa Occidental e Oriental; na Asia Occidental; na China, e na Oceania* (Lisbon, 1844), ii, Part I, XIV.

[6] D.R., p. 362.

Dambe Island was still the most important Mpongwe centre. The other kings probably were leaders of more recently arrived clans.

Barent Erikszoon, the probable source for the description in Linschoten's book, also mentions three kings in the Gabon River. One lived in a large village upstream from the islands, on what was probably the Como River. The Dutch, being the first whites to come this far from the sea, got a rousing reception here.[1] Another king was encountered on a tree-covered island near the mouth of the Gabon called Caracombo. This might be D. R.'s Caiombo on the north shore, except that the description in Linschoten more closely resembles the island-studded south shore. Possibly Caracombo was Nengue Awoga Island, an early Ndiwa centre.[2]

The strongest king on the river lived on the island which D. R. called Pongo. Erikszoon and his men got a much more impressive reception from this ruler than from the other two. The Dutchmen were brought into a crowded hut and seated on mats on the floor. Then

the black people did nothing but tapping them on the shoulder and indicating to them to look up, while they uttered the words 'Mani Gabam'. And not knowing what they meant, they looked upwards, where they saw a Negro sitting several steps up higher, just about totally motionless, like a statue of a god. He had many strings of bones and rings around his neck—it was a horrible sight. He had some women lying at his feet, who fanned him fresh air and chased away the flies with tails of elephants. From this they gathered that he must be the King of the island, and they fell on their knees paying him homage after the fashion of the country, clapping their hands until the Mani or King signalled to them by clapping his hand. Then they got up and they were honoured with royal gifts: some lovely little mats made from bark.[3]

The King of Cape Lopez was also surrounded by ceremony as the following account from D. R. indicates.

Their King, called Mani, eateth his meate out of a Tinne Platter, but the rest in woodden Platters . . . .. The King hath a faire House greater than any in all the Towne, he it is called Golipatta, he is bravely set out with many Beads made of beanes and shels, which are dyed red, and hanged about his necke, and upon his armes and legs, they strike their faces with a kind of

---

[1] Linschoten, *Beschryvinghe*, p. 10. The Portuguese had been in the river previously, but had never come up as far as this village.

[2] See above, p. 7. The text is not clear on the location of 'Caracombo'. It could even have been Nengue-Nengue Island near the mouth of the Como.

[3] Linschoten, *Beschryvinghe*, pp. 8–9.

white colour, they are very much subject to their Kings, and doe him great honour, when they are in his presence: before his House there lyeth an Iron Peece, with certain Bases which he bought in former time of the Frenchmen.[1]

Another official, apparently a village level chief, was also encountered at Cape Lopez. At dawn the people

goe to salute their Commander, or Chaveponso, and bid him good morrow, and when they come to him they fall downe upon their knees, and clapping both their hands together, say *Fino, Fino, Fino*,[2] whereby they wish peace, quietnesse and all good unto him.[3]

The political situation in the Gabon seems to have remained about the same until after the middle of the century. The King of Pongo Island was now called *Mani-Pongo*, and he was still much stronger than the two rulers on the mainland.[4] His palace, a large but 'very mean' house, was called Goli-Patta; significantly this was said to be in imitation of the name used at Cape Lopez.[5] The *Chave-Pongo* was a village judge appointed by the *Mani-Pongo* and was greeted in the manner described by D. R. for Cape Lopez. Although the kings were war leaders, they and the chiefs received little respect from the people, and 'neither have those dignified persons any shew of state or grandeur'.[6] Bosman also observed that the 'king' and the 'prince' had no real power. The King earned a living by blacksmithing and by hiring out his 'wives' to Europeans 'at a reasonable price'; but he was as poor as his subjects.[7]

Barbot encountered a far different situation in Cape Lopez. A *Chave-Pongo* was at the Cape itself to regulate day by day trade. As discussed above, the king personally controlled the important camwood trade. Barbot crossed the bay to 'Olibatta' town, near the Nazareth mouth, where Prince Thomas, the son of the king, lived; and then proceeded several leagues up the river by canoe to see the king. After passing several villages, each with its own *Chave-Pongo*,

[1] D.R., p. 365.
[2] Possibly from the Portuguese *fino*, 'sharp'; 'clever'. See P. E. H. Hair, 'The Earliest Vocabularies of Cameroons Bantu', *African Studies*, xxviii (1969), p. 51. According to Barbot (*Coasts of North and South Guinea*, p. 393), *fino* meant 'good' in the local trade jargon. However, an earlier source gives the form *fuio* (Linschoten, *Beschryvinghe*, pp. 6, 11).   [3] D.R., p. 367.
[4] Olfert Dapper, *Beschreibung von Afrika* (1670 German translation, reprinted New York, 1967), pp. 503–4.
[5] Barbot, *Coasts of North and South Guinea*, pp. 390–1.   [6] Ibid., p. 393.
[7] Bosman, *New Description*, p. 510. Iron working was also associated with royalty in Kongo and Ngola.

the party arrived at the capital, a town of some 300 houses. The king himself, dressed in white and blue striped cloths, was preceded by an entourage of drummers, trumpeters, bearers of Dutch flags, and men firing guns. When the king drank, the musicians played and the musketeers let off a volley. The people showed great deference to their ruler, although Barbot speculated that this was partially to impress the European visitors. The king spoke 'broken Portuguese' and owned several French cannons.[1]

It seems that at least by the late seventeenth century the Adyumba monarchy at Cape Lopez was more powerful than those in the Gabon. One possible explanation is that the Mpongwe ruler at the Cape was able to assert a greater control over trade. The evidence is far from conclusive, but the only clear reference to royal control of trade in the Gabon is in Erikszoon's account.[2] In the absence of a royal monopoly, commoners competed for business in the Gabon. And, as the northern Mpongwe were divided into three political units, competitive pressures might have prevented ambitious rulers from taxing or otherwise interfering with commerce. Two other factors may help explain the differences in political systems; the influence of the powerful kingdom of Loango, and struggles for ascendancy among the kingdoms in the Gabon.

Several lines of evidence suggest that the influence of Loango reached as far as the northern Gabon coast. Loango was centred on the coast of what is now Congo–Brazzaville, but its frontiers extended, at least at times, as far north as Cape St. Catherine. Cape Lopez was less than a hundred miles further north and was more exposed than the Gabon itself to influence from Loango. It is significant that D. R.'s brief account lists the terms *Chaveponso* and *Golipatta* only at Cape Lopez. These terms were only later applied to Gabon, and *Golipatta* at least was borrowed from Cape Lopez.[3] The title *Mani*, ascribed to rulers at both places, is of course the same as in Kongo and Loango. *Chaveponso* or *Chavepongo* could be derived from the Portuguese *chefe*, chief; while *Pongo* probably meant Mpongwe. *Golipatta*, and the term *Olibatta* for the Nazareth river and the nearby village, are probably derived from the Ki-Kongo *libatta* meaning town.[4]

[1] Barbot, *Coasts of North and South Guinea*, pp. 395–7. Barbot called the official a *Chave-Ponso*.   [2] Linschoten, *Beschryvinghe*, p. 11.

[3] Barbot, *Coasts of North and South Guinea*, p. 390.

[4] The Vili language spoken in Loango is closely related to Ki-Kongo and the same or a similar word may mean 'town' in Vili.

Several other words noted by early travellers suggest possible contacts with the south. These include *epacaça* (buffalo) noted at Cape Lopez in 1584;[1] *mallafa* or *malaffo*, given as 'wine' or 'mead' at Cape Lopez[2] and *melasso* (mead) at Gabon;[3] and *matombe* (bark cloth) at Gabon.[4] A few other vocabulary items were collected in the seventeenth century, but these words are generally common Bantu roots, borrowings from Portuguese, or untraceable to any modern language.[5]

The same language was spoken at Gabon and Cape Lopez;[6] it was distinct from both the language of the Rio d'Angra to the north[7] and a dialect of the Vili language of Loango which was spoken as far north as Sette-Cama.[8] Although none of the early authors even hint that Vili, a language well known to the Dutch because of their extensive trade with Loango, was spoken further north than Sette-Camma, Avelot has used the evidence of three 'Fiotte' words (*Mani*, *malaffo*, and *matombe*) as the basis of his thesis that northern Gabon was inhabited by Vili-speakers until *c*. 1800.[9] This hypothesis is rendered completely untenable by Mpongwe traditions, as well as the fact that Loango's frontiers were well to the south and there is no evidence of settlement further north. However, inter-African trade contacts could easily explain the presence of these words in the north, especially as *matombe* cloth was an important export from Loango.[1] Political titles in use as far north as Vili-speaking Sette-Cama could easily have been borrowed by the chiefs of Cape Lopez as they consolidated their power.[2] Long distance trade, possibly

[1] Brasio, *Monumenta*, vol. iii, p. 277.

[2] Brun, *Schiffarten*, p. 34; and D.R., p. 362.

[3] John Ogilby, *Africa, Being an Accurate Description* (London, 1670), p. 486. This work is essentially a translation of Dapper's *Beschreibung*.

[4] Dapper, *Description*, p. 319.

[5] Barbot, *Coasts of North and South Guinea*, p. 398, lists 22 words used in trade at Cape Lopez. Three or four are probably derived from Portuguese; one, *jango* (little), seems peculiarly Omyene, while most of the rest appear to be from roots common to many languages in the general Congo–Cameroun area. Due to the paucity of modern linguistic data, positive identifications are difficult. This vocabulary was first published by De Marees in 1602. See Hair, 'Earliest Vocabularies', p. 54.

[6] Dapper, *Beschreibung*, p. 505.   [7] D.R., p. 361.

[8] Ogilby, *Accurate Description*, p. 493.

[9] Avelot, 'Recherches', p. 364. 'Fiotte' means Vili-like.

[1] Gautier, *Étude*, p. 18; Martin, *External Trade*, pp. 38–9.

[2] Ogilby, *Accurate Description*, p. 493, and Andrew Battell, *The Strange Adventures of Andrew Battell of Leigh, in Angola and the Adjoining Regions*, ed. E. G. Ravenstein (London, 1901), p. 58.

with Loango as well as Europe, and the example of Loango probably both played a role in the development of the stronger monarchy at Cape Lopez.

An alternative, if generally less persuasive, explanation for the presence of words from the Kongo–Vili language group in this area is that the Europeans, already familiar with the southern coast, simply assigned Kongo–Vili words to things they saw elsewhere. Sailors may well have assumed that all kings on the coast south of Guinea were called *Mani* and conveyed this and other terms to the early Mpongwe. The title 'Mani Gabam' recorded in Linschoten's late-sixteenth-century work almost certainly originated in this manner, as 'Gabon' was a word coined by the Portuguese. The use of *epacaça* for wild cow or buffalo at Cape Lopez could also be explained in this way.[1]

In addition to the admittedly tentative linguistic evidence, the large numbers of copper bracelets worn by Mpongwe women[2] may suggest early trade contacts between northern Gabon and the Loango kingdom. The sole sources of copper in the region were the mines in Teke country. Copper was traded to Loango, and from there presumably up the coast at least as far as the Gabon estuary.[3] However, since the Portuguese were selling copper and brass rings (*manillas*) in Benin by the early sixteenth century,[4] it is conceivable that they furnished some or all of the Mpongwe supply.

There is no doubt that the Africans inhabiting the equatorial coast had vessels capable of sea-going traffic. Mpongwe canoes were made from long hollowed trees and could hold up to eighty men.[5] With such craft they ranged the coasts between Cape Lopez and the Cameroun River, and perhaps farther.[6] Even if, as in the nineteenth century, rounding Cape Lopez was difficult,[7] the creeks of the

---

[1] Brasio, *Monumenta*, vol. iii, p. 277. Cf. Vili *m-pakasa*, but Mpongwe and Orungu *ny-are*. However, the text ('vaça montezina, a que chamão epacaça') seems to specify that the word was used by the local inhabitants. Perhaps the Portuguese encountered a Vili hunting or raiding party, or modern Mpongwe has lost this word.

[2] e.g., D.R., p. 364.

[3] Martin, 'Trade of Loango', p. 143, *External Trade*, pp. 41–2. Battell, *Strange Adventures*, p. 43, confirms the sale of copper rings of apparently indigenous manufacture in Loango.

[4] Ryder, *Benin*, pp. 40, 42.   [5] Brun, *Schiffarten*, pp. 32–3.

[6] Barbot, *Coasts of North and South Guinea*, p. 393.

[7] Abbé Walker, *Notes*, p. 78. The Mpongwe were sailing as far as Cape St. Catherine by, and probably before, the 1850s. Paul B. Du Chaillu, *Explorations and Adventures in Equatorial Africa* (New York, 1861), p. 39.

Ogowe delta provided a safe and easy route south to the Fernan Vaz lagoon. On the southern coast, African boats carried dyewood and probably ivory from Sette-Cama to Mayumba and Loango.[1] Mpongwe seafarers were as competent and daring as any on the Guinea Coast.[2] While the evidence is thin, the 'maritime factor' is perhaps a neglected aspect of the early history of Western Africa.[3]

The seventeenth century seems to have been a period of some turmoil for the Mpongwe. Several wars are recorded by European observers and the growing trade, besides being a new source of conflict and rivalry, supplied weapons to supplement the old arsenal of spears, knives, bows and arrows, and shields.[4] Firearms were introduced by 1600 and, as D. R. observed, 'they are verie subtill to learne how to use all kinds of Armes; specially, our small Gunnes'.[5]

The Mpongwe of the Gabon, in addition to being more likely to attack European vessels, seem to have been more aggressive towards other Africans than their counterparts at Cape Lopez. By c. 1600 the northern Mpongwe were, besides sacking the Dutch fort near Corisco, engaged in skirmishes with the Rio d'Angra people.[6] The powerful king of Pongo Island and his ally on the north bank were hostile to the people of the south and Cape Lopez.[7]

The King of Pongo still dominated the river at least until c. 1668.[8] Between perhaps 1620 and c. 1650, he launched a series of far-reaching naval attacks with the apparent motive of seizing trade goods for sale to the Europeans. The first victims were the Mpongwe of Cape Lopez. After an unsuccessful defence, the southerners abandoned

---

[1] Barbot, *Coasts of North and South Guinea*, p. 468; Ogilby, *Accurate Description*, p. 492.

[2] See Robert Smith, 'The Canoe in West African History', *Journal of African History*, xi, No. 4 (1970), pp. 515–33.

[3] The possibility of pre-European sea trade between the Congo region and the Guinea coast has been suggested by Daniel F. McCall in his review of Lionel Casson's *Ships and Seamanship in the Ancient World* (*International Journal of African Historical Studies*, v, No. 4 (1972), p. 670. If such trade existed, copper from Teke mines may have been used in Benin and elsewhere in southern Nigeria. Spectrographic analysis of early metal objects might reveal the source of the copper. David Birmingham has made a similar suggestion in 'The African Response to Early Portuguese Activities in Angola', in Ronald H. Chilcote, ed., *Protest and Resistance in Angola and Brazil: Comparative Studies* (Berkeley and Los Angeles, 1972), p. 17, n. 14.

[4] Linschoten, *Beschryvinghe*, p. 8.

[5] D.R., p. 365. Brun, as described above, found the Mpongwe eager to get ammunition and a gunnery instructor.

[6] Perhaps the ancestors of the Benga and/or Shekiani.

[7] D.R., p. 362.   [8] Dapper, *Beschreibung*, p. 503.

Olibatta and its stores of ivory, slaves, and bees–wax to the invaders. This venture was profitable enough to cause the king of Pongo to plan a new raid, but he was dissuaded by the Dutch, who successfully arranged a truce which resulted in a long period of peace. Some years later, the *Mani-Pongo* led an attack on the people of Cameroun River area, 'who had formerly affronted him, and his subjects'. Fifty or sixty large canoes ravaged the Cameroun River estuary, the Ambosies Islands, and even reached the Rio del Rei in the Niger delta. The raiders returned with a rich booty in slaves and ivory; other peoples sent gifts to placate the *Mani-Pongo*.[1]

Bosman found a very different situation when he visited the river in 1698. The kingdoms of the north and south banks, still mentioned by Dapper and Barbot (although perhaps they were still just copying D. R.) were no longer in existence. The kingdom of the *Mani-Pongo* had fallen far from its mid-century glory. Civil war had broken out and the two island strongholds of the Ndiwa were abandoned. The 'king' and the 'prince' had fled to creeks on opposite sides of the estuary, from whence they harried each other by night raids. A third group of Mpongwe 'troubled themselves with neither, but live quietly'.[2] Other Mpongwe clans were ready to seize control of the coast from the weakened Ndiwa.

Events at Cape Lopez are not so well documented. The southern Mpongwe clans, headed by the Adyumba, seem to have devoted themselves to peaceful commerce and, by the time of Barbot's visit, had profited considerably from this policy. But, while the weakness of the established clans on the Gabon made them vulnerable to new challengers from the interior, the very success of the southern Mpongwe also attracted powerful rivals.

The peoples of the northern Gabon coast still engaged in subsistence agriculture, fishing, and hunting at the end of the seventeenth century, but the demands and offerings of European traders had created an entirely new economic situation.[3] Significant changes in

1 Barbot, *Coasts of North and South Guinea*, p. 393. Generally similar accounts are given in Dapper, *Beschreibung*, p. 504; and Ogilby, *Accurate Description*, p. 487. Even at twenty warriors per canoe, this would seem to be a very large raiding force, compared to an estimated Mpongwe population of *c*. 6,000 in the mid-nineteenth century. Dapper and Ogilby state that a new attack on Olibatta followed this expedition.

2 Bosman, *New Description*, p. 508.

3 Even if there had been some pre-colonial trade with Loango, the volume must have been comparatively low and the type of goods exchanged quite different.

the political and social spheres must have occurred. It would seem that the monarchy at Cape Lopez had been strengthened while political fragmentation and strife had taken place in the Gabon. Gathering ivory, wax, and wood and transporting them to the ships were tasks requiring considerable time and effort; perhaps the imported slaves were used for some of this work, or this new social group could have freed Mpongwe men from food-production so they could devote more time to trade. Imported metals, metal goods, and cloth adversely affected local craftsmen, while firearms certainly aided hunters. The periodic arrivals of large numbers of lonely sailors probably caused strains on family life, regardless of whether they were viewed as honoured guests or paying customers. American food crops and new diseases were almost certainly introduced during these early years of European contact.

Bosman, the merchant, was impressed with more superficial aspects of Mpongwe society; the fondness of the Mpongwe for adopting Dutch names and titles, their love of European garments, and their inordinate craving for alcoholic beverages, which far surpassed anything he had seen on the Guinea Coast.[1] Comparing the northern Mpongwe with coastal West Africans, Bosman wrote that 'these people are the most wretchedly poor and miserable that I think I ever saw . . . .. In short, these are men which no otherwise differ from beasts than in shape.'[2] It may be concluded that, perhaps partly due to civil strife, the people of the Gabon were less well off than other coastal Africans, that trade was not as well regulated, and that Bosman really detested the Mpongwe. His writings, and those of his contemporaries, leave many important questions unanswered and unanswerable; but eighteenth-century sources are such that one wishes in vain for a new D. R. or Barbot.

[1] Bosman, *New Description*, pp. 508, 509, 513.
[2] Ibid., pp. 508, 510.

CHAPTER II

Population Shifts and the Rise of the Slave Trade: 1700–1815

IMPORTANT changes took place on the northern Gabon littoral during the eighteenth century. The established Mpongwe clans were challenged and eventually displaced by new groups which were attracted to the coast by the riches brought there by the boats of the white men. In the south, an entirely new tribe, the Orungu, wrested control of Cape Lopez and its trade from the Mpongwe; while around the Gabon new clans, the families of the nineteenth-century kings, were displacing the 'Ndiwa' on both banks of the estuary. In addition to these changes in the ethnic composition of the coastal people, new trade patterns began to emerge around mid-century. The slave trade began in earnest shortly after mid-century. Commercial contacts with Europe and with the nearby Portuguese islands became more intense towards the end of the century.

Unfortunately, this period is very poorly documented. Bosman's account of northern Gabon in 1698 is the last description of any detail until T. E. Bowdich visited the estuary in 1818.[1] Only scant references to trade are found in the European sources, but oral traditions shed some light on internal developments.

The Orungu, originally called the Ombeke, were probably a northern offshoot of the Eshira, who are in turn related to the Vili of Loango.[2] The Galoa of the Ogowe valley, like the Orungu an 'Omyene-ized' matrilineal people who originally spoke a language related to Eshira and Vili, claim to have a common mother with the

[1] For example, a comprehensive geography of Africa published in 1763 was dependent on seventeenth-century works for information on Gabon and Cape Lopez. Thomas Salmon, *Hedendaagsche Historie of Tegenwoordige Staat van Afrika* (Amsterdam, 1763), pp. 543–6.

[2] Père Gautier, *Étude historique sur les Mpongoués et tribus avoisinantes* (Brazzaville, 1950), pp. 19, 22; and Abbé André Raponda Walker, *Notes d'histoire du Gabon* (Brazzaville, 1960), p. 70. For a contrary view, see J. Ambouroué Avaro, 'Le Bas-Ogowé au dix-neuvième siècle', unpublished doctoral dissertation (University of Paris, Sorbonne, 1969), pp. 69–72.

Orungu.[1] The cluster of northern Eshira clans who were to become the Orungu of Cape Lopez moved down the lower Ogowe and settled behind the coastal creeks, especially the upper Gange, probably during the early seventeenth century. They were presumably suppliers of ivory and wood to the Adyumba clan of the Mpongwe who, as we have seen, were settled along the Nazareth River and on the coast at Mpembe (Olibatta).[2] The Orungu, recognizing the technological superiority of the Adyumba, sent their children to the coast to learn crafts like boat building and iron working. These children returned home speaking Mpongwe, and tradition maintains that this eventually led the whole tribe to adopt the new language.[3] In addition, Mpongwe was doubtlessly useful in dealing with the coastal traders. About 1700 the Orungu made a bid for control of the coast and direct access to European trade.

According to traditions collected by Walker, the immediate *causus belli* was the disappearance of an Orungu hunter named Djengue. The Adyumba were held responsible, and war broke out. At first the Adyumba were victorious and drove their enemies into the hinterland. Here the Orungu rallied under the leadership of the sorcerer Ogang Orungu (lit. 'Orungu sorcerer'). They painted themselves white, covered themselves with feathers, and, thus disguised as pelicans, surprised the Adyumba sentries. King Repeke tried vainly to rally the defenders, but they were crushed and only a handful escaped to form a new settlement in the interior on Lake Azingo. This war, which may well be a traditional 'telescoping' of a long series of events, resulted in Orungu supremacy on the coast. The Orungu, under the leadership of their king Ndongo (or Retodongo) then consolidated their position by driving two other Mpongwe clans, the Adoni and Angwengila, northwards along the coast toward Point Pongara, and thus became masters of the country between the Awanie River in the north and Cape Lopez in the south. Ndongo moved to the former Adyumba town of Mpembe (or Izambe).[4]

[1] Hubert Deschamps, *Traditions orales et archives au Gabon* (Paris, 1962), p. 106.

[2] Abbé Walker, *Notes*, p. 60; Gautier, *Étude*, p. 43; Avaro, 'Bas-Ogowé', pp. 154–6. Olibatta is called Mpembe or Izambe in the traditions.

[3] Gautier, *Étude*, p. 22.

[4] Abbé Walker, *Notes*, p. 71; Deschamps, *Traditions*, pp. 114–15. Avaro, 'Bas-Ogowé', pp. 157–66, ascribes the conquest of the coast to the end of the fifteenth century, but his argument is poorly documented and unconvincing.

Once established on the coast, the Orungu seem to have reorganized their political structure to meet the demands of their new economic situation. Hitherto, all clan heads had been equal in authority, but now Ndongo, head of the powerful Aboulia clan, was made king by a tribal assembly and his clan was given control over maritime commerce and relations with Europeans. The king gained the power to tax trade, and he only could open trade and act as host to traders who came ashore. The royal title, *Agambwinbeni*, 'judge of the sea', indicated the king's control over trade with Europeans.

Another clan, the Avandji, was given the title 'defender of the land' and seems to have controlled inland commerce. The clan head had rights to one tusk of every elephant killed or found dead. The remaining clans were given rights over the lands they occupied.[1]

It is impossible to assign an exact date for the replacement of the southern Mpongwe by the Orungu, but Soret's suggestion of *c.* 1700 seems reasonable.[2] The Adyumba war seems clearly to have been after the visit of Barbot, but there are no later European sources which would allow a precise dating. The Orungu king list given below would be compatible with an early eighteenth century date for Ndongo, the first ruler.[3]

LIST I

1. Ndongo
2. Ndebulia-Mburu (son of 1)
3. Re-Nkjangue-Ndongo (son of 1, brother of 2)
4. Re-Nkondje (nephew of 3)
5. Ngwerangui (brother of 4)
6. Ndombe (son of 5)
7. Reombi-Mpolo (son of 5, brother of 6)

The seventh monarch, Reombi-Mpolo, came to power about 1790[4] after winning a civil war against his brother Ndombe, who had succeeded against their father's wishes. Assuming that Ndombe's tenure was short, there were five rulers between the Orungu conquest of the coast and *c.* 1790. Although the lengths of the reigns of these rulers are unknown, and there is no date given for any of them in contemporary European sources, it seems reasonable to assume that the dynasty originated early in the eighteenth century.[5]

1 Abbé Walker, *Notes*, p. 72.
2 Marcel Soret, 'Introduction', in Abbé Walker, *Notes*, p. 16.
3 Abbé Walker, *Notes*, pp. 71–5; Deschamps, *Traditions*, p. 116.
4 Abbé Walker, *Notes*, p. 72.
5 This estimate is in accord with an average length of reign of 13 ± 5 years and

A similar displacement of the Mpongwe clans who had been dominating the coast and its lucrative trade was under way at the same time in the Gabon estuary, but in this case the newcomers were other Mpongwe groups who had been living on the creeks and rivers of the hinterland. The overthrow of the earlier arrivals, whom we can lump under the term 'Ndiwa', was not entirely pacific, but it seems to have been a more gradual and less spectacular process than the sudden emergence of the Orungu.

Earlier writers erroneously ascribe the collapse of the Ndiwa to a disastrous defeat inflicted upon them by the Dutch in 1698. Supposedly the Dutch devastated the islands of the 'king' and the 'prince' at that time in reprisal for Mpongwe attacks on the Dutch in 1600 and 1601.[1] While it is conceivable that there were some unrecorded skirmishes between the two parties during the seventeenth century, there is absolutely no evidence for a *répression hollandaise* in 1698. Bosman clearly states that the islands were deserted because of a war between the 'king' and the 'prince'.[2] At any rate, it is most implausible that the Dutch would wait a century to avenge themselves for the events of 1600–1. A power vacuum on the coast was not suddenly created in 1698 as Gautier and Walker assert, although the struggle recorded by Bosman probably does indicate a serious weakening of the Ndiwa. Traditional accounts support Bosman's observation that the Ndiwa had fled from the islands, and sought refuge on creeks on both banks of the estuary.[3] The causes of the downfall of the Ndiwa are not clear; it can be surmised that struggles to keep other groups away from the Europeans and internecine conflicts, perhaps over trade, may both have played a role. Another possible source of weakness could have been a population decline caused by the influx of new diseases, such as smallpox or syphilis.

By the late seventeenth century it seems that conditions were propitious for new groups to move to the coast. Traditional genealogies indicate that the three clans who were to dominate the estuary until well into the nineteenth century first reached the coast about the beginning of the eighteenth century.

---

an average length of dynastic generation of 30 years found in a recent survey of African dynastic lists. D. H. Jones, 'Problems of African Chronology', *Journal of African History*, xi, No. 2 (1970) pp. 165–6.

[1] Gautier, *Étude*, p. 35; Abbé Walker, *Notes*, pp. 58–9.

[2] Willem Bosman, *A New and Accurate Description of the Coast of Guinea* (Pinkerton ed., London, 1814), p. 508.

[3] Gautier, *Étude*, p. 35; Abbé Walker, *Notes*, pp. 42, 58.

The Agoulamba clan, headed by 'King George' in the nineteenth century, had originally been in the group of clans which had followed the Ndiwa down the left bank of the Como. They had settled south of the estuary along the Mbilangone and Remboue creeks.[1] At this time, according to the testimony of King George in 1851, the Ndiwa still controlled the river, and the Agoulamba were still in the bush, thinking that the sight of salt water would be fatal to them.[2] The clan reached the coast about five or six generations before the coming of the French (1843).[3] Walker, in a later work, gives a genealogy showing only four generations in the pre-French period, but Gautier furnishes one earlier name. A composite genealogy is presented below. Either Re-Nene or Re-Nkangu founded the first coastal settlement.

LIST II

Re-Nene[4]
|
Re-Nkangu[5]
|
Re-Seno
|
Re-Ndongula-Ekanda
|
Rassondji (George)

George was a middle-aged man at the time of Bowdich's visit (1818).[6] Allowing about twenty-five years for a generation, it seems probable that the Agoulamba settled on the shore near Ngango by c. 1700-25.[7]

The other leading clan on the south shore in the nineteenth century was that of 'King Denis', the Assiga. Walker gives the following genealogy for King Denis:[8]

[1] Abbé Walker, *Notes*, p. 38.

[2] Rev. Rollin Porter to Rufus Anderson, 1 Oct. 1851, American Board of Commissioners for Foreign Missions Letterbooks, A.B.C. 15.1, vol. iii, No. 325.

[3] Abbé André Raponda Walker, 'Les Tribus du Gabon', *Bulletin de la Société des recherches congolaises*, iv (1924), p. 59.

[4] Gautier, *Étude*, p. 46.

[5] Abbé Walker, *Notes*, p. 38.

[6] T. E. Bowdich, *Mission from Cape Coast Castle to Ashantee* (3rd ed., London, 1966), p. 425.

[7] The Mpongwe lists are genealogies, and cannot be handled like the Orungu king-list material.

[8] Abbé Walker, *Notes*, p. 24.

LIST III

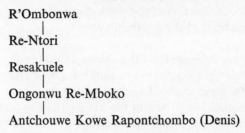

R'Ombonwa
|
Re-Ntori
|
Resakuele
|
Ongonwu Re-Mboko
|
Antchouwe Kowe Rapontchombo (Denis)

R'Ombonwa apparently led the clan to the coast,[1] and since Denis was born *c.* 1780,[2] we can assume that this took place about 1700. The defeat of the Adoni and Angwengila clans by the Orungu also occurred about this time and perhaps these clans had already been beaten and were too weak to resist the Assiga. Conversely, the Assiga might have weakened the others for the Orungu onslaught.

'King Louis' and 'King Glass', who were leaders on the north shore of the Gabon in the first half of the nineteenth century, were both members of the Aguekaza clan. This clan had been in the party which had followed the right bank of the Como. They had first settled on the upper Ikoi Creek, between the Moondah and the Gabon. After some fighting and apparently serious reverses,[3] Re-Ndoukoue established a village on the estuary. Walker gives the following genealogies for Louis and Glass:[4]

LIST IV

Re-Ndoukoue

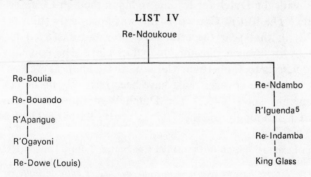

Re-Boulia
|
Re-Bouando
|
R'Apangue
|
R'Ogayoni
|
Re-Dowe (Louis)

Re-Ndambo
|
R'Iguenda[5]
|
Re-Indamba
|
King Glass

[1] Abbé Walker, *Les Tribus*, p. 59.
[2] Abbé Walker, *Notes*, p. 24.
[3] Tradition collected in 1906 by Gautier, *Étude*, p. 48.
[4] Abbé Walker, *Notes*, pp. 34–5. Similar data is given in Gautier, *Étude*, pp. 48–50.
[5] Little is known of R'Iguenda's descendants. There may have been another generation between Re-Indamba and 'King Glass'.

Louis was born about 1800,[1] which would suggest that the Aguekaza clan began its domination of the north shore of the Gabon River in about the first third of the eighteenth century.

Documentary evidence from the eighteenth century is very slender and sheds little light on the events outlined above. However, some details can be gleaned about the rise of the slave trade and other European contacts, especially in the last part of the century. Trade with European vessels continued throughout the eighteenth century, and significant economic changes took place during this period. Dutch trade suffered from increased competition from England, while Portugal and France began to play a larger role. Most importantly, significant slave exports from northern Gabon began in the mid-eighteenth century.

At the end of the seventeenth century, a Portuguese company was established on Principe to trade for slaves on the Costa da Mina (Slave Coast) and in the area of Gabon.[2] This company failed, but a new Companhia do Corisco was established by royal decree in 1723 to furnish slaves for Bahia and the mines of Minas Gerais. The Portuguese crown was eager to develop the coast opposite the colony of São Tomé e Principe as an alternative slave supply, free from the restrictions imposed by the Dutch on the Costa da Mina. The new company was in conflict with the Brazilians, who were quite willing to deal with the Dutch for trading rights in the rich Costa da Mina markets.[3] The fort at Corisco Island was apparently still operating in 1723; in that year the establishment was transferred to Cape Lopez by its French director, João Dessaint.[4] The company sent slaving vessels to Cameroun, Corisco, and Gabon as well as Cape Lopez, but these voyages must have been relatively unsuccessful as the company soon failed.[5] The Dutch West India Company still claimed a monopoly on the Guinea coast; its harassment of the

---

[1] John Leighton Wilson to Prudential Committee, 2 July, 1842, A.B.C. 15.1, vol. ii, No. 121.

[2] Pierre Verger, *Flux et reflux de la traite des nègres entre le Golfe de Bénin et Bahia de Todos os Santos du XVIIᵉ au XIXᵉ siècle* (Paris, 1968), pp. 66–7.

[3] Ibid., pp. 75–6.

[4] José Joaquim Lopes de Lima, *Ensaios sobre a Statistica das Possessões Portuguezas na Africa Occidental e Oriental; na Asia Occidental; na Chine, e na Oceania* (Lisbon, 1844), ii, Part I, p. 38A; and Archives nationales, Colonies, C⁶, 10, 1728. Compaigne des Indies, Extract.

[5] Lopes de Lima, *Ensaios*, ii, Part I, p. 25.

Portuguese at Cape Lopez probably contributed to the company's downfall.[1]

Another factor contributing to the demise of the plan to trade slaves at the Cape Lopez factory was the apparent unwillingness of the newly-established Orungu to deal in people. John Atkins visited Cape Lopez in 1722 and left the only description of the area until the visit of Lt. Boteler in 1826. Wood could be obtained cheaply; water was free; plaintains, goats, fowls, and grey parrots were all cheap, and a little ivory and gold was offered for sale. The principal trade items were honey and cakes of wax, which were exchanged for linen, calico, knives, and pewter spoons. Europeans had to give small presents before opening trade. But, said Atkins, 'they never sell one another'.[2]

The people lived a little inland, as they had in the previous century, and were too afraid of kidnapping to venture aboard ship.[3] As in former times, many of the people had taken European names and the chiefs, to Atkins's amusement, often wore fancy hats, wigs, and breeches. A cloth was held up to conceal 'King Jacobus' when he drank.[4] Finally, it appeared to Atkins that the people had very few guns.[5]

European references to the northern Gabon coast increase dramatically after mid-century and especially by the 1760s. This fact alone suggests an abrupt increase in commercial contacts, an inference which is supported by the sources themselves. The remainder of this chapter will be devoted to documenting and describing the growth and nature of African–European trade during the last half of the eighteenth century and the first years of the nineteenth.

Evidence presented to the British Parliament in 1789 strongly suggests that the Gabon slave trade was still in its infancy in the 1760s. John Newton visited the area in 1747 on the *Greyhound* and spent a month in the Gabon river. Forty-three years later he recalled that 'the most humane and moral people I ever met with in Africa were on the River Gaboon, and at Cape Lopas [sic]; and they were

---

[1] Archivo Histórico Ultramarino, São Tomé, caixa 4, 1726, 'Letter of complaint to governor of São Tomé'.

[2] John Atkins, *A Voyage to Guinea, Bresil and the West Indies, in H.M.S. the Swallow and Weymouth* (London, 1735), p. 197.

[3] Ibid. This may have been a temporary fear, as Atkins was surgeon on a British warship which had just captured the pirate Roberts and his three vessels at Cape Lopez.

[4] The custom, also observed by the Mpongwe rulers, was very widespread in Sub-Saharan Africa.   [5] Atkins, *A Voyage*, pp. 198–200.

the people who had the least intercourse with Europe at that time.'[1] Newton, a repentant slaver testifying before a parliamentary commission which he hoped would abolish the trade, stated that there had been no slave trade in Gabon at the time of his visit and that people had spoken to him against slaving, condemning it as an act which, like murder, could never be undone. The *Greyhound*, the only ship in the river, had traded for bees-wax and ivory.[2]

David Henderson had been a sailor on two Liverpool vessels which sailed to Gabon 1767–9, and was on another ship which sailed to Gabon from New York in 1770. All of these voyages were 'for wood and other articles'. On one of his voyages he had gone up twenty-five miles beyond 'Parrot Island' (Mbini) where he had seen 'eight or fourteen' of 'King Abraham's'[3] people, armed with muskets and spears, setting out to capture slaves. They returned about two weeks later with five or six prisoners. Henderson was told by African traders that this was the usual method of getting slaves; their statements were confirmed by several slaves who claimed that they had been kidnapped. On his 1770 voyage, one of Henderson's shipmates was the son of one of the kings in the river. The young man had spent a year in New York, and hoped to use his education to become a slave dealer.[4]

The fact that the Mpongwe were attempting to capture slaves rather than trade for them probably indicates that they were just beginning to learn the slaving business.[5] A French report of 1761 would tend to confirm this view. 'Few slaves are traded at the River Cameroun. The principal commerce there consists of ivory, wax, and honey, and the Dutch do almost all the trade. It is the same in the Gabon and at Cape Lope.'[6] Negative evidence is of course not very satisfactory, but the available data give no indication of English slaving in the area before the 1760s. The earliest reference I can find

---

[1] Minutes of Evidence on the Slave Trade, Parliamentary Papers, Commons, 1790, xxx, p. 138, Testimony of the Rev. John Newton.

[2] Ibid., pp. 138–9, 144.

[3] Probably the predecessor of King George Rassondji.

[4] Report of Lords' Committee, Parliamentary Papers, Commons, 1789, xxvi, No. 649a, Pt. 1, Evidence of David Henderson.

[5] By the nineteenth century the Mpongwe trading network drew slaves from far in the interior. Once such a system was established, the coastal people could leave the dirty work of procurement to others and concentrate on the orderly marketing of slaves.

[6] Archives nationales, Colonies, C[6], 14, Sénégal 1761, 'Considerations sur le commerce d'Affrique', p. 8.

is 1769, when the *Shark* landed a cargo of slaves from the 'Gabon Coast' in South Carolina.[1]

Trade in ivory, wax, honey, and wood attracted merchants to Gabon and Cape Lopez at about the same time as the opening of large-scale slaving. In addition to direct voyages from Europe, by about 1770 there was an established British coasting trade to Gabon conducted by small boats based at Cape Coast.[2] The Danes sent a few vessels from the Gold Coast for Gabonese ivory.[3] The Portuguese on São Tomé seem to have resumed, or at least increased, their commerce with the neighbouring coast about 1780. Wax and *evano* wood (ebony) were bought in Gabon by small schooners from the islands.[4] Gabon continued to attract Dutch vessels, and by 1776 at least one American ship had visited the river.[5]

The trade of Cape Lopez was sufficient to justify the erection of an English factory there by the early 1770s. Richard Brew, an Irish trader based at Anomabu on the Gold Coast, established trading posts at Whydah, Popo, Lagos, Benin, and Cape Lopez. His agents bought local slaves and shipped them to Anomabu for re-export.[6] Some slaves were dispatched directly to the Americas; in 1776 the factor at Cape Lopez was ordered to send a cargo of 120 slaves to the West Indies.[7] The Cape Lopez factory, which also drew trade from the Gabon River, was abandoned after Brew's death in 1776.[8]

Trade could be hazardous for both Africans and Europeans. Captains often gave out trade goods on credit and in return were sometimes given 'pawns', people to be held on shipboard until the cargo had been loaded. In case of non-payment, the pawns could be kept

[1] Elizabeth Donnan, *Documents Illustrative of the History of the Slave Trade to America* (4 vols., Washington, D.C., 1930–5), iv, p. 428. 'Negroes Imported Into South Carolina.'

[2] Donnan, *Documents*, ii, p. 543. 'Certificate of Issac Garrick, 1771.'

[3] Georg Nørregård, *Danish Settlements in West Africa, 1658–1850* (Boston, 1966), p. 125; Paul Erdman Isert, *Voyages en Guinée et dans les Îles Caraïbes en Amerique* (Paris, 1793), p. 132, n. 1. According to Mpongwe tradition there was a Danish factory at Nengue-Awoga Island, on the south bank near Denis. (Gautier, *Étude*, p. 40.)

[4] Archivo Histórico Ultramarino, São Tomé, caixa 10, 1783, 'Petition of Gregorio Alvarez Pereira'; 'João da Mattos Sa to the Queen', 7 Feb. 1786.

[5] A New York ship was reportedly there hiding from British cruisers. Donnan, *Documents*, iii, p. 315. Captain Peleg Clark to John Fletcher, 20 Feb. 1776.

[6] Margaret Priestly, *West African Trade and Coast Society: A Family Study* (London, 1969), p. 72. The factory at Cape Lopez, which along with Lagos was the most important out-station in the Brew network, may have been founded in 1769 or even a few years earlier.

[7] Ibid., p. 77.   [8] Ibid., pp. 88–90.

as slaves.[1] Outright kidnapping was not unknown. Once when David Henderson was at Gabon, a Liverpool vessel kidnapped twenty-five Mpongwe who had come on board to trade. A Dutch ship in the river, its trade ruined by the resultant furor, vainly pursued the kidnappers.[2] Captain Mathews of Bristol once made off with a few Mpongwe boys, perhaps unredeemed pawns, and experienced some difficulty upon his return in 1771-2. Although 'John' and 'Smack Abram' threatened violence if he landed, Mathews succeeded in getting a cargo of about 150 slaves. The Orungu ruler, the so-called 'King of Nazareth', killed an innocent English crew in retaliation for Mathew's kidnappings at Gabon and Cape Lopez.[3]

Not all contact between Africans and Europeans in this period was commercial. A mission station was set up by Italian Capuchins in the Gabon estuary in the 1770s. However, Pombaline decrees against foreign clergy in Portuguese colonies forced the Capuchins to leave their hospice on Principe and the missionary effort in Gabon had to be abandoned.[4] There was apparently little success, and later observers found no memory or trace of this pioneering effort.

France displayed very little interest in the region until the 1780s. There were isolated contacts; an abortive scheme to establish a trading base on Corisco Island;[5] a voyage to the Gabon in 1741 by a Nantes vessel.[6] A Captain Gaugy of Nantes made a map based on his 1769-72 voyages to Angola with some details on Cape Lopez; he probably stopped there for supplies.[7] Captain Labrière, who bought 240 slaves in Gabon about 1786, admitted that 'this part of Africa is still almost unknown to us'.[8] An anonymous report of 1784 described the trade of Gabon and Calabar,

---

[1] Report of Lords' Committee, Evidence of David Henderson.

[2] Ibid. The resort to kidnapping would suggest a low slave supply and is perhaps another indication that the Gabonese slave trade was still in an embryonic stage of development.

[3] Minutes of Evidence on the Slave Trade, Parliamentary Papers, Commons, 1790, xxx, Testimony of James Morely, pp. 156, 159, 163.

[4] Père J-B. Piolet, S. J., Les Missions catholiques françaises au XIXᵉ siècle, vol. v, Missions d'Afrique (Paris, 1902), p. 219.

[5] Archives nationales, Colonies, C⁶, 3, 1701, 'Sur un comptoir à établir aux Côtes de Guinée'.

[6] Gaston-Martin, Nantes au XVIIIᵉ siècle, l'ère des négriers (1714-1774) (Paris 1931), p. 218.

[7] Bibliothèque nationale, Cartes et plans, Porte-feuille 114, 3, No. 16, 'Carte de la Côte d'Angolle'.

[8] Archives nationales, Colonies, C⁶, 24, Cabinde, divers pièces, 'Mémoire sur le commerce à faire au Gabon', 22 June 1787.

where one makes commerce like at Benin, that is to say by merchandise. But the people are ferocious and it is necessary always to be on guard in the vessels so as not to be surprised. Slaves, wax and ivory are traded there. The captives of this country are little esteemed in America; those of Benin are a little better.[1]

Captain Labrière disagreed with this assessment of Gabonese slaves. He thought that he could buy 600 slaves and sell them in the colonies for a 400 per cent profit;[2] but Labarthe, who investigated trading opportunities on the African coast in 1788, was more sceptical. While admitting that Gabon had some potential, he repeated Landolphe's warning that the coast between Benin and Cape Lopez was so unhealthy that the slave trade there was in effect 'an exchange of whites for blacks'.[3]

Labarthe's pessimism was not shared by all of his countrymen. Aware that Britain and Holland were successfully trading in the Bight of Biafra, and that the inhabitants of São Tomé and Principe were trafficking on the coasts for ivory, wax, slaves, and hides,[4] a group of Bordeaux merchants set up a factory on Principe in 1791 to conduct trade with Gabon, Cape Lopez, Benin, and Calabar. This foreign factory, although illegal under Portuguese law, was aided by a number of natives of Principe.[5] Slaves were purchased in Gabon by the factors and, despite the protests of Principe merchants hurt by the competition of the French 'contrabandists', the authorities on the island did nothing to enforce the law.[6] The French company apparently ceased operations about 1800.[7]

English trade with the Gabon coast became increasingly important

[1] Archives nationales, Colonies, C⁶, 24, 'Mémoire sur le commerce des Côtes d'Afrique'.

[2] Archives nationales, Colonies, C⁶, 24, Cabinde, divers pièces, 'Mémoire sur le commerce à faire au Gabon', 22 June 1787.

[3] P. Labarthe, *Voyage à la côte de Guinée, ou description des côtes d'Afrique depuis le Cap Tagrin jusqu'au Cap de Lopez Gonzalves* (Paris, 1805), pp. 185, 182.

[4] Archives nationales, Colonies, C⁶, 27, Guinée, Juda, divers pièces, 1771–1818, 'Établissements et forts qui les françaises, anglais, hollandaises, danois et portugais possedent aux Côtes d'Afrique', 1791.

[5] Archivo Histórico Ultramarino, São Tomé, caixa 13, 'Report of João Baptista da Silva, Capitão-Mor of São Tomé', 30 Sept. 1792.

[6] Archivo Histórico Ultramarino, São Tomé, maço 17, 1798, 'Petition of Gregorio Lucas de Matos'.

[7] In 1801 the governor of São Tomé reported that the French had formerly traded to the coast from Principe. (Archivo Histórico Ultramarino, São Tomé, caixa 14, 31 Mar. 1801). The bulk of the company's trade had been in Benin and the Niger Delta. See Alan F. C. Ryder, *Benin and the Europeans, 1485–1897* (London, 1969), pp. 227–8.

toward the end of the century. Dyewood and ivory were still significant,[1] but the slave trade was growing. By 1788 Gabon and Cape
Lopez were authoritatively estimated to be exporting five hundred
slaves annually.[2] Although slaves from Gabon were considered
'a miserable race of beings' and were 'held in but little esteem in the
West Indies',[3] many were in fact sent there. West Indian authorities
reported the landing of 990 slaves from Gabon and 497 from Cape
Lopez between 1791 and 1800.[4] These totals were not complete and
no African sources were given for many of the cargoes landed.

Although the English data are incomplete and the volume of
French and Portuguese slave exports are not known, Norris's esti-
mate of 500 slaves a year seems reasonable for the pre-war period.
The volume in the 'nineties was perhaps somewhat higher.

The Napoleonic Wars had an adverse effect on European trade to
Africa, but neither English nor French trade with the Gabon area
was completely halted by the hostilities. In 1803 a French schooner
which had loaded 315 slaves at Cape Lopez sought refuge at São
Tomé from English cruisers;[5] an English brig with a cargo of
Gabonese ivory and wax entered São Tomé harbour in 1804 to avoid
French attack.[6] British vessels bought dyewood in large quantities
during the war;[7] indeed the army's demand for red dyes for uniforms
created something of a boom for Gabonese dyewood.[8]

---

[1] John Adams, *Remarks on the Country Extending from Cape Palmas to the
River Congo, Including Observations on the Manners and Customs of the Inhabitants*
(London, 1823; new impression, 1966), p. 145. Adams was active on the coast
1786–1800.

[2] Report of Lords' Committee, Parliamentary Papers, Commons, 1789,
xxvi, 649a, Pt. I, 'Estimate of Robert Norris'. A 1783 French estimate gives
3,000 a year for Gabon and 300 for Cape Lopez, but this seems too high, and as
discussed above, the French had little first-hand knowledge of the area. The
document gives detailed information on the coast between Senegal and Benin,
and for Angola, but only bare numbers for the Bight of Biafra. Archives nationales, Colonies, C⁶, 18, Sénégal 1783, 'Remarques. État en aperçu des esclaves
que peuvent retirer les nations de l'Europe de la côte occidentale d'Afrique'.

[3] Adams, *Remarks*, p. 144.

[4] For further details, see K. David Patterson, 'The Mpongwe and the Orungu
of the Gabon Coast 1815–75: The Transition to Colonial Rule', unpublished
Ph.D. dissertation (Stanford University, 1971), pp. 84–5.

[5] Archivo Histórico Ultramarino, São Tomé, caixa 14, 'Reports of 27 Dec.
1803', No. 7.

[6] Archivo Histórico Ultramarino, São Tomé, caixa 15, folder 4, 'Report of
31 Jan. 1804'.

[7] Archivo Histórico Ultramarino, São Tomé, caixa 20, 'Report of Governor
of São Tomé, 3 Apr. 1812'.

[8] Thomas Boteler, *Narrative of a Voyage of Discovery to Africa and Arabia,*

However, the wars do seem to have caused enough of a trade depression to alarm the Mpongwe and Orungu, and to create new opportunities for Portuguese traders from the offshore islands. In 1800, Liumba Pasol (Reombi), the king of Cape Lopez, sent a letter to the governor of São Tomé. The king reported selling ivory and slaves to one João da Sa and asked the governor to send other islanders to trade with him.[1] The governor, João Baptista e Silva, received a similar letter from the ruler of 'Great Gabon' or Point Pongara.[2] Baptista e Silva seized this opportunity to open, or more exactly expand trade with the entire coastal area between Calabar and Cape Lopez.[3] The kings of 'Little Gabon' (Cape Lopez) and 'Great Gabon' were eager to sell slaves, wax, ivory, and ebony, as they formerly had done to the French traders from Principe and still did to the English. The monarchs reportedly remembered trade from the islands 'in the time of their ancestors' and, professing to prefer the Portuguese to other Europeans, asked for Portuguese flags. The ruler of Cape Lopez sent a large tusk as a sample of his wares, while the Mpongwe king asked to send a son to Lisbon for an education. Governor Baptista e Silva sent samples of Gabonese ebony to Lisbon and suggested it would be excellent material for ship-building. Furthermore, he declared, the islands could be a valuable depot for the Brazilian slave trade. Small vessels could go to the coast to gather slaves, which could then be picked up at São Tomé or Principe by large ships from Lisbon.[4] Baptista e Silva obtained permission to build a factory in Gabon and, in summing up the achievements of his administration, listed one of his major accomplishments as the 'discovery' of trading points on the African coast.[5]

Performed in His Majesty's Ships, Leven and Barracouta, from 1821 to 1826, Under the Command of Captain F. W. Owen, R. N. (London, 1835), ii, p. 394.

[1] Archivo Nacional da Torre do Tombo, Junta do Comercio, maço 20, 'Liumba Pasol to Governor of São Tomé, 9 Dec. 1800'.

[2] Archivo Nacional da Torre do Tombo, Junta do Comercio, maço 20, 'João Baptista e Silva to the King, 31 Mar. 1801'. The Gabonese ruler was almost certainly Re-Mboko, the father of Denis.

[3] Archivo Histórico Ultramarino, São Tomé, caixa 14, 'João Baptista e Silva to the King, 7 Sept. 1802'.

[4] Archivo Histórico Ultramarino, São Tomé, caixa 14, 'Letter of 31 Mar. 1801'. Signature obliterated, but the letter appears to be an expanded version of the Torre do Tombo letter cited in n. 2.

[5] Archivo Histórico Ultramarino, São Tomé, caixa 14, 'João Baptista e Silva to the King', n.d. [1802], 'Outline of the Progress Made in Agriculture, Navigation, and Commerce in São Tomé e Principe'.

Trade with the Gabon area flourished. Customs records for São Tomé show the arrivals of seven island schooners from Gabon between November 1802 and February 1804 with cargoes of ivory, balls of wax, ebony, redwood, and a few slaves. Data are not complete for all of the arrivals, but four boats brought in a total of 224 arrobas of wax in balls, 553 arrobas of ivory (apparently including one cargo of hippopotamus teeth), some wood, and eleven 'new slaves'.[1] Between August 1802 and August 1803 ten vessels cleared São Tomé for Gabon and Cape Lopez.[2] Goods traded for these products included, at least on one occasion, aquardente (a form of rum), paper, oil, vinegar, wine, hats, and cloth.[3]

In 1805, when the 'princes of the kingdoms of the Gabon' were reportedly closing their ports to vessels from the islands, nine merchants blamed the 'extinction' of this 'very useful trade which had been opened up by the Governor João Baptista e Silva' on the attempt of the new governor to monopolize the trade for himself.[4] Merchants also complained about high import duties. Twenty slaves brought from Gabon in 1806 were allegedly taxed at an exhorbitant rate, and 149 slaves died on ship in the Gabon River, supposedly because the owner could not raise funds to pay the taxes.[5] Governor Luis Joaquim Lisboa responded to royal queries about these complaints by asserting that, despite the end of the English slave trade, the islands had never been so prosperous.[6] To prove that the Gabon trade was not 'extinct', he later submitted a list of ten Principe and three São Tomé schooners which were employed in the Gabon trade.[7] Lisboa further ingratiated himself with his superiors by sending a Gabonese 'Ourang-Outang' to the royal museum.[8]

[1] Archivo Histórico Ultramarino, São Tomé, caixa 15, folder 5, 'Report on Customs Duties', 22 Feb. 1804, document 6. An arroba equals thirty-two pounds.

[2] Ibid., document 20. Neither of these reports includes Principe and they are probably not complete for São Tomé.

[3] Archivo Histórico Ultramarino, São Tomé, caixa 15, 21 Oct. 1805, No. 7, 'Cargo list of the Maria Apolonia'. As it seems improbable that there was much of an Mpongwe market for oil, vinegar, or paper, this may not have been a typical cargo.

[4] Archivo Histórico Ultramarino, São Tomé, caixa 15, folder 36, 'Petition', 29 Dec. 1805.

[5] Archivo Histórico Ultramarino, São Tomé, maço 5, 'Complaint of José Antonio Pereira', 18 Apr. 1809.

[6] Archivo Histórico Ultramarino, São Tomé, caixa 18, 'Reports of Luis Joaquim Lisboa', 24 Sept. 1808, No. 11.

[7] Archivo Histórico Ultramarino, São Tomé, caixa 18, 'List of Ships from São Tomé Employed in the Trade . . . at Gabon', 30 June 1810, No. 9.

[8] Archivo Histórico Ultramarino, São Tomé, caixa 18, 'Letter of Governor

Customs House records, which are available for both islands for most years between 1809 and 1818, support Governor Lisboa's contention that there was a lively trade between the Gabonese coast and the Portuguese islands. These records, however, must be used with some caution. While the officials at Principe usually gave detailed cargo lists and stated where in Africa the cargo was loaded, the São Tomé books often just listed 'goods' of a particular value coming from the 'Coast of Africa'. Also, there probably was a great deal of tax-evasion, both by under-declaring cargoes and by clandestine landings. For example, an American captain calling at Principe in 1811 found himself confronted with unexpectedly high tariffs on his cargo. But, 'from this dilemma a little finesse and the expense of a few small articles in the way of presents to those in office extricated me, and saved from 12 to 1500 dollars in duties'.[1] Other captains undoubtedly reduced their expenses in the same way.

The British slave trade ended, in law and largely in fact, in 1808, and the island merchants appear to have taken advantage of this to increase their own slave purchases. Ship arrivals from Cape Lopez and Gabon between 1810 and 1815 average fifteen a year at Principe; of these about twelve paid taxes only on slaves. However, three or four ships a year brought in ivory, wax, and wood, with perhaps a few slaves to complete the cargo.[2]

The table below indicates the dimensions of Gabonese slave imports into the islands, and can be used to give some indication of the total exports from Gabon and Cape Lopez for this period. However, in addition to the possibility of exports by other nations and an unknown death rate of slaves en route to the islands, the limitations noted above for the customs records must be considered in attempting to reach an estimate of the magnitude of human exports from the Gabon coast. Evasion of the 3·5 milreis per head tax is impossible to measure and, while slave sources are almost always given for slaves reaching Principe, such notations are rare in the São Tomé records. An estimate of São Tomé imports from Gabon and Cape Lopez is made in column 6, on the assumption that the proportion of Gabonese slaves brought in was similar to that of Principe.

Lisboa', 22 Dec. 1807. The animal was probably a chimpanzee, but conceivably it was a gorilla, a beast then regarded by Europeans as mythological.

[1] Samuel Swan to Brothers, Aug. 1811, Samuel Swan Letter Book, Peabody Museum.

[2] See sources for Table I.

TABLE I

Imported Slaves Taxed at Principe and São Tomé, 1809–1815

PRINCIPE

Year	1 Total[a]	2 From[b] Gabon	3 From[b] Cape Lopez	4 Sum, 2 & 3
1809	1,641	—	—	(170)[e]
1810	2,622	113	35	148
1811	(3,200)[c]	—	—	(328)[e]
1812	2,622	(290)[d]	(215)[d]	(505)[d]
1813	2,309	278	77	355
1814	1,744	232	54	286
1815	3,591	227	62	289
Totals	17,729			2,081

[a] Slave totals are from the annual 'Mapas da Reçeita do Cofre da Fazenda Real' for each island. Calabar, Cameroun, and Benin were the other major sources recorded.

[b] Slave sources are from the annual 'Livro da Real Fazenda' for each island. Records for 1809 are in Archivo Histórico Ultramarino, São Tomé, caixa 19, 1810 folder; for 1810 in caixa 20, 1811 folder; for 1812 in caixa 21, 1813 folder; for 1814 in caixa 21, 20 abril 1814 folder; for 1814 in maço 7, 1815 folder; for 1815 in maço 8, 20 octobre 1816 folder.

[c] Since the only Principe data available for 1811 was a figure for total revenue, this is an estimate based on 77 per cent total revenues collected, divided by the per capita slave tax of 3,500 reis. For all other years, slave taxes consistently supplied about 77 per cent of the island's locally-raised revenues.

[d] Figures were not given for a few vessels landing slaves; the estimate is based on the average number of slaves on known voyages.

The data, incomplete and uncertain as they are, suggest that something in the order of 4,000 slaves from the Gabon coast reached the Portuguese islands between 1809 and 1815. Total exports, assuming a low level of transatlantic exports due to English and American anti-slave trade legislation and the effects of the war on French and Dutch shipping, would equal this figure, plus deaths *en route* to the islands, plus direct exports to Brazil and possibly Cuba.[1] A conserva-

[1] Later, during the clandestine period of the trade, Cuba was a major market for Gabonese slaves. Direct trade to Brazil is an unknown factor, but the estimate

TABLE I—(cont.)

SÃO TOMÉ

| | 5 | 6 | 7 |
| | | Est. slaves[f] from Gabon & Cape Lopez | Est. Total Gabon & Cape Lopez (Cols. 4 & 6) |
Year	Total[a]		
1809	1,758	(183)	353
1810	1,680	(94)	242
		(67 known Gabon)	
1811	4,308	(450)	778
1812	2,798	(290)	795
1813	837	(128)	483
1814	2,137	(349)	635
		(46 known Gabon)	
1815	1,358	(109)	398
Totals	14,876	1,603	3,684

[e] Calculated from the average of Cape Lopez' and Gabon's contribution to the 1810, 1813, 1814, and 1815 totals (10·4 per cent).

[f] Calculated from the percentage of Principe's imports from Cape Lopez and Gabon for that year (1810, 1812, 1814 and 1815) or the 10·4 per cent Principe average (1809 and 1811).

tive guess of an annual export of about 1,000–1,500 persons from the Gabon estuary and Cape Lopez in this period seems reasonable and is comparable with estimates for the late eighteenth century.

Like the British, the Portuguese sometimes became embroiled in disputes with the Mpongwe and Orungu. The most spectacular broke out in mid-1805 when Captain Manoel Marques Camacho kidnapped the son and two slaves of 'Gula' (Ogoul 'Issogoue), the king of Cape Lopez, and headed for Maranhão with a cargo of 180 slaves. The king, infuriated and apparently aware that his son was further endangered by an epidemic raging aboard Camacho's ship, retaliated by closing trade to all Portuguese and by seizing a ship, crew, fifty-nine slaves, and seven hundred arrobas of wax belonging

is almost certainly too low rather than too high. Brazil's imports continued at a high level during the whole war period. Philip D. Curtin, *The Atlantic Slave Trade: A Census* (Madison, 1969), p. 211.

to a black São Tomean, João Viegas de Abreu.[1] The incident ended relatively happily when the boy was returned a year later. Abreu's men and goods were released and trade was re-opened, which pleased Governor Lisboa because 'the slaves are very fine there'.[2] The only loser in the affair was Abreu. Camacho's employer, José Antonio Pereira, claimed that, as the king's son was never kidnapped but had only been his houseguest in Maranhão, the Cape Lopez people had just looked for an excuse to seize Abreu's ship. Pereira declined any responsibility for the conduct of these 'savages and robbers' and refused to indemnify Abreu.[3]

Gula became involved in another controversy in 1810 when he allegedly seized the unarmed Bahian brigantine *Flor da America* and massacred the entire crew. The stolen boat was sold to a Sr. Gomes who was apprehended and sent to Bahia to be investigated by the vessel's insurers.[4] Governor Lisboa noted the frequency of attacks by African war canoes on merchant vessels and ordered the arming of all ships trading at Cape Lopez, Gabon, Benga [Corisco Island], Bembe [Rio Muni Coast], Cameroun, Old Calabar, Bonny, New Calabar, Warri, and Benin.[5] Vessels going to Gabon were to have at least six cannons.[6]

Despite Lisboa's fears of Mpongwe hostility, Portuguese sailors seem to have been relatively safe among them. In 1805 a São Tomé ship anchored off Quaben's town on the north bank of the Gabon was lost, together with its cargo, when the ship dragged anchor and ran aground while the crew slept. The beached vessel was robbed by the local inhabitants 'in accordance with their laws, not even leaving the nails'. By the time King Quaben reached the scene, the vessel had been reduced to scraps of wood.[7] The only recorded incidence of

1 Archivo Histórico Ultramarino, São Tomé, caixa 17, 19 Oct. 1805, No. 3, 'Luis Joaquim Lisboa to the King'; ibid., 'Gula to Lisboa', Aug. 1805; ibid.; 'Abreu (?) to Kreigar', 3 Aug. 1805. The kidnapped youth may well have been the future King Ombango Passol.

2 Archivo Histórico Ultramarino, São Tomé, caixa 17, 1806, 'Lisboa to Visconde de Anadia', 27 Aug. 1806, No. 17.

3 Archivo Histórico Ultramarino, São Tomé, maço 5, Apr. 1809, 'Petition of José Antonio Pereira, 1806'.

4 Archivo Histórico Ultramarino, São Tomé, caixa 19, 'Lisboa to Conde das Galvaez', 15 Oct. 1810, No. 59; ibid., caixa 18, 'Lisboa to Conde das Galvaez', 30 June 1810, No. 30.

5 Ibid., caixa 19, 'Lisboa to Conde das Galvaez', 15 Oct. 1810.

6 Ibid., caixa 18, 'Lisboa to Conde das Galvaez', 30 June 1810.

7 Archivo Histórico Ultramarino, São Tomé, caixa 15, folder 37, 'Report of Governor Lisboa', 24 Dec. 1805.

Mpongwe violence toward the islanders was the robbery of a slaving ship in 1809 and the murder of two of its crew.[1]

American trade on the African coast benefited from the wartime dislocation of British shipping, and a few New England vessels visited Gabon for redwood and other cargoes.[2] One, the *Tropic Bird*, had obtained a cargo at least of 100 sticks of ebony, 315 sticks of redwood, 6 bags of wax, 2 bags of gum, 3 tusks, and 70 screvellos,[3] when it ran into serious trouble. The master, Captain Skinner, had traded with King George, 'a native who commands the territory round the mouth of the river Gabon'.[4] George, by claiming that war had broken out between America and Britain and that English cruisers were in the area, tricked Skinner into coming in the narrow creek to his village and landing the cargo. Skinner and most of his men were then poisoned, but the supercargo, a Mr. Fabian, escaped to Cape Coast on an English ship. Fabian later found the *Tropic Bird* at Principe. It had been purchased by Sr. Neugara,[5] a Principe merchant having 'great influence' with George. Neugara, described as rich and powerful, but none too honest, may perhaps have instigated the affair.[6]

Thus, despite the ending of the British slave trade and the adverse

---

[1] Archivo Histórico Ultramarino, São Tomé, caixa 18, 'Petition of Joaquim Pedro Lagrande', 2 Mar. 1809.

[2] A Boston ship was in Gabon for redwood in 1811 (Swan to Brothers, 1811). See also n. 4 below.

[3] Small tusks, sometimes also including hippopotamus teeth.

[4] This passage presents some difficulties, as King George was at the eastern end of the Gabon, near where it splits into the Como and Remboue branches. However, at this time, and in contrast to later decades, some ships ventured a few miles up these streams. Swan probably meant that George lived at the mouths of these rivers, as elsewhere he states that King George lived upriver from Konig Island ('Captain Samuel Swan's Memoranda on the African Trade', MS., Library of Congress, dated *c.* 1810, published in George E. Brooks, Jr., *Yankee Traders, Old Coasters and African Middlemen: A History of American Legitimate Trade with West Africa in the Nineteenth Century* (Boston, 1970), p. 337.) Or, he could have been talking about King Denis. American missionaries later found a number of trade documents in the possession of a chief on the Como, including evidence of an American visit in 1804. J. L. Wilson, 'An Excursion to the Head Waters of the Gaboon River', 25 Aug. 1842, A.B.C. 15.1, vol. ii, No. 117.

[5] Antonio Henrique Noguiera, who owned three of the ten Principe schooners used in the Gabon trade. Archivo Histórico Ultramarino, São Tomé, caixa 18, 30 June 1810, No. 9.

[6] Samuel Swan to Thomas F. Wharton, 28 Dec. 1810, Samuel Swan Letter Book. Swan, who brought Fabian to Principe and reported the whole matter to Wharton, the ship's owner, does not directly accuse Noguiera of complicity with King George.

effects of the European war on their export opportunities, the Mpongwe and Orungu were able to open new markets in the offshore islands. Although direct voyages from Europe and the Americas did not altogether cease, the islands became important entrepôts for the trade of the northern coast of Gabon. São Tomé and Principe merchants bought manufactured goods from European and American vessels[1] and exchanged them on the coast for African commodities. Wax, ivory, and wood were purchased at the islands by foreigners who wished to avoid the dangers and delays of coastal trading;[2] the slaves could be re-exported to Brazil.[3] Thus the Mpongwe and the Orungu were in both direct and indirect contact with their trading partners in Europe and America.

Peace in Europe brought more ships to the African coast and freed the British navy for more intensive action against the Atlantic slave trade. Both of these factors tended to reduce the role of the Portuguese in the commercial affairs of the coast. As early as 1813 a British frigate had taken a São Tomé slaving boat in the Gabon river and several other Portuguese vessels elsewhere on the coast;[4] the island schooner *Madelena* was caught in the Gabon in 1815.[5] The slave trade temporarily declined, throwing the islands into a depression. Governor Lisboa complained that merchants were now stuck with large quantities of cloth purchased at Benin, most of which 'used to be exported to Gabão Grande [Gabon River], but at this port we now trade only a little ivory, gum, and wood'. Lisboa suggested that the islanders try to buy gum copal and sell it to the English.[6] The Real Fazenda reports for 1817 showed only 1,142 slaves reaching the islands, all supposedly from the legal zone south of the equator. The financial report noted the 'commercial decadence' of the islands.[7]

The Mpongwe and Orungu, now having direct access to European

1 Samuel Swan to Brothers, Aug. 1811.

2 Samuel Swan to Captain John Wood, 26 Dec. 1815, Samuel Swan Letter Book; Brooks, *Yankee Traders*, p. 283.

3 Archivo Histórico Ultramarino, São Tomé, caixa 14, 'João Baptista e Silva to the King', n. d. [1802], 'Outline of the Progress Made in Agriculture, Navigation, and Commerce in São Tomé and Principe'.

4 Archivo Histórico Ultramarino, São Tomé, caixa 21, 'Governor of São Tomé to the King', 28 Nov. 1813.

5 Archivo Histórico Ultramarino, São Tomé, maço 7, 1815 folder, 'Report of 1 May 1815, No. 3'.

6 Archivo Histórico Ultramarino, São Tomé, maço 8, 'Governor of São Tomé to Marques d'Aguias', 2 Oct. 1816, No. 21.

7 Archivo Histórico Ultramarino, São Tomé, maço 9, 20 July 1818 folder, 'Real Fazenda Reports for 1817'.

trade, had little need for the island middlemen to handle their ivory, wax, and wood. But later, as the Anti-Slavery Patrol grew in strength and effectiveness, they discovered that they increasingly needed the islanders as slave runners. Rickety schooners packed with chained slaves were to link the peoples of the Gabon coast to the Portuguese islands for several decades to come.

The period from the replacement on the coast of the Adyumba and Ndiwa groups of Mpongwe until the new trading conditions after 1815 was a crucial epoch in the history of the coast. Nineteenth-century Gabon, as will be shown in the next chapter, had undergone many changes since the days of Barbot and Bosman. Unfortunately, almost nothing can be gleaned from the available sources on changes that were taking place in African social, political, or economic life. An attempt will be made in the following chapters to examine some of the factors which helped shape the contrasting Mpongwe and Orungu societies of the nineteenth century.

CHAPTER III

The Mpongwe and Legitimate Trade: 1815–1838

THE vital role of trade in the early history of the northern Gabon coast has been documented in the first two chapters. Patterns evolving during the seventeenth and eighteenth centuries, and especially after the opening of the slave trade, had reached full development by the nineteenth century when they were first described by literate observers. The period between 1815 and 1840 was in many ways the high point for Mpongwe and Orungu middlemen. Trade soared after the conclusion of the Napoleonic wars; French colonialists and American missionaries had not yet appeared in the Gabon and the British navy had made only tentative efforts to control the slave trade in equatorial waters.

Although the quality and quantity of nineteenth-century sources increase dramatically in comparison with material available for earlier periods, many important questions are impossible to treat adequately. Most literate observers were concerned with conducting profitable trade, developing a French *comptoir*, fighting the commerce in slaves, or spreading Christianity, and their writings naturally reflect their own interests. Since few European visitors took any real interest in the internal affairs of the Africans, relatively little can be said about local politics or economic activities not connected with long-distance trade. Mpongwe political and economic life between 1815 and 1838 will be discussed in this chapter and, as the Mpongwe were the leading traders in ivory and forest products, 'legitimate' trade will also be discussed here. Since the Orungu were the region's leading slave traders, a detailed account of the traffic in human beings will be given in the next chapter, together with a sketch of Orungu political history.

The political situation on the Gabon River was quite different from that at Cape Lopez. By the nineteenth century and probably earlier, the Mpongwe were divided into four major political communities, each with its own ruler. However, while some of the Mpongwe monarchs were wealthy and influential men, their power in no way approximated to that of the Orungu kings. The 'kingdoms' were invariably called by the European names given to their kings; Denis and George on the south bank, and Quaben and Glass on the north. These names were given to successive rulers in a dynasty without further description. For example, 'King Glass' may refer to six or more nineteenth-century figures. To further complicate matters, most early observers failed to give the kings' proper Mpongwe names.

King Denis, called William by the English and Americans, was of the Assiga clan. His villages were located near Point Pongara, at the mouth of the Gabon. Antchouwe Kowe Rapontchombo, to give his African name, was born about 1780, the son of King Re-Mboko.[1] He is said to have served on a Spanish slaving ship at some time between 1800 and 1810.[2] Perhaps because of this valuable business experience, Re-Mboko passed over his older sons to select Denis as his successor.[3] He ascended the throne about 1810 and ruled until his death in 1876.[4]

Denis became the leading slave dealer in the Gabon and enjoyed such close relations with the merchants of the Portuguese islands that his main village became known as São Tomé.[5] By the 1840s, Denis had gained a widespread reputation for honesty and wisdom and was the most influential and respected man on the river. European visitors, even the missionaries who damned him for his slaving activities, invariably described Denis in the most favourable terms. The Reverend John Leighton Wilson paid a visit in 1842 and enjoyed, along with excellent conversation, a fine meal served with two French wines. At this time, Denis's main town had about 150 houses with about 700–800 people, plus a Spanish-run barracoon. He also ruled two slightly smaller towns, and had forty or fifty wives and 300–400 slaves. All in all, the missionary found Denis to be 'one of the most remarkable men I have met in Africa'.[6]

[1] Abbé André Raponda Walker, *Notes d'histoire du Gabon* (Brazzaville, 1960), p. 24.

[2] Abbé André Raponda Walker and Robert Reynard, 'Anglais, Espagnols et Nord-Américains au Gabon au XIXᵉ siècle', *Bulletin de l'Institut d'études centrafricaines*, N.S., xii (1956), p. 256.

[3] Père Gautier, *Étude historique sur les Mpongoués et tribus avoisinantes* (Brazzaville, 1950), p. 49.   [4] Abbé Walker, *Notes*, pp. 24, 29.

[5] Archives d'Outre-Mer, Sénégal, iv, 37, a, 'Rapport de M. de Peroune', 18 Apr. 1838.

[6] J. L. Wilson, 'Excursion to King William's Town', 8 July 1842 American Board of Commissioners for Foreign Missions Letterbooks, A.B.C. 15.1, vol. ii, No. 122.

The other major Mpongwe centre on the south bank of the estuary was that dominated by the Agoulamba clan, presided over by Rassondji, or King George. In the early nineteenth century, George was the wealthiest and most influential of the Mpongwe kings. The date of his accession to the throne is unknown, but he is mentioned in documents as early as 1809[1] and 1810.[2]

T. E. Bowdich, while returning home after his visit to Kumasi, was a passenger on an English ship which spent seven weeks trading redwood and ebony at George's town in 1818. He described George as a middle-aged man, hospitable and intelligent, who, like all the leading Mpongwe traders, spoke good English.[3] Ngango, George's capital, consisted of

one street, wide, regular, and clean. The houses are very neatly constructed of bamboo, and afford a ground floor of spacious and lofty apartments. They sleep on bedsteads encircled with mosquito curtains of bamboo cloth. The manner of the superiors is very pleasing and hospitable, and a European may reside amongst them, not only with safety, but with comfort and dignity. I do not think that the old and new town together contain 500 inhabitants between them.[4]

Ngango was located at the entrance of the Remboue River into the Gabon, about forty miles from the open sea. The Remboue was the major route for products coming from the hinterland south of the Gabon and from the Ogowe River. George's village was strategically located to command these routes.

King George, recognizing the value of literacy and desiring to improve his relations with European traders, sent two of his sons to Europe to be educated. One went to France and arrived uneventfully. The other, an eight- or twelve-year-old boy named Richard, was sent to England on the *Juno* in 1809. However, the *Juno* was taken by a French privateer and young Richard apparently spent the next several years at Caen.[5] Both boys had returned to Gabon by 1818,

[1] Archives nationales, Colonies, C[6], 24, Cabinde, divers pièces 1785–1809, 'Affaire de jeune nègre fils du prince du Gabon, pris sur le navire anglais la Junon'.

[2] Samuel Swan to Thomas F. Wharton, 28 Dec. 1810, Samuel Swan Letter Book, Peabody Museum.

[3] T. E. Bowdich, *Mission from Cape Coast Castle to Ashantee* (London, 1819; repr. 1966), p. 425.

[4] Ibid., p. 439.

[5] Archives nationales, 'Affaire de jeune nègre', encls. 1–4. Interestingly, the boy had to be interrogated with the help of one of the English prisoners, a veteran trader who was fluent in Mpongwe.

and were able to speak and write French well. They found life in Gabon 'disgusting' and were both anxious to return to France.[1]

By the early 1840s George Rassondji's prosperity was clearly on the wane. Slaves from the upper Ogowe were more and more being sent directly down river to the Orungu. Fewer European vessels came up to Ngango; the captains found it more convenient to anchor off the towns closer to the mouth of the estuary. Goods from George's people had increasingly to be carried in canoes to the ships trading at Glass or Denis.[2]

Four minor Mpongwe settlements should also be mentioned. 'Abraham's' town, apparently a dependency of Denis, was located on the south bank half way between Point Pongara and Ngango.[3] 'Tom Larsen', evidently a brother of George, had a small town in the same area.[4] 'King Duka', perhaps also a relative of King George, had 150 people in a village about ten miles up the Remboue.[5] Dambe or Konig Island, the old Ndiwa centre, was resettled in the early nineteenth century by part of the Adoni clan. The Adoni, after being driven from the coast by the Orungu c. 1700 in the aftermath of the Adyumba war, had lived on the creeks on the south bank. Some of them later moved to Dambe under their chief, Antchouwe Re-Dembino or 'François'.[6] There were about 300 people in two villages on the island in 1842.[7]

[1] Bowdich, *Mission*, p. 425.

[2] J. L. Wilson, 'Some General Remarks in Relation to the Situation of the Gaboon River', 1842, A.B.C. 15.1, vol. ii, No. 119.

[3] Bowdich, *Mission*, p. 423, n.; Archives d'Outre-Mer, Sénégal, iv, 40, b, 'Lt. A. Bouët to Comm. Gabon', 1 Aug. 1852.

[4] William Walker to Prudential Committee, 28 Dec. 1843, A.B.C. 15.1, vol. ii, No. 28.

[5] William Walker to Rufus Anderson, 29 May 1843, A.B.C. 15.1, vol. ii, No. 174.

[6] Abbé Walker, *Notes*, pp. 42–4.

[7] J. L. Wilson, 'Excursion to Konig Island', 12 Aug. 1842, A.B.C. 15.1, vol. ii, No. 123. Wilson found four corroded cannons on the top of the hill on Dambe. The people told him that the Dutch had once bought the island. Bowdich (*Mission*, p. 422) was told that there were ruins of an old Portuguese fort on the island. Winwood Reade saw the guns in 1862 and was told that they were Dutch (*Savage Africa; Being the Narrative of a Tour in Equatorial, Southwestern, and Northwestern Africa* (New York, 1864), p. 117). Robert Reynard thought these guns were left after an abortive attempt by São Tomé prospectors to set up a base in Gabon ('Recherches sur la présence des Portugais au Gabon (XV–XIXe siècles)', *Bulletin de l'Institut d'études centrafricaines*, N.S., ix (1955), p. 30. This view is supported by Manuel Ferreira Ribeiro (*A Provincia de S. Thomé e Principe e suas Dependencias* (Lisbon, 1877), p. 18), who claims that in 1723 some Portuguese built a fort on the island, but left when they failed to find rumoured

Both of the kingdoms on the north bank of the Gabon were ruled by families of the Aguekaza clan. The cluster of villages ruled by King Glass was a few miles up the river from Quaben's domains. The genealogy of the Glass dynasty is not known with any certainty after the first few individuals.[1] Samuel Swan observed about 1810 that King Glass was 'not to be trusted too much' and Bowdich referred to a 'Prince Glass' in 1818.[2] Lieutenant Boteler visited 'King Glass', apparently the same individual, in 1826. The king, a pleasant man of about fifty-five who spoke good English, possessed a ship's bell which, according to its inscription, had been presented to King Glass in 1787 by Sydenham and Company of Bristol, England. Boteler implies that the recipient was the immediate predecessor of the monarch that he met.[3]

Glass was a popular trading point for English and American vessels in the nineteenth century, as it had apparently been in earlier years. When the first American missionaries arrived in 1842, King Glass (Ravonya) had about 600–800 subjects.[4] This number grew rapidly in later years, when several European factories were built and Glass gained commercial ascendancy over its rivals.

The political situation in King Quaben's villages was quite complex. The name Quaben is first recorded in 1805.[5] In 1810 Captain Swan referred to Quaben as 'the first man in the way of trade' in the river.[6] Like 'William', 'George', and 'Glass', it had probably been coined by eighteenth-century sailors and passed down to successive

---

gold deposits. Another possibility is that the guns originally belonged to the Mpongwe themselves. According to John Barbot (*A Description of the Coasts of North and South Guinea and of Ethiopia Inferior, Vulgarly Angola* (London, 1732), p. 487) the King of Pongo had several cannons, although he seems to have kept them on Mbini Island. At any rate, these cannons remain one of the minor mysteries of Gabonese history.

[1] See ch. II.

[2] 'Captain Samuel Swan's Memoranda on the African Trade', MS., Library of Congress, dated *c.* 1810, published in George E. Brooks, Jr., *Yankee Traders, Old Coasters and African Middlemen: A History of American Legitimate Trade in West Africa in the Nineteenth Century* (Boston, 1970), p. 337; Bowdich, *Mission*, p. 432 n.

[3] Thomas Boteler, *Narrative of a Voyage of Discovery to Africa and Arabia, Performed in His Majesty's Ships, Leven and Barracouta, from 1821 to 1826, Under the Command of Captain F. W. Owen, R.N.* (London, 1835), ii, p. 395.

[4] Reverend Benjamin Griswold to Rufus Anderson, 4 July 1842, A.B.C. 15.1, vol. ii, No. 153.

[5] Archivo Histórico Ultramarino, São Tomé, caixa 15, folder 37, 'Report of Governor Lisboa', 24 Dec. 1805.

[6] Samuel Swan, 'Memoranda', p. 338. He called Quaben's Kingdom 'Batavia'.

monarchs. King Quaben, who was about sixty years old in 1842,[1] was the sovereign of all the north bank settlements toward the sea from Glass. Louis, usually considered by the French as a *chef*, but sometimes listed as a *roi*,[2] belonged to a junior branch of the royal family. He and Kringer's villages seem to have enjoyed considerable autonomy from Quaben. The chart below shows the dynastic situation.[3]

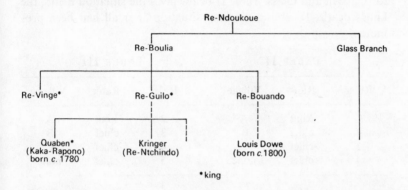

The population of the four villages acknowledging Quaben was about 3,000 in 1842, of whom approximately one-half were foreign slaves.[4]

Royal succession, as with the Orungu, generally went to the eldest surviving brother of the deceased king and then to his eldest son. However, the old king successfully designated a younger son on at least two occasions.[5] The deceased ruler was buried along with a few slaves to serve him in the afterlife[6] and, after a few days, the new ruler was formally chosen by election. It is not clear who the electors were. One source identifies the kingmakers as 'all the gentlemen',

[1] J. L. Wilson, 'Various Excursions Performed in the Vicinity of the Gaboon River', 2 July 1842, A.B.C. 15.1, vol. ii, No. 121.

[2] *Chef* in Archives d'Outre-Mer, Sénégal, iv, 32, b, 'Cadeaux pour rois et chefs du Gabon', 28 Dec. 1847 and 1848; the 1855 *cadeaux* list (ibid., 32, d) calls Louis a *roi*.

[3] Compiled from Gautier, *Étude*, pp. 49–51; and Abbé Walker, *Notes*, p. 35. See also ch. II.

[4] Wilson, 'Various Excursions'.

[5] Bowdich, *Mission*, p. 437; Gautier, *Étude*, p. 49.

[6] Archives d'Outre-Mer, Sénégal, iv, 39, a, 'Comm. Gabon to Comm. Gorée', 20 Oct. 1847.

perhaps meaning family heads and men of means.[1] According to Abbé Walker, the elders had the powers to veto the natural heir and to nominate another candidate.[2] Minor fights sometimes broke out among the contenders.[3]

A curious system for the replacement of village chiefs within a kingdom, reminiscent of the 'Rota' system of Kievan Rus or the promotional succession to office in early Loango,[4] has been described for Quaben and Glass. Table II below gives the situation before the king's death; III shows the final situation after all had been promoted.

	TABLE II			TABLE III	
Ruler	Rank	Village	Ruler	Rank	Village
1	king	A	2	king	A
2	chief	B	3	chief	B
3	chief	C	4	chief	C
4	chief	none	5	chief	none

The senior chief replaced the king, the junior chiefs moved up to govern the village next in the hierarchy, and one new chief (5) entered at the bottom.[5] However, only one authority even hints at an organized succession scheme like this, and there is no evidence that such a plan was ever actually followed. It is possible that such a system had once been tried, or at least was considered the norm by some Mpongwe.

During an interregnum, the throne was literally occupied by a sister or daughter of the old ruler. The duly elected king was informed of his good fortune a few days after the interment of his predecessor. He was then subjected to verbal and even physical abuse from all the people for a few hours until the actual coronation. Finally, the new

[1] William Walker Diary, iii, 12 June 1843, William Walker Papers, Box 2, State Historical Society of Wisconsin.

[2] Abbé Walker, *Notes*, p. 54.

[3] Wilson, *Western Africa: Its History, Condition, and Prospects* (New York, 1856), p. 276.

[4] Phyllis M. Martin, *The External Trade of the Loango Coast 1576–1870: The Effects of Changing Commercial Relations on the Vili Kingdom of Loango* (Oxford, 1972), p. 25.

[5] Archives d'Outre-Mer, Sénégal, iv, 39, c, 'Mémoire sur le lever à vue des environs du poste du Gabon', by Capt. Parent, 12 Oct. 1849.

king replaced the female relative of the old one on the throne. He had to stay on the throne and in the palace for five or six days, while the people came to congratulate him and to take part in the revelry going on around their seated sovereign. At length, the celebrations and ceremonies completed, the new ruler was free to go about his duties.[1]

The Mpongwe king, like many traditional African rulers, could not be seen drinking, as at that time he was vulnerable to the witchcraft of his enemies.[2] The king's house, larger than those of his subjects was unique in being built perpendicular to the street. He had a throne (*eka*) covered with white cloth, a royal bell (*nkendo*), and other emblems of power such as an ebony cane (*nkogu*), and a fly-switch (*elanga*) made from the tail of a buffalo or an elephant.[3]

Such royal insignia were more impressive than actual royal power. As a French admiral remarked of the Mpongwe kings, 'ils ne sont redoutable, ni redouté'.[4] Major decisions were made in meetings at which most or all free adult males were eligible to speak. Lesser questions, including judicial decisions, were decided by a council of elders or family heads. The king could theoretically veto any decision, but he in practice never did.[5] An influential and respected king like Denis could guide affairs, but could not rule against the opposition of the elders or the population at large. One of the few absolute powers enjoyed by a ruler was the granting of asylum. Persons guilty of murder or manslaughter could flee to the house of his own, or preferably another king, confess, mark his forehead with chalk, and then sit on the throne. He was then safe, presumably until his protector could arrange some sort of settlement with the victim's relatives.[6]

Mpongwe kings were often wealthy traders, although this was generally a qualification for attaining office rather than a consequence of it. It was customary to give the king a small present before open-

[1] Wilson, *Western Africa*, p. 276; Wm. Walker Diary, iii, 12 June 1843; Paul B. Du Chaillu, *Explorations and Adventures in Equatorial Africa* (New York, 1861), pp. 42-4. Similar ritual insults were practised by the Orungu (see next chapter) and the Apindji of central Gabon (Du Chaillu, *Explorations*, p. 496).

[2] Bowdich, *Mission*, p. 438; Wilson, *Western Africa*, p. 310.

[3] Abbé Walker, *Notes*, pp. 53-4.

[4] Archives d'Outre-Mer, Afrique, i, 5, 'Adm. Montaignès de la Roque to Ministère de la Marine', 25 Oct. 1846.

[5] Wilson, *Western Africa*, p. 273; Abbé Walker, *Notes*, p. 54.

[6] William Walker, 'Mpongwe Laws or Customs', unpublished MS., n. d., p. 4. William Walker Papers, Box 1.

ing trade at his town,[1] and the king got one-third of any 'dash' given
to speed up the loading of a ship.[2] However, any Mpongwe man could
deal with the Europeans without reference to the wishes of the king.
In 1818 the wealthiest trader in Gabon was said to be Tom Lawson
(or Larsen); he enjoyed 'as much, if not more influence than his
brother', King George.[3] At Glass, the trader Toko was wealthier
than the monarch; Europeans sometimes dealt with him immediately
on arrival, without even a courtesy call on King Glass.[4]

Although the Mpongwe were divided into several political communities, they had a strong sense of solidarity as a people. They were
in constant communication across the placid waters of the estuary
and their kings were generally on excellent terms.[5] Every August
there was a meeting of clan heads on Mbini Island.[6] The Mpongwe
regarded themselves as civilized men, far superior to the savage
peoples of the hinterland who had no contact with the Europeans.
Women from 'bush' tribes were acceptable as wives, but Mpongwe
women did not marry outside the tribe.[7] The interior peoples who
supplied the ivory, wood, and slaves were considered by the coastmen
as a barbaric and sometimes even cannibalistic lot, who were fortunate to have such sophisticated people as the Mpongwe to deal
with the Europeans for them.[8]

The institution of domestic slavery was highly developed by the
nineteenth century. Its origins are unknown. Probably the rise of trade
in the seventeenth century created a need for labourers to replace the
Mpongwe men, who increasingly became trade specialists. Slaves

[1] Louis Edouard Bouët-Willaumez, *Commerce et traite des noirs aux côtes
occidentales d'Afrique* (Paris, 1848), p. 153. A typical present for a king consisted
of two large and two small cloths, two bottles of 'eau-de-vie', and twenty-five
heads of tobacco.
[2] Wilson, *Western Africa*, p. 277. The usual dash was $20–30 in goods for load-
ing redwood and $60–90 for ivory. The remaining two-thirds were divided by the
elders.
[3] Bowdich, *Mission*, pp. 432, 436.   [4] Griswold to Anderson, 4 July 1842.
[5] Wm. Walker to Prudential Committee, 28 Dec. 1843.
[6] André Hauser, 'Notes sur les Omyene du Bas-Gabon', *Bulletin de l'Institut
français d'Afrique noire*, B, xvi (1954), p. 408. The exact purpose and proceedings
at these meetings are unknown.
[7] Except perhaps to the Orungu, with whom the Mpongwe were on excellent
terms and who were also a sophisticated coastal people. Wm. Walker, 'Mpongwe
Laws', p. 2.
[8] See for example, Marquis de Compiègne, *L'Afrique équatoriale: Gabonais,
Pahouins, Gallois* (Paris, 1875), p. 185.

were first obtained from the Dutch and, no doubt, from wars and purchases from interior peoples. The spread of the Atlantic slave trade to Gabon in the eighteenth century led to the opening of new sources of supply in the hinterland, as will be discussed in the next chapter. Those slaves not sold to Europeans could be used to meet local needs.

Little is known about domestic slavery among the Orungu, but the Mpongwe system has been fairly well described. Mpongwe society was divided into classes which were defined by the relative degrees of 'pure' Mpongwe and foreign ancestry. Du Chaillu described five groups.[1] Pure Mpongwe numbered only about 300, while the next most prestigious group, the descendants of Mpongwe men and their free Benga, Shekiani, or Bakalai wives were estimated at 800. Children of Mpongwe men and slave women, about 1,000 in all, were considered free, but the males could not marry Mpongwe women.[2] Children of slaves, also estimated at about 1,000, were also free among the Mpongwe, although a person with one slave grandparent was still counted a slave by the Orungu.[3] Du Chaillu estimated the number of slaves held by the Mpongwe at 3,000–4,000.

Slaves, like wives, were an important index of wealth. Some prominent Mpongwe owned twenty or even a hundred slaves.[4] Most European observers thought that slaves were generally well treated, although they had to do much of the hard work, such as farming, house-building, and the collection and transport of dyewood.[5] Slave women were often used as prostitutes.[6] Some of Denis's slaves lived in a farming village in the hinterland and were usually left alone as long as they supplied produce to their master.[7] Economically, slave labour freed Mpongwe men from farming and other tasks, allowing them to be full-time traders.

---

[1] Du Chaillu, *Explorations*, p. 41. These numbers are only guesses; the figure for 'pure' Mpongwe seems very low.

[2] Wm. Walker, 'Mpongwe Laws', p. 7.

[3] Hubert Deschamps, *Traditions orales et archives au Gabon* (Paris, 1962), p. 118.

[4] 'Letter of J. L. Wilson', *The Missionary Herald*, xxxix (1843), p. 233; 'De l'esclavage au Gabon', letter of R. P. LeBerre, 31 Oct. 1873, *Bulletin général de la Congrégation du Saint-Esprit*, ix, No. 92 (1873), p. 757.

[5] Lestrille, 'Note sur le comptoir du Gabon', *Revue coloniale* (Oct 1856), p. 440. Wilson on the other hand, accustomed as he was to the slave system of the American south, thought that Gabonese slaves did very little work ('Letter of J. L. Wilson', p. 233).

[6] Lestrille, 'Comptoir', p. 437; LeBerre, 'De l'esclavage', p. 759.

[7] Du Chaillu, *Explorations*, p. 165.

Slaves also filled social functions. Mpongwe marriage was by exchange. If a man wished to marry but had no eligible female relative to give in exchange, he could substitute a slave.[1] Slaves could also be given as fines in murder and bodily injury cases.[2] Some slaves were always sacrificed at the funeral of a king or other person of substance.[3]

Mpongwe slaves were not entirely powerless against their masters. Domestic slaves were rarely sold outside the tribe, and masters could not put slaves to death except in certain murder cases.[4] Slaves, like all people from faraway places, were thought to possess unusual magical powers. While slaves were more frequently condemned as witches than free people, their supposed supernatural powers acted as a check on the master. Mistreated slaves often fled into the nearby forest, occasionally in armed groups which successfully resisted attempts at recapture.[5] A few slaves were able to achieve wealth and prestige, including slave ownership, within the Mpongwe system. Although there was no provision for manumission,[6] slaves could hope for social and economic advancement, both for themselves and for their children.

The Mpongwe economy can be divided into 'indigenous' and 'European' sectors. The indigenous sector included food production, crafts, and local trade with other Africans; the European sector involved the procurement, transport, and sale of export commodities. In general, women and slaves were occupied with the former, while virtually all of the men devoted their efforts to commerce.

Agriculture had been enriched since the seventeenth century by the introduction of new crops from America. The men cleared the fields during the dry season, leaving the women and slaves to tend the plantations, which were often located several miles from the towns. The staple crops of cassava and plantains were supplemented by sweet potatoes, peanuts, maize, sugar-cane, pumpkins, peas, and beans. Goats and chickens were kept in large numbers. Fishing and hunting supplemented the protein supply,[7] while the people of Glass

---

[1] Wm. Walker, 'Mpongwe Laws', p. 1.   [2] Ibid., p. 3.
[3] Lestrille, 'Comptoir', p. 447.   [4] Wm. Walker, 'Mpongwe Laws', p. 3.
[5] 'Letter of J. L. Wilson', p. 233.
[6] Wm. Walker, 'Mpongwe Laws', p. 7.
[7] 'Letter of J. L. Wilson', p. 231; Du Chaillu, *Explorations*, p. 46; Archives de la Congrégation des Pères du Saint-Esprit, Boîte 167, vii, 1863, 'Rapport sur les cultures du Gabon', 16 Nov. 1863, by R. P. Le Berre.

netted sea turtles at Cape Santa Clara. Salt was made by boiling sea water.[1]

Trade goods supplied most of the Mpongwe demand for manufactured items. European cloth was in general use; cooking ware, furniture, alcohol, and many metal goods were all imported. Knives, spears, and mats were bought from the Bakalai for European goods.[2] Dyes were made from wood and from clay deposits located three days south of the river,[3] and there were a few local blacksmiths.

The major export commodities handled by the Mpongwe were slaves, dyewood, ebony, ivory, and rubber. Small amounts of beeswax and gum copal were exported from time to time. Except for some of the wood, these products were collected by the Shekiani, Bakalai, and, in later years, the Fang, all of whom dealt with the Europeans only through the Mpongwe.

Wax, gum, and ivory were collected in the forests, mostly by the Shekiani.[4] The Shekiani sold both wax and honey to the Mpongwe, who kept the honey and sold the wax.[5] Elephants no longer roamed the shores of the estuary, as they had in Bosman's time. Bakalai and Fang hunters supplied the Mpongwe with tusks, often from quite far inland. Mpongwe boatmen also bought ivory in the Rio Muni area and brought it back to the Gabon for resale to Europeans.[6]

Ebony was difficult to harvest. The trees grew in scattered stands of three or four on high ground, often far from any navigable waterway. Cutters had to roam the forest looking for trees large enough to cut, and then faced the difficult problem of getting the logs to a creek to float them down to the estuary.[7]

Dyewood, also known as redwood or barwood, grew near the creeks and swamps of the Gabon and Moondah. Much was cut in the north bank of the Gabon and then floated down to one of these rivers. As the useful dyestuff was concentrated in the heartwood, the surrounding layer of sapwood had to be carefully cut off. The wood then had to be cut into three-foot sticks weighing fifteen or twenty pounds each before being offered for sale.[8]

---

[1] Rev. Benjamin Griswold, 'Tour to Corisco', 6 June 1843, A.B.C. 15.1, vol. ii, No. 169; Abbé André Raponda Walker, 'Les Tribus du Gabon', *Bulletin de la Société des recherches congolaises*, No. 4 (1924), p. 70.

[2] Bowdich, *Mission*, p. 427.   [3] Ibid., pp. 440, 448.

[4] S. Aubry, 'Note sur le commerce du Gabon et de ses dépendances', *Revue coloniale*, xiii (1854), p. 469.

[5] 'Letter of J. L. Wilson', p. 231.   [6] Samuel Swan, 'Memoranda', p. 337.

[7] Du Chaillu, *Explorations*, pp. 323–4.   [8] Ibid., pp. 154–5.

Rubber exports began in 1853 and within two years had become one of the major exports from the Gabon.[1] The Mpongwe had used rubber for drum heads and balls long before they became aware of its commercial possibilities.[2] J. L. Wilson, one of the American missionaries, was quick to realize the potential value of Gabonese rubber and the trade was developed by another American, Captain Richard E. Lawlin.[3] Africans gathered latex from vines growing in the forest, hardened it in wooden cylinders, and brought it to the coast for sale.[4]

In addition to buying goods in the hinterland, tradesmen range the coasts for saleable items. Mpongwe seamanship had not declined since the seventeenth-century expedition to Cameroun. The canoes, sixty-foot vessels capable of carrying eight or ten tons of cargo, were often equipped with masts and sails copied from European models. They were made from the trunk of a special type of tree which generally grew several miles inland. After cutting the tree, the boat-builder burned out a hollow in the log and shaped it with an adze. A path for the prepared hull had to be cut through the forest. Rollers were placed in front of the canoe at two-foot intervals to facilitate its progress toward the sea.[5] In these boats the Mpongwe sailed the coast from Cape St. Catherine in the south to Batanga, on the Cameroun coast, in the north; buying ivory and redwood in small lots, and bringing it back for sale to the Europeans.[6]

Goods produced in the interior usually passed through several

[1] Archives d'Outre-Mer, Sénégal, iv, 40, c, 'Rapport sur la situation au Gabon pendant le 1ère trimestre 1853', 3 July 1853; Archives d'Outre-Mer, Gorée, iv, 3, b, 'Rapport pour 1ère trimestre 1855', 1 Apr. 1855.

[2] Bowdich, *Mission*, p. 446.

[3] Wilson, *Western Africa*, p. 245; Captain Vignon, 'Le Comptoir français du Gabon sur la côte occidentale d'Afrique', *Nouvelles Annales des voyages*, iv (1856), p. 286.   [4] Du Chaillu, *Explorations*, pp. 155-7.

[5] Ibid., pp. 39, 167. Boats with sails were significantly called 'santomés' (J. Ambouroué Avaro, 'Le Bas-Ogowé au dix-neuvième siècle', unpublished doctoral dissertation, University of Paris, Sorbonne, 1969, p. 225). The use of rollers may have been a recent innovation. Boteler said that unfinished canoes had to be carried to the shore by as many as 100 people (*Narrative*, ii, p. 397). On the other hand, Robert Smith believes that the use of rollers was a traditional technique in Yorubaland ('The Canoe in West African History', *Journal of African History*, xi, 4 (1970), p. 520; and personal communication). In this letter, Smith raises the inevitable question; if rollers were used, why was the wheel unknown?

[6] Du Chaillu, *Explorations*, p. 39; J. L. Wilson to Rufus Anderson, June 1847, A.B.C. 15.1, vol. iii, No. 469; Wilson, *Western Africa*, p. 297. See also n. 6, p. 59 above.

hands before reaching a ship's hold in the estuary. Each group tried to control the access to the Europeans and their goods to everyone further inland. Thus the Mpongwe permitted nobody else to deal directly with the whites, but they in turn were not allowed far into the hinterland. For example, the major ivory suppliers on the Como were Fang. They sold ivory to the Bakalai, who in turn passed this ivory, plus the fruits of their own hunting, on to the Shekiani. The Shekiani traded these tusks, along with their own production, to Mpongwe traders, who sold it to a ship in the river.[1] The ethnic groups did not function as a trading block; several Shekiani or Bakalai might have been involved in the chain. Each group protected its middleman position by force and by guile. The Mpongwe, for example, told grisly tales about the 'bush' people to the Europeans, and vice versa.[2]

Naturally, each tier of middlemen took a cut of the profits. A French officer estimated that the Mpongwe kept one-half of the goods paid for a tusk and passed the rest on to the Shekiani. They and the Bakalai each got a share, leaving a rather meagre reward for the Fang hunter.[3] Goods which changed hands four times generally went up about six times in price.[4]

Trading was further complicated by the widespread use of credit. If the Fang hunter had sold his tusk on 'trust', as he often had to, endless delays and disputes might ensue. Even given good faith on all sides, the absence of records, transport problems, losses due to climate or warfare, and fluctuations in the quality and quantity of trade goods obtainable from the Europeans all could and did cause disputes. Traders of course tried to establish good relations with their customers and suppliers, but these often broke down. Some, like Toko of Glass, relied on personal reputation.[5] Many Mpongwe contracted marriages with foreign women to create or solidify trade connections.[6] King Duka's people all spoke Bakalai and cultivated relations with the Bakalai living south-east of the Gabon.[7]

[1] Lt. Pigeard, 'Exploration du Gabon, effectuée en août et septembre 1846', *Revue coloniale* (1847), pp. 275, 278.

[2] Du Chaillu, *Explorations*, p. 27; Griffon du Bellay, 'Le Gabon', *Le Tour du monde*, xii (1865), p. 285.

[3] Aubry, 'Commerce du Gabon', p. 468.

[4] Archives Cong. St. Esp., Boîte 172, ii, Derano to his brother, 21 Feb. 1850.

[5] 'Letter of J. L. Wilson', p. 234.

[6] Wm. Walker Diary, ii, 13 Feb. 1843.

[7] 'Letter of William Walker, February 18, 1844', *The Missionary Herald*, xl (1844), p. 248.

Creditors often attempted to speed up payment of debts by seizing a relative, slave, or even an unrelated townsman of the debtor.[1] This generally forced a settlement or led to a war. Gabonese wars, while short, localized, and not particularly deadly by European standards,[2] did take a toll in life, property, and trade disruption.

Trading vessels came to the Gabon from a number of countries. Spanish and Portuguese slavers were active, especially at Denis. A few French and American merchantmen called, but the bulk of the 'legitimate' trade was in the hands of the British. There was a tendency for English and American vessels to trade at Quaben (which had the advantage of being closest to the open sea) and Glass, while the French, Spanish, and Portuguese were more active on the south bank, but there were many exceptions to this generalization.[3]

As soon as a ship had anchored, it was besieged by Mpongwe anxious to become the captain's 'trademan'. Each candidate had 'books', or letters of recommendation from previous captains.[4] According to one American sailor, most of these books reflected little credit on their bearers. 'Nearly all of them cautioned other Captains from trusting them. . . . [the books] said they would rob if the opportunity offered them.' The captain selected one or more of the applicants as his agent and dismissed the others with a glass of rum.[5] The ship was not considered the 'property' of the village where it anchored; tradesmen from other villages were free to compete for its business.[6]

Mpongwe traders worked independently or with informal agreements with colleagues; there was no organization comparable to the 'house' system of the Niger Delta. Although kings and 'princes' were sometimes given small presents before trade was opened, and were dashed for a quick loading job, trade was not subject to governmental control or taxation. The king and his relatives generally were, however, prominent traders with many good 'books'.

Since the arrival of a ship was such an important, but apparently

1 Wm. Walker, 'Mpongwe Laws', p. 6.

2 Boteler, *Narrative*, ii, p. 384; Bushnell to Anderson, 24 May 1851, A.B.C. 15.1, vol. iii, No. 79.

3 Boteler, *Narrative*, ii, p. 394; 'Letter of J. L. Wilson', p. 231.

4 A sample 'book' is given in the 'Journal of the Brig *Neptune*', 21 Mar. 1841 entry, Peabody Museum.

5 John R. Congdon, 'Private Journal Kept on the Bark *Montgomery* of Providence, R.I., 28 August 1846–9 June 1847', entry for 27 Dec. 1846, p. 125. MS., Rhode Island Historical Society.   6 Boteler, *Narrative*, ii, pp. 379–81.

capricious event, it is not surprising that the Mpongwe often sought to lure vessels and to thwart their competitors by supernatural means. A brother of King Glass once spent eighty dollars for a powerful fetish from Corisco which was guaranteed to attract ships;[1] Toko of Glass had a man drowned for using witchcraft to drive ships away from trade rivals.[2]

Most trade with Europeans in the Gabon was, as in West Africa generally, conducted on a credit basis. As there seldom were sufficient quantities of wood or ivory on hand to load a ship, the Mpongwe middlemen had to be 'trusted' with enough goods to secure a cargo. These advances were sometimes worth as much as $4,000.[3] While the ship waited at anchor, the tradesmen used goods, credit, or a combination of both to buy products from their suppliers. They often used mnemonic devices such as notches on a piece of wood to help keep track of the complex transactions.[4] It usually took several weeks to complete a cargo and for the captain and his trademan or trademen to reach agreement over prices.[5]

The trust system, generally deplored by European observers, was quite advantageous to the Mpongwe. The pledging of pawns as security for trust goods was still demanded by slave ships and some legitimate traders as late as 1810, the pawns generally being the children of prominent Mpongwe.[6] However, this custom was soon ended and the African merchants then had the opportunity to abscond with the trusted goods, a practice by no means unknown. More importantly, the Mpongwe were well aware that in any transaction, time was on their side. Time spent at anchor was money lost for the Europeans, who also had to contend with malaria and other deadly tropical diseases. Some ships were loaded quickly,[7] but presents

[1] Wm. Walker Diary, ii, 28 Dec. 1842.

[2] Ibid., ix, 1 Aug. 1858. Two Mpongwe trade 'medicines' are described in Robert H. Nassau, *Fetishism in West Africa: Forty Years' Observation of Native Customs and Superstitions* (New York, 1904), pp. 181–2.

[3] 'Letter of J. L. Wilson', p. 231.

[4] A missionary described a system of marking tusks by weight. A vertical line indicated ten pounds; a horizontal mark stood for one pound. Hence a sixty-three pound tusk was marked ||||||≡. (Griswold to Anderson, 4 July 1842.) Boteler (*Narrative*, ii, p. 396) described the use of notches on a piece of wood as a device to help remember the value equivalents of different kinds of goods.

[5] Samuel Swan, 'Memoranda', pp. 337–9, describes trade etiquette as of *c.* 1810. See also Du Chaillu, *Explorations*, pp. 35–8; Bouët-Williaumez, *Commerce et traite*, pp. 152, 155–6.   [6] Samuel Swan, 'Memoranda', p. 338.

[7] The *Neptune* loaded 100 tons of dyewood bought on trust in only twelve days ('Journal of the Brig *Neptune*', 6 June 1841).

were often solicited to speed up the flow of goods from the interior and, as Bosman had found in 1698, the Mpongwe were in no hurry to come to a final price settlement.

European merchants tried to counter the trust system in various ways. Perhaps the most common was simply to establish a good and continuing relationship with an honest and efficient Mpongwe trader such as Denis, Glass, or Toko.[1] Some captains made trust arrangements in Gabon and then left to trade elsewhere until the goods were assembled. Since wood was cheap at Corisco, the Muni, and the Moondah, it was common to pick up an Mpongwe pilot who knew these treacherous waters, and make the short trip north.[2] Other ships made coasting voyages north to Cameroun, stopping at villages along the way for small transactions.[3] English merchants with established trade connections often left an advance and returned on a later voyage to complete the transaction and to leave a new advance. An alternative plan was to arrange for another vessel of the same company to pay for and collect the cargo.[4] By the 1840s, legitimate merchants were beginning to follow a tactic pioneered by the slave dealers of northern Gabon. The slavers, faced with the necessity of loading cargoes quickly to avoid the naval patrols, erected barracoons on the coast where they bargained for and stored slaves. Ships could simply anchor and load up, without waiting for slaves to be assembled and purchased. However, since the factory system, while certainly no novelty elsewhere in West Africa,[5] did not reach Gabon until the eve of the colonial era, it will be discussed in a later chapter.

Despite a post-1815 slump in dyewood prices,[6] the Mpongwe enjoyed considerable prosperity in the first half of the nineteenth century. The demand for ivory remained high and, as will be shown in the next chapter, the slave trade flourished into the 1840s. The river was almost never empty of ships seeking slaves, wood, or the highly regarded Gabonese ivory.[7]

---

[1] Archives d'Outre-Mer, Sénégal, iii, 5, b, 'Esquisse commerciale de la côte occidentale d'Afrique', 6 May 1839, by M. Broquant, p. 87.

[2] Bouët-Willaumez, Commerce et traite, p. 154.

[3] 'Log of the Bark Reaper', 3-31 Dec. 1843. Essex Institute.

[4] Broquant, 'Esquisse commerciale', p. 91.

[5] e.g., the Gold Coast. The relative advantages of 'ship-trade' and 'factory-trade' in Senegambia are discussed in K. G. Davies, The Royal African Company London, 1957), pp. 216-18.

[6] Boteler, Narrative, ii, p. 394.

[7] Bowdich, Mission, p. 452; 'Letter of J. L. Wilson', The Missionary Herald, xxxix (1843), p. 157; Bouët-Williaumez, Commerce et traite, p. 151.

These eagerly-awaited vessels brought a large variety of manufactured goods to the Gabonese. The Mpongwe sold wood and ivory for an assortment of goods, called a bundle by the English and a *paquet* by the French. In 1826, Boteler saw an English trader buy two tusks totalling 130 pounds for a bundle made up of 4 muskets, 2 neptunes (shallow brass basins), 2 iron kettles, 4 pieces of cloth, some nails, assorted fish-hooks, pottery beads, copper bars, and one jar of rum[1]. A few years later the price of ivory had risen considerably. For 100 pounds of ivory, the following *paquet* was suggested as an example for French merchants: 8 large and 8 small cloths, 7 neptunes, 7 kettles, 8 basins, 20 pots, 7 guns, 20 iron bars, 20 copper bars, 2 storage chests, 4 small metal barrels, 2 fine hats, 2 trade hats, 2 vests, 2 cotton umbrellas, 4 wheelbarrows, 2 lead bars, a 20 pound barrel of gunpowder, 2 fathoms of red cloth, 8 knives, 4 padlocks, 4 snuffboxes, 4 mirrors, 20 heads of tobacco, 20 pipes, 4 razors, 4 scissors, 4 tinder-boxes, 4 'demimasses' of glass beads, 4 large and 6 small bells, 4 machettes, 20 gun flints, and 4 bonnets.[2]

One hundred sticks of dyewood (about 1,500 kg) was worth much less; most of the same items were included, but in lesser quantities. No guns, kettles, or neptunes were recommended to French traders, but a spoon, fork, 2 plates, 2 glasses, and a red sash were suggested. A hundred sticks of ebony (about 1,200 kg) cost twice as much as dyewood.[3] In 1854, wax sold for about 2 francs a kilo, rubber for half that, and gum copal for 5 francs per 12·5 kg; all paid in goods.[4]

The use of the assorted bundle of goods helped insure that both the coastal people and the interior middlemen and producers received a wide range of manufactured goods, rather than a glut of, say, hats or cauldrons. A bundle could be easily divided into smaller but still balanced assortments to be passed along to the next link in the commercial chain.

Despite widespread conceptions to the contrary, a glance at the above lists shows that Mpongwe, like most other Africans, imported some very useful merchandise.[5] Metal containers were still as superior

[1] Boteler, *Narrative*, ii, p. 395.

[2] Bouët-Willaumez, *Commerce et traite*, p. 154. Broquant ('Esquisse commerciale', p. 89) gives a very similar *paquet*.

[3] Bouët-Willaumez, *Commerce et traite*, p. 154; Broquant, 'Esquisse commerciale', pp. 89–90.   [4] Aubry, 'Commerce du Gabon', pp. 468–9.

[5] Basil Davidson, *The African Slave Trade: Pre-Colonial History 1450–1850* (Boston, 1961), pp. 278–82. Whether or not these goods were fair compensation for African products and people is of course another question.

to pottery kitchenware as imported cloth was to indigenous bark cloth, which had been replaced by Benin and Yoruba cloth imported by European traders, and later by cloth of European manufacture.[1] Guns and knives could be put to productive use; metal bars were used to make tools as well as arm and leg rings for Mpongwe ladies of fashion.[2] The Mpongwe, like all consumers, did buy non-productive and apparently frivolous items such as beads and mirrors. While such purchases did not contribute to African economic progress, they did help make life easier and more interesting. It is hard to begrudge the Mpongwe merchant a relaxing glass of rum or the pleasure of his favourite pipe after a long day's bargaining in the equatorial sun.

The Gabonese trading system, while perhaps not very elegant, did work. Despite the complaints of European observers,[3] a constant flow of goods emerged from the forest. Wars might disrupt trade in one area, but this was only a temporary obstacle and goods could still come in from unaffected regions. All parties were victimized on occasion by the trust system, but all profited enough to keep using it. A simpler and more economically efficient trade network might well have increased the volume of trade at least temporarily; but, since elephants and dyewood trees were exhaustible commodities, too great a volume would be damaging in the long run.[4]

Mpongwe traders, like other nineteenth-century African middle-men, were regarded by most Europeans as economic parasites who stood uselessly between them and the producers. In Gabon, as elsewhere in western Africa, European traders were anxious to cut out the middlemen and get into direct commercial contact with the supposedly wealthy interior. However, the African middleman did perform valuable economic functions. He brought goods from the interior, assembled them into large enough lots to interest a European buyer, and started the flow of manufactured goods back into the hinterland, at a time when Europeans were unable or unwilling to venture inland. To be sure, he kept as much as possible for himself; but, being a full-time trading specialist, he knew how to extract the

[1] Samuel Swan ('Memoranda', pp. 316, 334) recommended that 'Jebboe' (Ijebu Yoruba) cloths be purchased at Lagos for the Gabon market, 'particularly the large ones, with the large blue stripes of a bright colour'. These cloths could also be sold at the Portuguese islands, mostly for re-export to Gabon.
[2] 'Letter of J. L. Wilson', p. 232.
[3] Du Chaillu, *Explorations*, pp. 34–5; Pigeard, 'Exploration du Gabon', p. 289.
[4] Bellay, 'Le Gabon', p. 278.

highest possible prices from the Europeans. His bargaining talents helped bring higher profits to the intermediate middlemen as well as to the producers.

Mpongwe and Orungu middlemen were able to meet European demands for African products until after the mid-nineteenth century. Then, when European traders broke through to the interior and began to set up factories there, colonial rule followed right behind, just as it did in Senegal, Nigeria, and points between.

Any description of the Mpongwe in the nineteenth century would be very incomplete without a discussion of the slave trade. However, as the Mpongwe slave trade was closely connected to the more extensive traffic at Cape Lopez, this topic will be treated as a unit in the next chapter.

CHAPTER IV

The Orungu Kingdom and the Northern Gabon Slave Trade to *c*. 1860

DOCUMENTATION on the Orungu kingdom is much less adequate than that on the Mpongwe. Most European visitors to the Cape Lopez area were involved in the clandestine slave trade and of course did not wish to draw attention to their activities. This, together with the fact that colonial rule and missionary activity began much later in the Cape Lopez region than in the Gabon estuary, means that less is known about the Orungu in nineteenth century. This is especially regrettable since the Orungu had the only real state on the entire coast between the Cameroun River and the northern marches of the Loango kingdom at Mayumba and Sette-Cama. Since the Orungu were the major slave exporters in this region, the whole northern Gabon slave trade will be discussed in this chapter, together with what can be discerned about Orungu history from *c*. 1790, when Reombi-Mpolo's reign marked the increasing centralization of the Orungu state, to the death of King Ombango-Rogombe about 1860.

The royal dynasty of the Orungu provides a convenient chronological framework and political focus for their history. As was discussed in chapter two, this dynasty began *c*. 1700 with Ndongo's conquest of the coast. Almost nothing is known about the individual rulers or internal Orungu developments until about 1790. Orungu kings are listed in Table IV.

Ngwerangui-Wono, the fifth ruler, had selected his son Reombi to succeed him, but Ndombe usurped the throne. Ndombe, aided by two other brothers, had to fight a civil war against Reombi. Apparently because of Ndombe's belligerent behaviour towards them, some Spanish and Portuguese slave dealers eventually took Reombi's side. Ndombe and his two loyal brothers were soon captured and sold to the Spaniards, who carried them off as slaves.[1]

---

[1] Abbé Walker, *Notes*, p. 72.

TABLE IV

Orungu Monarchs[a]

King	Relation to predecessors	Dates
1. Ndongo or Retondogo	—	c. 1700
2. Ndebulia-Mburu	Son of 1	
3. Re-Ndjangue-Ndongo	Brother of 2	
4. Re-Nkondje	Nephew of 3, son of 2	
5. Ngwerangui-Wono	Brother of 4	
6. Ndombe	Son of 5	
7. Reombi-Mpolo	Son of 5, brother of 6	c. 1790–c. 1802/4[b]
8. Ogoul' Issogoue (Rogombe, Passol)	Son of 7	c. 1802/4–c. 1840
9. Ombango-Rogombe (Passall, Pascal, Ikinda)	Son of 8	c. 1840–c. 1860
10. Ndebulia-Rogombe	Brother of 9	c. 1860–c. 1865[c]
11. Ntchegue	Brother of 9 and 10	c. 1865– (in office 1882)

[a] Data from Abbé André Raponda Walker, *Notes d'histoire du Gabon* (Brazzaville, 1960), pp. 71–5; and Hubert Deschamps, *Traditions orales et archives au Gabon* (Paris, 1962), p. 116; except as noted.

[b] Abbé Walker, *Notes*, pp. 72–3, gives 1790–1810; but, as will be shown below, his successor was in power by 1805.

[c] Archives d'Outre-Mer, Gabon, i, 6. d. Aube to de Langle, 21 Dec., 1866.

Thus, after several years of turmoil, Reombi, surnamed Mpolo, 'the Great', gained the throne about 1790. He moved his residence to Apomande Island, on the left bank of the Nazareth, because it was a convenient place for the traders, and is said to have governed wisely and successfully. During his reign the position of the Orungu monarchy was greatly strengthened. The king was no longer a relatively weak figure presiding over a group of clans, but a powerful and often despotic ruler who controlled and grew wealthy on the growing maritime trade. As was described in a preceding chapter, Reombi opened commercial relations with the Portuguese islands.

The 1800 letter signed 'Liumba Pasol' was obviously sent by Reombi with the aid of a literate merchant.[1]

Reombi was succeeded, perhaps with Spanish aid,[2] between this date and 1805 by his son Ogoul 'Issogoue, who was later better known as Rogombe or Passol. This ruler was the 'Gula' whose son was kidnapped in 1805 by an island merchant.[3] Ogoul 'Issogoue was said to be a powerful and tyrannical ruler who, in contrast to his predecessor, took part in many wars.[4]

The Orungu at this time had to face the competition of the Nkomi, who lived south of Cape Lopez near the Fernan Vaz lagoon and were beginning to develop a centralized form of kingship. The Nkomi were apparently a group of Ashogo and Apindji clans who had become 'Omyene-ized' on the lower Ogowe, in the same manner as the Galoa, Enenga, and the Orungu.[5] They probably reached the coast c. 1780–1800 and settled in the region between Cape Lopez and Cape St. Catherine.[6] Trade rivalries soon triggered off a series of wars between the Orungu and Nkomi. In 1805 a chief Petiquinbe wrote to the Governor of São Tomé asking for trade and assistance against 'the thief Gulla', who had forced him to leave his old village of 'Sarame' and move to the San Mexias mouth of the Ogowe.[7]

[1] Archivo Nacional da Torre do Tombo, Junta do Comercio, maço 20, 'Liumba Pasol to Governor of São Tomé', 9 Dec. 1800. The liquid consonants *L* and *R* were often confused by Europeans recording words from Bantu languages. 'Passol', a common praise name for kings in the whole Gabon area, is from the English 'pass-all'. Reombi's power surpassed all others in the area. See J. Ambouroué Avaro, 'Le Bas-Ogowé au dix-neuvième siècle', unpublished doctoral dissertation (University of Paris, Sorbonne, 1969), pp. 105, 246, 253, for the role of Reombi in political centralization.

[2] Abbé André Raponda Walker and Robert Reynard, 'Anglais, Espagnols et Nord-Américains au Gabon au XIXᵉ siècle', *Bulletin de l'Institut des études centrafricaines*, xii (1956), p. 255.

[3] See ch. II. T. E. Bowdich referred to this ruler as 'King Ogoola or Passall' in *Mission from Cape Coast Castle to Ashantee* (3r ed., London, 1966), p. 431.

[4] Abbé Walker, *Notes*, p. 73.

[5] Avaro, 'Bas-Ogowé', p. 341. The incipient Nkomi state had fragmented by 1840. See also Abbé André Raponda Walker, 'Les Tribus du Gabon', *Bulletin de la Société des recherches congolaises*, iv (1924), p. 71, n. 2.

[6] On the Nkomi, see Auguste Forêt, 'Le Fernan-Vaz', *Bulletin de la Société de géographie*, xix (1898), p. 308; the Rev. J. L. Wilson's account in *The Missionary Herald*, xliii (1847), p. 258; and the Rev. Albert Bushnell's description, ibid., xlvii (1851), p. 145. Avaro ('Bas-Ogowé', p. 312) believes that the Nkomi reached the coast about 1650 and are probably of the same stock which gave rise to the other Omyene-speaking peoples.

[7] Archivo Histórico Ultramarino, São Tomé, caixa 15, folder 37, 'Petiquinbe to Lisboa', 15 Dec. 1805; and ibid., 'Report on Petiquinbe', 24 Dec. 1805.

Petiquinbe may possibly have been a dissident Orungu chief, but this episode was more likely an early event in the Orungu–Nkomi encounter. After several years of intermittent struggle, the Orungu emerged completely victorious.[1] The traditional naval war in which the Orungu routed a Benga fleet from the Corisco area may also have taken place about this time.[2]

'King Passol' was visited in January 1826 by British officers making a survey of the African coast. One of these men, Lieutenant Thomas Boteler, has left a valuable description. The Orungu capital, a sprawling and sandy place, was still at Apomande Island. An Orungu official, who called himself the Duke, led the English party to Passol's residence.[3] This structure was an impressive two-storey building, about fifty feet long and twenty feet wide, built of fir planks imported from England. Each storey was divided into two large and two small rooms. The walls were hung with mirrors, prints, and watercolours, and the king had a number of 'antediluvian' English chairs. The royal residence had been built by a local carpenter who had carefully studied the construction of the European ships he had visited.[4]

The king himself was described as 'a tall, muscular, ugly-looking black, apparently about fifty years of age, but his appearance by no means indicated that ferocity of disposition which report said he indulged in, much to the detriment of his subjects' heads'. King Passol understood French and English but spoke through an interpreter. Refreshments were served and the king urged the officers to tell the English to come for trade.[5]

Orungu prosperity in the nineteenth century was almost entirely based on the slave trade, which will be discussed later in this chapter. However, items of 'legitimate commerce' were also traded. Captain Swan wrote about 1810 that 'Cape Lopaz and River Nazareth' were

said by some to be the first places in Africa for procuring large quantities of wax, small ivory and sea horse [hippopotamus] teeth, not being much frequented by ships. The King, who calls himself Passall, will teaze [sic]

---

[1] Deschamps, *Traditions*, p. 73.   [2] Abbé Walker, *Notes*, p. 97.
[3] Thomas Boteler, *Narrative of a Voyage of Discovery to Africa and Arabia, Performed in His Majesty's Ships, Leven and Barracouta, from 1821 to 1826, Under the Command of Captain F. W. Owen, R.N.* (London, 1835), ii, p. 365. Extensive quotes from Boteler's account of Cape Lopez are given in W. F. W. Owen, *Narrative of Voyages to Explore the Shores of Africa, Arabia, and Madagascar* (London, 1833; reprinted 1968), ii, pp. 301–9.
[4] Boteler, *Narrative*, ii, pp. 368–9.   [5] Ibid., p. 366.

for presents; it is best to make a friend of him and you may go ashore at
his town in safety. The country is healthy and pleasant. Trade Goods are
Cloth, Dominie and mock coral beads, Hats, caps, plates, mugs, knives,
razors etc., in short all small articles. Iron bars, neptunes, kettles and guns
are not much required.[1]

As was discussed in chapter three, Portuguese traders bought wax
and ivory at Cape Lopez, as well as slaves. In 1826 King Passol
assured his naval visitors that he could supply large quantities of
ivory, dyewood, ebony, gum-copal, and wax. A few British vessels
came for these articles even before the naval visit. Lieutenant Boteler
met a fourteen-year-old English boy at Cape Lopez who had jumped
ship there because of harsh treatment. He was thoroughly Orungu-
ized and refused to go home.[2] The Liverpool firm of Horsfall and
Tobin had 'a very promising trade at Cape Lopez' by 1831. However,
a British naval attack against some Spanish pirates who had sought
asylum among the Orungu so angered King Passol that he barred
all English traders.[3]

King Ogoul 'Issogoue was succeeded about 1840 by his son
Ombango-Rogombe, also known as Passol, Pascal, and, because
of his reputed generosity, Ikinda or 'bountiful table'. Ombango
had to defeat his brothers, who also aspired to the throne; he was
able to do this with support from the Spanish slavers who operated
the Cape Lopez barracoons.[4]

The new Orungu monarch had an unusual background, which in
some ways prepared him for his position as leader of a tribe of middlemen in the slave trade. He had been to Brazil, and was probably the
son of 'Gula' taken to Maranhão in 1805. He had also spent two
years in Lisbon, where he learned to speak and read Portuguese.[5]

[1]'Captain Samuel Swan's Memoranda on the African Trade', MS. Library of
Congress, dated c. 1810, published in George E. Brooks, Jr., *Yankee Traders,
Old Coasters and African Middlemen: A History of American Legitimate Trade
in West Africa in the Nineteenth Century* (Boston, 1970), p. 339.

[2] Boteler, *Narrative*, ii, p. 370.

[3] Parliamentary Papers, Commons, 1847–8, xxii, Third Report of the Select
Committee on the Slave Trade, p. 112, Testimony of Thomas Tobin. Christopher
Lloyd described a dramatic attack on some Spanish pirates and the Orungu who
were sheltering them, but says this happened in 1833. Some of the pirates were
captured and the Orungu town was destroyed after a long see-saw struggle.
Lloyd, *The Navy and the Slave Trade: The Suppression of the African Slave Trade
in the Nineteenth Century* (London, 1949), pp. 64–7.

[4] Abbé Walker, *Notes*, p. 74.

[5] Paul B. Du Chaillu, *Explorations and Adventures in Equatorial Africa* (New
York, 1861), p. 174. See also ch. II. Du Chaillu erroneously states (p. 218) that
Ombango was the brother of his predecessor.

Business contacts had given him some command of French and Spanish.[1]

Ombango's position as ruler of the Orungu was made increasingly difficult by the vagaries of the slave trade. Fluctuations in the supply of slaves from up the Ogowe and from the Gabon area were normal hazards, but the great reduction of Brazilian imports after 1850 and the persistent efforts of the naval patrols hurt the Orungu position as the major slave dealers between the Cameroun River and Loango. Profits were still to be made, but lean years became increasingly numerous during Ombango's reign.

Ombango was constantly harried by the British cruisers which regularly patrolled the Cape Lopez region. The Orungu capital had been moved to Sangatanga, on the coast north of the Nazareth, because the shallow offshore waters and winding channels prevented surprise raids by the Royal Navy. However, the town was still bombarded several times, forcing the Orungu to disperse their houses and farms over a wide area.[2] Commander Hall tried to get an anti-slavery treaty from the Orungu in 1851, but was rebuffed. Ombango, well aware of his precarious economic situation, hinted he might reconsider after two or three British merchant ships had come for ivory, dyewood, and other local products.[3] However, under continued pressure, Ombango did sign a treaty on 2 February 1853 and offered to sell ivory, gum, bees-wax, India rubber, ebony, dyewood, tortoise shell, and copper.[4]

Needless to say, this treaty was not honoured by the Orungu. The Reverends William Walker and Ira Preston of the Protestant mission station at Gabon visited Sangatanga in late August and early September of 1854, and were shown both the treaty and a collection of slaves awaiting shipment.[5] Ombango apparently had suffered a stroke shortly before the missionaries' arrival. The king had just returned with one hundred men from an attack against a rival, his brother, whom he thought had poisoned him.[6] The matter was

---

[1] Abbé Walker, *Notes*, p. 74.

[2] Du Chaillu, *Explorations*, p. 177.

[3] Parliamentary Papers, Lords, 1852–3, xxii, Class A, p. 266, No. 169, encl. 1, 'Commander Hall to Commodore Fanshawe', 11 June 1851.

[4] Parliamentary Papers, Commons, 1854, lxxiii, Class A, p. 154, No. 113, 'Rear Admiral Bruce to Secretary of the Admiralty', 29 Mar. 1853; encls. 1 and 2.

[5] William Walker and Ira Preston, 'Visit of Messrs. Walker and Preston to the River Nazareth', *The Missionary Herald*, li (1855), p. 35.

[6] Ibid., p. 33. Du Chaillu, *Explorations*, p. 175, states that Ombango was paralysed on his left side.

temporarily resolved, but the brother, Nchouga, was later defeated and forced to flee to Fernan Vaz and seek asylum among the Nkomi.[1]

The Franco-American traveller and raconteur Paul Du Chaillu visited Sangatanga in 1856 and found the partially paralysed monarch in low spirits despite his victory in the civil war. The two barracoons were full and Du Chaillu saw one ship being loaded, but Ombango complained that British patrols had hurt business and that the future outlook was very unfavourable. Nonetheless, Sangatanga, or at least its ruler, seemed quite prosperous. The king still lived in a two-storey palace, although Du Chaillu thought it was 'an ugly hole of a house'.[2] The Mafouga[3] led Du Chaillu to this residence, which was surrounded by the homes of several hundred wives and slaves of the king. Ombango possessed a sofa and a valuable golden crown presented by a Rio de Janeiro slaving firm. Most of his wives were dressed in silk, and rum, extorted as 'presents' from the Portuguese factors, seemed plentiful.[4]

Sangatanga was the largest Orungu town at this time. It actually consisted of many villages scattered around the king's village, which stood on a hill two miles from the sea and English firepower. The old capital site at 'Olibatta' was occupied by a prosperous fishing village.[5] Many people went from Sangatanga to Cape Lopez every dry season to catch fish and turtles and to make salt by boiling sea water.[6] Orungu power on the Ogowe extended about eighty miles upstream to Orovy and Ashouka.[7]

Ombango died about 1860, leaving his two brothers to contest the throne. The winner, Ndebulia, inherited an increasingly impoverished kingdom. The slave trade was sputtering to a close, and the early French voyages up the Ogowe challenged the Orungu control of the river mouth. Ndebulia, who abandoned Sangatanga and moved the

---

[1] Du Chaillu, *Explorations*, pp. 225–6.

[2] Ibid., p. 174. Du Chaillu's career is described in K. David Patterson, 'Paul B. Du Chaillu and the Exploration of Gabon, 1855–1865', to appear in 1974 in the *International Journal of African Historical Studies*.

[3] Evidently the successor of the 'Duke' encountered thirty years previously by Boteler. The title was originally used in Loango for the official in charge of European affairs, but it had spread widely by the early nineteenth century. Phyllis Martin, 'The Trade of Loango in the Seventeenth and Eighteenth Centuries', in Richard Gray and David Birmingham, eds., *Pre-Colonial African Trade: Essays on Trade in Central and Eastern Africa before 1900* (London, 1970), p. 160.

[4] Du Chaillu, *Explorations*, pp. 172–7.

[5] Ibid., p. 173.   [6] Ibid., pp. 216–17, 219.

[7] Abbé Walker, *Notes*, p. 72; Wm. Walker and Preston, 'Visit', p. 35.

capital back to the Ogowe delta, was forced to agree to a treaty ceding sovereignty to France in 1862.[1] Although the treaty was not enforced for several years, the Orungu were already in full decline.

The economic activities of the Orungu centred around the slave trade, which was their major source of wealth. Control of trade, especially the slave trade, was the basis of the king's power. Orungu kingship was very different from the institution prevailing in the Gabon. All Orungu were under the authority of one ruler, who, in striking contrast to the Mpongwe kings, had great political and economic strength. Indeed, Ogoul 'Issogoue (Rogombe) and Ombango were described as despots of a rather fearsome nature.[2]

As among the Mpongwe, royal succession generally passed to the deceased king's eldest brother, and, if there were no eligible brothers, to the ruler's son. The new monarch was supposedly elected by the heads of the twenty or so clans, although on occasion the old king seems to have had some influence on the choice of his successor. Civil wars among the contenders for power were the rule rather than the exception, at least by the late eighteenth century, and intervention by European slavers was sometimes decisive. The new king, however he was selected, had to sail up the Ogowe where the people ritually seized him, placed him on the throne, scattered cinders around, and proceeded to criticize his faults.[3] The newly enthroned ruler then returned to the coast, where he frequently erected a new royal village.[4]

Orungu kings were very powerful rulers by the nineteenth century. Surrounded by pomp and royal regalia, they enjoyed great wealth from their control over trade. This wealth enabled the monarchs to reward their faithful subjects and supporters; indeed the rulers were expected to be generous with the European goods they acquired. The king also had ritual and religious powers. He was believed to be able to predict disasters like epidemics, famines, and ant invasions, and prevent their occurrence by appropriate dances and offerings.[5]

[1] Archives d'Outre-Mer, Gabon, iv, 9, 'Didelot to Ministère de la Marine', June 1862.

[2] The Reverend John Leighton Wilson, *Western Africa: Its History, Condition, and Prospects* (New York, 1856), pp. 298–9; and Richard F. Burton, *Two Trips to Gorillaland and the Cataracts of the Congo* (London, 1876; reprinted New York, 1967), i, p. 142.

[3] Avaro, 'Bas-Ogowé', p. 248; Deschamps, *Traditions*, p. 116. The trip up the Ogowe may have represented a pilgrimage to the former Orungu homeland in the interior.   [4] Burton, *Two Trips*, i, p. 142.

[5] Deschamps, *Traditions*, pp. 115–16; Abbé Walker, *Notes*, p. 75.

The king was supposedly assisted by a council of clan heads and dignitaries, especially on judicial cases involving the death penalty;[1] but
rulers like Ombango were apparently unchecked by such a group.
Except for an official (the 'Duke' or Mafouga) who functioned as a
sort of minister for European affairs, almost nothing is known about
lower offices. The powers of clan elders and the sub-clan heads who
functioned as village chiefs were probably not very extensive.

The slave trade, as was described in an earlier chapter, did not
become important in the northern Gabon region until the last third
of the eighteenth century. However, because of the proximity of the
Portuguese islands, the Mpongwe and especially the Orungu exported
slaves well into the 1870s, long after the trade had ended elsewhere on
the West African coast. Slaves continued to be an important supplement to the trade in wood, ivory, and other forest products for the
Mpongwe until 1845. Even after that date, many slaves were smuggled
out, despite the presence of a French naval base at Gabon. The
Orungu never developed 'legitimate' commerce to any significant
extent and were economically dependent on slave exports. Despite
the best efforts of the British navy and sporadic action by the French,
coastal merchants reaped great profits from the sale of hinterland
peoples to supply the demand for labour in Brazil, Cuba, and after
about 1860, the Portuguese colony of São Tomé e Principe.

Slaves were recruited from most of the interior tribes. More
numerous groups like the Apindji, Adouma, Eshira, and Mitsogo
supplied the largest numbers; slaves were also drawn from the
Nzabi, Massangou, Shake, and other peoples. Some slaves from these
central Gabon groups were sold to Pounou and Lombou merchants
and eventually reached the Mayumba or Loango coasts. Large
numbers were shipped down the Ogowe and were eventually sold by
the Orungu or the Mpongwe. Slaves reached the Mpongwe by overland march from the Ogowe, by coastal shipping, and from the
immediate hinterland of the estuary. A few slaves were sent to the
southern mouth of the Ogowe, the Fernan Vaz, where they were
exported by the Nkomi people. The volumes of these various branches of the trade are difficult to estimate and certainly fluctuated greatly
over time. Except perhaps in the 1830s, the Nkomi trade was never
extensive. Slave exports from Mayumba and Loango may, at least
at times, have drawn more heavily on some central Gabon peoples

1 Deschamps, *Traditions*, p. 115.

than did the trade of Cape Lopez and the Gabon River. However, the Ogowe River seems to have been the major route for slaves from the entire northern half of modern Gabon.

Like the Mpongwe and Orungu, most of the interior tribes practised domestic slavery. Debtors, criminals, or war prisoners were enslaved within the tribe and exploited as farmers, wives, or sometimes even as trade agents. Domestic slaves were usually well treated and, unless they misbehaved, were generally not sold to other peoples.[1] However, the rising demand for salt and European goods, coupled with the growing market for slaves on the coast, acted as a stimulus both to the enslavement process and the rate of sale to tribes closer to the Europeans. Domestic slaves were more likely to be sold out of the tribe than freemen, at least in the early stages of involvement.

Individuals could be enslaved for any of several reasons. 'The criminal, the disorderly, the maimed, the idiotic, the orphan child, the useless woman, and the witch or wizard whose death penalty has been commuted' could all be sold,[2] but, in the absence of state systems in the interior, slaves were not procured in tribute payments. Although quantitative data are extremely weak, it seems clear that many slaves from Gabon were, in some way, misfits within their own societies.

Mechanisms of social control could easily be perverted into mechanisms for providing people for export. Deviant individuals became marketable commodities; a village could get cloth, guns, salt, or alcohol by ridding itself of thieves and witches. The demand for imported goods stimulated a rise in crime and witchcraft accusations.[3] Many persons were unjustly convicted, with enslavement and sale being an increasingly common penalty.[4]

People were sold on a variety of real or imagined pretexts. The Shekiani sold 'children when they were unhealthy or destitute of what they considered good sense. And also . . . their wives, when for certain reasons they became dissatisfied with them'.[5] The Adouma sold thieves and adulterers,[6] the Apindji sold disobedient children

---

[1] Du Chaillu, *Explorations*, pp. 379–80.

[2] Robert Hamill Nassau, *My Ogowe: Being a Narrative of Daily Incidents During Sixteen Years in Equatorial West Africa* (New York, 1914), p. 19.

[3] 'Rev. Bushnell's Journal', 5 Nov. 1855, *The Missionary Herald*, lii (1856), p. 108.   [4] Nassau, *My Ogowe*, p. 26.

[5] Bushnell to Anderson, 1 Jan. 1850, American Board of Commissioners for Foreign Missions Letterbooks, A.B.C. 15.1, vol. iii, No. 74.

[6] Deschamps, *Traditions*, p. 55.

and *femmes legères*,[1] the Nzabi and Sangou sold only their own disobedient slaves.[2] In a group of six slaves recaptured by the French
in 1851, four (including an eight-year-old girl) had been judged
criminals, one was a war prisoner, and one, a ten-year-old boy, had
been sold by his father for unspecified reasons.[3] Debtors or their
children were also sold on occasion.[4]

The amount of social disruption caused by the slave trade is difficult to assess. As will be discussed below, the region as a whole
suffered a population loss, but the effects were not identical for all
groups. For peoples still on the periphery of the system, the slave
trade provided a new, convenient, and profitable way to rid society of
undesirables. More heavily involved groups like the Apindji, Adouma,
and Shekiani sold the innocent as well as the guilty; the victim's
angry relatives sometimes tried to retaliate against the accuser. Some
slaves were obtained by kidnapping,[5] but the Bakalai seem to have
been the only group to indulge in large-scale slave raiding.[6] A large
percentage of the Sierra Leone recaptives of Gabonese origin were
Bakalai, who were probably captured and sold by other Bakalai
bands. Surprisingly, the second largest recaptive group were Orungu,[7]
who could be sold for crimes and debts as well as, perhaps, real or
imagined challenges to the rule of Rogombe Passol.[8]

Demographically, the slave trade was a small but significant drain
on the population of northern Gabon. The population of the slave
reservoir may be guessed at roughly 100,000–200,000; if, as seems
plausible, slave exports were in the range of 2,000–5,000 per year,
the demographic loss would have been from 1 per cent to 5 per cent
annually. Additional casualties of course occurred during the enslavement process and transport to the coast. The drain was in fact
even more serious because young, productive people were the most

1 Ibid., p. 36.
2 Ibid., pp. 47, 53. The impact of trade on one interior group is described by
Georges Dupré, 'Le Commerce entre sociétés lignagères; les Nzabi dans le
traite à la fin du XIXᵉ siècle', *Cahiers d'études africaines* (1972), No. 4, pp. 616–
58.
3 'Extrait d'un rapport de Commandant du Gabon', 23 Sept. 1851, Archives
d'Outre-Mer, Sénégal, xiv, 4.
4 Du Chaillu, *Explorations*, p. 380; Sigismund Wilhelm Koelle, *Polyglotta
Africana* (Graz, Austria, 1963; original ed. London, 1854), p. 13.
5 Koelle, *Polyglotta*, p. 11; Nassau, *My Ogowe*, p. 26.
6 Abbé Walker, *Notes*, pp. 133–4.
7 Philip D. Curtin and Jan Vansina, 'Sources of the Nineteenth Century
Atlantic Slave Trade', *Journal of African History*, v (1964), p. 202.
8 Avaro, 'Bas-Ogowé', p. 236.

likely to be sold. Children were often shipped; out of 172 slaves liberated by the British (Table V, p. 80 below, items 5 and 11), 87 were children. The data from this small sample also suggests that many women were exported.[1] Besides the loss of productive people, the trade of course exacted a heavy toll in human suffering and social disruption among the groups supplying slaves. But, such was the demand for trade goods, that few peoples of the Gabonese interior were able to resist the temptation to sell their fellows.

Slaves, like ivory and other products, passed through many hands before reaching the coast. The key intermediaries on the upper Ogowe were the Okande, who controlled the river from Lope, just below the Booué rapids, up to Adouma country. The Okande did not enslave their own people, but bought slaves from the Adouma, Shake, and other groups.[2] The slaves were brought downstream in fleets of canoes. Women and children were not confined, but the men were tied up in the boats and forced to wear heavy wooden stocks around their ankles when the flotilla made night camps on sandbars in the river.[3]

The Okande assembled slaves and some ivory every year in January or February at Lope for sale to Galoa and Enenga boatmen.[4] These Omyene merchants also bought Apindji and other slaves on the Ngounie River.[5] The Galoa and Enenga retained some of the slaves for use as farm labourers,[6] and sold the rest to either Orungu buyers who brought them to the Cape Lopez barracoons, or else to Mpongwe who marched them north to the Gabon.

The volume of overland trade between the Ogowe and the Gabon is unknown, but it is probable that many of the slaves and perhaps some of the tusks sold by the Mpongwe were obtained from this direction. Orungu and Mpongwe trade with the peoples of the Ogowe valley was greatly stimulated, but not initiated, by the rise of the slave trade in the late eighteenth century. In early times, the Orungu exchanged sea salt for raffia cloth and mosquito nets which

---

[1] Koelle's data on Sierra Leone recaptives also suggests that many women and children were taken from Gabon (*Polyglotta*, pp. 11, 13, 14, 19, 20).

[2] Deschamps, *Traditions*, p. 45.

[3] Alfred Marche, *Trois Voyages en Afrique occidentale; Sénégal, Gambie, Casamance, Gabon, Ogowé* (Paris, 1879), p. 326.

[4] Henri Brunschwig, *Brazza explorateur: l'Ogooué 1875–1879* (Paris, 1966), pp. 114, 149; Marquis de Compiègne, *L'Afrique équatoriale: Gabonais, Pahouins, Gallois* (Paris, 1875), p. 151.

[5] Marche, *Trois Voyages*, p. 197.   [6] Brunschwig, *Brazza*, pp. 100, 104.

TABLE V

Gabonese Slave Exports Known to the British

Date	Number of slaves	Where shipped	Remarks
1. 1815–16	265	Gabon	Landed at Martinique
2. 1822	152 shipped, 123 alive at capture	Cape Lopez	Taken by Navy on Port. slaver
3. 1824	17	Gabon	Rescued in starving condition by Navy in Principe harbour
4. 1827	144	Cape Lopez	Landed at Bahia
5. 1833	108— 34 men, 20 women, 39 boys, 15 girls	Cape Lopez	Taken by Navy from Port. vessel heading toward Principe
6. 1833	54	Cape Lopez	Taken by Navy from Port. vessel heading toward São Tomé
7. 1834	144	Gabon	Landed at Rio de Janeiro
8. 1843	460	Gabon	Landed in Brazil
9. 1847	60, 14 soon die	Cape Lopez	Taken by Navy
10. 1848	48, 8 soon die	Cape Lopez	Taken by Navy
11. 1851	64—9 men, 22 women, 23 boys, 10 girls	Sangatanga	Taken by Navy from Port. vessel heading toward São Tomé

Sources:
   Items 1, 4, 7, 8; P.P., Commons, 1845, xlix, No. 73.
   Item 2; ibid., 1824, xxiv, Class A, No. 4.
   Item 3; ibid., 1825, xxv, p. 706.
   Items 5, 6; ibid., 1835, li, Nos. 36 and 37.
   Items 9, 10; ibid., 1850, lv, returns pp. 2–14.
   Item 11; ibid., 1852–3, xxii, No. 206, encls. 2 and 3.

were made by peoples along the Ngounie River.[1] Commercial relations became so intensive that by 1818 the Galoa and Enenga had adopted the Omyene language.[2]

It is clear from Bowdich's account that the Mpongwe had well-established trade connections with the Ogowe peoples by the early nineteenth century. Mpongwe traders and slaves from the interior told him of a route leading from Ngango (George's Town) up a creek (the Mbilagone?) for one day, then for two and a half days across an uninhabited savanna called Woongawoonga to a point on the Ogowe one day's sail downstream from the Adyumba settlements on Lake Azingo. This route reached the river at or near Orovy which was, at least in the 1850s, within the Orungu domains. On the river above the Adyumba were the 'Gaelwa' (Galoa) and the Enenga, both of whom had already adopted the Mpongwe language. Still further upstream, according to Bowdich's informants, were the 'states' of the Okota and the Eshira. The Okande, who reputedly had a large kingdom, were the last of the riverine peoples known to the Mpongwe.[3]

Another overland route linked Denis and George with the Orovy region via the Remboue creek, but it had fallen into disuse by 1870.[4] A third and perhaps more important trail led from Ngango up the Remboue Creek and thence overland in a south-easterly direction for three or four days to the general region of the Ogowe–Ngounie confluence.[5] Yet another route led from the Remboue due south to Lake Azingo, which was connected to the Ogowe by navigable streams. The Reverend Robert H. Nassau, an American missionary, used this route twice to go from the Ogowe to Gabon. In December 1874, during the rainy season, the journey was difficult and took three full days; in the dry season of 1875 he found the path much easier and made the crossing in two days.[6] A French explorer in

---

[1] Avaro, 'Bas-Ogowé', p. 411.

[2] Bowdich, *Mission*, p. 429. If in fact they did not share a common origin with the Mpongwe. See ch. I.

[3] Ibid., pp. 429–30. Abbé Walker (*Notes*, p. 67), mistakenly assumed that Bowdich actually followed the route he described. The same error is repeated in Brunschwig, *Brazza*, p. 98, n. 2.

[4] Lieutenant A. Aymes, 'Exploration de l'Ogoway; recherches géographiques et ethnographiques sur le bassin du Gabon', *Revue maritime et coloniale*, xxvii (1870), p. 549.

[5] Abbé Walker, *Notes*, p. 39; Aymes, 'Explorations', pp. 560–1.

[6] Abbé Walker, *Notes*, p. 40; R. H. Nassau, 'Ogowe Report', Presbyterian Church in the U.S.A., Board of Foreign Missions, Correspondence and Report Files, Africa, vol. x, No. 136, Microfilm Reel 72, and Nassau to Rev. Lowrie, 3 July 1875, ibid., No. 243.

1862 met a party of twenty-five Mpongwe, mostly women, heading
south from George's town with loads of cloth, iron bars, and other
European goods. The Mpongwe, he observed, had several routes to
the Ogowe.[1]

In 1843 the American missionary William Walker got a garbled
account of the middle Ogowe and the routes linking it to the Gabon
from Antonio, a Spanish slaver living at Cape Lopez. Antonio
claimed to have travelled far up the Ogowe to towns called 'Ogobe'
and 'Idemibe' or 'Idembe', which were said to be on a branch of the
river called 'Galwa'. Galwa of course refers to the Galoa people;
Ogobe is a variant of Ogowe. Idembe may refer to N'dambi, a
village on the north bank of the Ogowe just above the Ngounie
confluence; more likely it is Odembe Island, opposite Orovy.[2]
According to Antonio, a land route connected Idembe with Denis's
town (he may well have meant George). An all-water route was said
to connect the Galwa branch to the Gabon. Perhaps Antonio meant
the Ogowe–Lac Azingo–Gabon route, although of course this or
any Gabon–Ogowe route involved some land travel.[3]

The antiquity of these routes and the volume of traffic they carried
are impossible to determine; but by the early 1870s, with the demise
of direct slave exports from the Gabon estuary and the encroachment
of the Fang into the region north of Lake Azingo, they had been
virtually abandoned.[4] The lower Ogowe became the sole commercial
outlet for the far interior; merchants in the estuary could now only
tap their own immediate hinterland.

Trade along the Ogowe was conducted by a *courtier* system similar
to that described for the Gabon hinterland. Each riverine group
dominated a section of the Ogowe and acted as middleman for goods
passing up or downstream. Orungu control of access to the sea was
ensured both by force and by guile. The king himself accompanied
trading expeditions up to the Galoa–Enenga markets,[5] and he

[1] Lieutenant P. Serval, 'Reconnaissance d'une des routes qui mènent du
Rhamboe à l'Ogo-wai', *Revue maritime et coloniale*, ix (1863), pp. 314–15.

[2] Brunschwig, *Brazza*, p. 102.

[3] William Walker Diary, iii, 10 Apr. 1843, William Walker Papers. Antonio's
testimony is published in K. David Patterson, 'Early Knowledge of the Ogowe
River and the American Exploration of 1854', *The International Journal of African
Historical Studies*, v (1972), p. 80.

[4] Aymes, 'Explorations', p. 561; Marche, *Trois Voyages*, p. 252.

[5] Abbé Walker, *Notes*, p. 24. The Galoa and Enenga inhabited successive
segments of the river but, at least on occasion, cooperated in trade.

exercised military control of the river as far up as Orovy.[1] The Orungu also discouraged attempts at direct trade contacts by convincing the up-river people that the whites were dangerous cannibals.[2] On the other hand, the Orungu were glad to leave navigation of the enchanted waters of the upper Ogowe to powerful magicians like the Enenga.[3] The Okande controlled Lope and the fearsome Booué rapids, but they had no desire to encounter the one-eyed, one-legged, one-armed white giants of whom the middle-Ogowe people told such grisly tales.[4] By such sanctions, as well as by physical force, each group protected its own trade monopoly on a segment of the river.

Although the peoples of the hinterland were familiar with domestic slavery, they found it difficult to understand why the whites wanted blacks in such numbers. One widespread explanation for this demand was that the whites fattened up the slaves and ate them.[5] Paul Du Chaillu, the first European visitor to the Gabonese hinterland since Andrew Battell's early seventeenth-century wanderings, was offered a slave for his supper by an Apindji chief eager to cater to the supposedly cannibalistic tastes of his mysterious visitor. The villagers were astonished, and perhaps a little relieved, when Du Chaillu declined the slave and dined instead on plantains and other local fare. The traveller had little success in explaining the notion that slaves were used as plantation labourers, not as food.[6] Another widespread theory was that the whites themselves were not cannibals, but merely the agents of textile-producing anthrophages. In the Ashango version, people called Mindongos lived on an island in the sea, where they made cloth. The whites carried this cloth to the blacks in their boats, and brought back in return blacks for the Mindongos to eat. Dealings with the Mindongos were by dumb barter; the whites rang a bell, landed the slaves and then went away. The Mindongos took the slaves, left cloth in payment, and rang the bell to signal the

[1] Wm. Walker and Preston, 'Visit to the River Nazareth', p. 35. The Americans actually got this far in canoes and thus preceded the first French penetration of the Ogowe by several years. Their exploits are discussed in Patterson, 'Early Knowledge of the Ogowe'.

[2] Marquis de Compiègne, L'Afrique équatoriale: Okanda, Bangouens, Osyeba (Paris, 1875), p. 129.

[3] Aymes, 'Explorations', p. 541.

[4] Marche, Trois Voyages, pp. 278, 339.

[5] Compiègne, Okanda, Bangouens, Osyeba, p. 129.

[6] Du Chaillu, Explorations, p. 491.

whites to come back for it.[1] Other peoples, including the coastal Nkomi of Fernan Vaz, thought that the cloth-making Mindongo had one eye in the centre of their heads.[2]

Even though the slaves were not in fact doomed to be eaten, their prospects were unenviable to say the least. A relatively fortunate few were retained as domestic slaves by the Orungu and Mpongwe, but a grimmer fate awaited the majority. The victims were packed into barracoons where they awaited shipment to plantations across the sea.

Fear of the British navy's patrols had caused the slavers to shift from 'ship trade', which involved a long and risky wait at anchor while slaves were assembled, purchased, and loaded, to a factory or barracoon system. European dealers maintained stockades at the Orungu capital, at Denis, and prior to the 1840s, at Glass. These agents, usually Spaniards or Portuguese, bought slaves from African merchants and held them until a ship arrived. The ship quickly unloaded merchandise to replenish the factor's supply of trade goods, embarked the slave cargo, and set sail.

Slaves, like ivory and dyewood, were usually bought at the barracoons with a bundle of assorted goods, but credit was less widely used. Although little can be said about the economics of the trade because of its clandestine nature, it is clear that the coastal peoples made large profits. According to Sir Richard Burton, in 1862 a slave worth four dollars in goods in Apindji country sold on the coast for nine times that price.[3] Du Chaillu saw an Orungu trader buy a boy from the Apindji for ten pounds of salt;[4] a fourteen-year-old boy was sold to the Portuguese at Sangatanga for twenty gallons of rum, beads, and a few fathoms of cloth. He also witnessed the sale of two young women. The factors gave a gun, a neptune, 30 fathoms of cloth, 2 iron bars, 2 cutlasses, 2 looking glasses, 2 files, 2 plates, 2 bolts, a keg of gunpowder, a few beads, and some tobacco for each of them.[5] As was described in the previous chapter, the goods from such bundles were passed down the chain of middlemen, leaving the 'producer' with a comparatively small profit. For example, a Mitsogo merchant told Abbé Walker that he used to buy Ashango slaves

[1] Abbé Walker, 'Les Tribus', p. 92.
[2] Du Chaillu, *Explorations*, p. 493; Abbé Walker, *Notes*, p. 129.
[3] Burton, *Two Trips*, i, p. 74.
[4] Du Chaillu, *Explorations*, p. 508. Orungu sea salt supplemented European trade goods for slave buying in the interior.
[5] Ibid., p. 180.

with the dregs of the bundle; a sack of salt, an iron bar, and a large neptune.[1] Galoa merchants bought slaves on the Ngounie for half the price paid to them by the Orungu.[2]

The coastal middlemen and their suppliers were able to trade slaves for the same range of goods that they got for ivory, dyewood, or any other local product. European demand and the available supply determined profits; the Mpongwe and Orungu sold indiscriminately whatever they could make money on. Elephants, dyewood trees, and people were alike in that they were exhaustible commodities which could not be over-harvested without producing economic collapse. Slaves, like other tropical commodities, were subject to periodic booms and busts related to market conditions beyond the control of the African coastal merchants. However, the trade in human beings had one disadvantage not associated with commerce in tusks and timber; it drew the wrath of the British fleet. Warships seized slaves and slavers, burned coastal villages, raided barracoons, blockaded trading places, and otherwise harassed the buyers and sellers of people.

The Mpongwe, as well as the Orungu, exported slaves and it appears that Denis became the major slave market in the Gabon after 1815, when British naval pressure made leisurely ship trading too dangerous. In addition to the stream of slaves arriving overland from the Ogowe, Shekiani, Bakalai, and Fang slaves were traded down from the interior along with ivory and other forest products. Spanish buyers based at Denis visited the other Mpongwe towns to collect these slaves.[3] Other slaves were recruited at Cape Santa Clara and brought by canoe to Denis or to Cape Lopez.[4] During periods of naval pressure, the Spanish factors marched slaves overland from Denis to Sangatanga for safer shipment,[5] a practice which became increasingly common after 1845 when the French naval base made really blatant slaving risky in the Gabon.

Two writers have left descriptions of Gabonese slave depots. One, the Reverend John Leighton Wilson of the fledgling Protestant

---

[1] Abbé Walker, 'Les Tribus', p. 91.

[2] Avaro, 'Bas-Ogowé', pp. 412–13. The bundle cited included cloth, firearms, salt, metal goods, and beads.

[3] Wm. Walker Diary, ii, 10 and 11 Feb. 1843; iii, 21 Mar. 1843.

[4] Reverend Benjamin Griswold, 'Tour to Corisco', 6 June 1843, A.B.C. 15.1, vol. ii, No. 169.

[5] Lt. Darricau to Governor of Senegal, 29 May 1844, Archives d'Outre-Mer, Sénégal, iv, 38, b.

mission in Gabon, visited the barracoon at Denis in July 1842. A Spaniard suffering from a severe skin disease ran the place and had collected four hundred and thirty-two slaves in three months. The captives, all expecting to be eaten by the whites, were closely guarded in the stockade. Men were chained in pairs by the ankles, the women were confined in neck rings and chained in large groups. Children under ten were not chained, but all the infants were killed.[1] Wilson was appalled by conditions in the barracoon. 'Suffice it to say', he wrote to his wife, 'my curiosity will never prompt me again to visit a similar scene of human degradation.'[2]

A month after Wilson's visit, the prisoners in the Denis barracoon revolted. H.M.S. *Rapid* had entered the river in an attempt to surprise the slavers, but they were able to escape and hide their prisoners in the forest. Here the slaves rebelled, and many managed to run away. The remainder were rounded up and two ringleaders were executed. A few days later a mass escape attempt failed and two more leaders were killed. The British continued to harass slaving vessels in the river; by October they had made four captures, including the ships which had loaded the survivors of the revolt. The sickly Spanish factor apparently never got the last successful voyage he needed to retire to a life of ease in Havana.[3]

Paul Du Chaillu visited the Sangatanga barracoons in 1856. Portuguese agents maintained two stockades of slaves, a few of whom managed to put up a cheerful front even though convinced that they were doomed to be eaten. Men were chained in collars in groups of six, but women and children were allowed to wander at will within the well-guarded compound. The slaves subsisted on rice and beans while awaiting shipment. When the slave ship arrived, the terrified captives were taken out to it in canoes and crammed aboard. Du Chaillu claims to have seen six hundred people loaded onto a schooner in two hours, haste being necessary to avoid capture by the British.[4]

Slaves embarked on the northern Gabon coast were sent to several

[1] J. L. Wilson, 'Excursion to King William's Town', 8 July 1842, A.B.C. 15.1, vol. ii, No. 122. Wilson's account was reprinted as 'Traite des noirs au Gabon' in the *Revue coloniale*, iii (1844), pp. 408–11, where it was readily accessible to French naval officers.

[2] Hampden C. Du Bose, *Memoirs of the Reverend John Leighton Wilson, D.D.* (Richmond, Va., 1895), p. 217.

[3] Wilson, 'Excursion', postscript of 13 Oct. 1842.

[4] Du Chaillu, *Explorations*, pp. 177–83.

destinations. Brazil, Cuba, and the Portuguese islands were the major markets, although some Gabonese slaves were taken to the French West Indies in the 1820s.[1] São Tomé and Principe continued to function as slave entrepôts after 1815. Slaves were run from the coast in small boats and held on the islands until it was safe to ship them to Brazil.[2]

The volume of slave exports is impossible to determine with any degree of certainty. Exports varied from year to year depending on supply, market conditions, and the effectiveness of the naval patrols. As was discussed in chapter two, something in the order of 1,500 slaves were exported annually between 1800 and 1815. Virtual closure of the Brazilian market after 1850, coupled with intensified British patrolling in the mid-1840s and some French efforts to halt the traffic in the Gabon after 1845, hurt the slave dealers badly, but the opening of new markets in the Portuguese islands caused a new boom after 1860. Table V lists slave landings known to the British as well as some captures made near Gabon. Captures of empty slavers in the area are not included; three were taken in late 1847–early 1848 alone. Many other slaving voyages were known to the Navy, or mentioned by the missionaries or others.[3]

These figures of course represent only a fraction of total human exports from the Gabon River and Cape Lopez. The number of Gabonese slaves known to have been landed in Brazil and Cuba seems very low, especially since British intelligence was quite efficient in the 1820–40 period.[4] However, between 1817 and 1843, at least 12,500 slaves reached Brazil from the Portuguese islands and 4,950 slaves from the islands were landed in Cuba.[5] Many of these people must

[1] P.P., Commons, 1828, xxvi, p. 90, 'Commodore Bullen to J. W. Croker, 18 Dec. 1825'; ibid., 1829, xxvi, p. 124, 'French Slavers Boarded, 22 July 1827'; ibid., 1831, xix, No. 94, 'Slavers Boarded, 1829'.

[2] Bowdich, *Mission*, p. 452; 'Captain George Howland's Voyage to West Africa, 1822–3', in Norman R. Bennett and George E. Brooks, Jr., eds., *New England Merchants in Africa: A History Through Documents 1802 to 1865* (Boston, 1965), p. 122.

[3] See P.P., Commons, 1850, lv, pp. 2–14, 'Returns Relative to the Slave Trade; Captures 1840–48'.

[4] The most recent authority on the dimensions of the Atlantic slave trade estimates that British agents were aware of about 80 per cent of Brazilian landings and 27 per cent of Cuban in this period. Philip D. Curtin, *The Atlantic Slave Trade: A Census* (Madison, 1969), p. 238.

[5] Ibid., pp. 240, 247. Many other ships brought unrecorded numbers of slaves from São Tomé and Principe. For this reason, as well as ships escaping British attention, the total must be considerably higher.

have been taken to the island entrepôts by the small craft trading at Gabon and Cape Lopez. In 1848 a French officer estimated that small boats brought about 2,000 slaves to the islands annually.[1] As will be discussed below, very few slaves were kept in São Tomé or Principe at this time; they were held for re-export. Travellers' accounts would also suggest a higher volume of trade in this period than the British figures indicate. Bowdich saw six slaving vessels in the Gabon during his seven-week visit in 1818; three were small Portuguese schooners which ran slaves to the islands, where they were held 'until the coast is clear for shipping them to America'.[2] French slavers were active at Cape Lopez in 1826; at the same time the Mpongwe were trading slaves 'on a grand scale with the French, Spaniards, and Portuguese'.[3] In 1843, a missionary estimated that about 2,000 slaves a year were exported from Denis, then the centre of the Mpongwe trade.[4] A colleague thought that at least one hundred persons a month were shipped from the Gabon, mostly in small Portuguese schooners.[5] The Orungu trade always seems to have been larger than that of the Mpongwe; this was certainly true in the 1840s when slaves were being sent overland for export from Sangatanga.[6] Total slave exports from the region must have averaged several thousand a year between 1815 and 1850.

British, and to a lesser extent French, naval pressure began to be a serious inhibiting factor in the mid-'40s. The British fleet began more extensive patrols south of the equator in 1842 after the Portuguese had been forced to outlaw the slave trade south of the equator and agree to an equipment clause treaty. As will be discussed in a subsequent chapter, the French ended large scale slaving at Denis in late 1845, forcing a concentration of the traffic at Sangatanga. Admiral Edouard Bouët-Willaumez planned a raid on the Orungu capital in 1849, but this was called off when the slavers fled after learning of his successful attacks on barracoons on the Guinea Coast.[7] H.M.S.

---

[1] Edouard Bouët-Willaumez, *Commerce et traite des noirs aux côtes occidentales d'Afrique* (Paris, 1848), p. 221.

[2] Bowdich, *Mission*, p. 452. Two Spanish and one French slave ships were also in the river.

[3] Boteler, *Narrative*, ii, pp. 364, 394.

[4] Wm. Walker Diary, iii, 6 May 1843.

[5] Benjamin Griswold to Rufus Anderson, 8 May 1843, A.B.C. 15.1, vol. ii, No. 163.

[6] Bouët-Willaumez, *Commerce et traite*, p. 206.

[7] Bouët-Willaumez to General Lahitte, 26 Jan. 1850, in P.P., Commons, 1851, lvi, Class A, No. 279, encl. 2 and Archives d'Outre-Mer, Sénégal, iv, 4.

Britomart visited Sangatanga in June 1849 and found the three barracoons abandoned because of low profits and the fear of a French raid. Two Brazilian ships had carried off the factors and slaves in May, but the Orungu were confident that the barracoons would soon be in use again.[1]

Orungu optimism was well founded, at least in the short run, as within months the trade was bustling.[2] Catholic missionaries from Gabon visited King Passol in June 1850 to ask permission to establish a station. This request was quickly denied; the Orungu and the newly re-established Spanish and Brazilian factors naturally feared that the priests would act as spies for the French navy.[3] However, British cruisers soon forced the Orungu to evacuate slaves from hidden creeks south of Sangatanga[4] and, as was described above, King Passol was forced to agree to an anti-slaving treaty in 1853. This pressure, together with the effective abolition of slave imports into Brazil after 1850, cut deeply into Orungu exports, as Passol complained to Du Chaillu in 1856. The British were now concentrating on slaving south of the equator and a warship frequently cruised off Sangatanga.[5] The trade appeared to be sputtering to a close. King Passol died about 1860; his successors faced a growing political and economic crisis which threatened the very existence of the Orungu state.

[1] Commander Chamberlain to Commodore Fanshawe, P.P., Commons, 1850, lv, Class A, No. 182, encl. 2.

[2] Commodore Fanshawe to the Secretary of the Admiralty, 10 Apr. 1850, P.P., Commons, 1851, lvi, Part I, Class A, No. 191.

[3] Cong. St. Esp., 148, iii. Notes sur la mission du Gabon–Rapport par R. P. Lossedat.

[4] Commodore Fanshawe to the Secretary of the Admiralty, 29 Apr. 1851, P.P., Lords, 1852–3, xxii, Class A, No. 147.

[5] Commodore Wise to Rear-Admiral Sir F. Grey, 19 May 1858, P.P., Commons, 1859, Session 2, vol. 34, p. 177.

CHAPTER V

The Mpongwe and the Onset of Colonial Rule: 1838–1845

THE growth of trade, which had enabled the Mpongwe to achieve a prosperous and distinctive way of life, eventually led to their downfall as an independent economic and political entity. Commercial prosperity brought the Gabon and its fine natural harbour to the attention of both the French Navy and American missionaries. The Mpongwe faced missionary penetration as early as 1842 and the beginnings of colonial rule only a year later; other, less conspicuous peoples in the region did not have to confront either of these problems for several decades.

The first official contact between France and the Mpongwe communities occurred in March 1838, when two French warships, the *Triomphante* and the *Fine*, visited the river. Captain Peroune anchored off King Denis's town, 'São Tomé' or 'village français', where he was impressed to learn that some of Denis's people spoke French and that several had in fact been to France. Indeed, one of King Denis's brothers had even served in the French army. According to Peroune, Denis was eager for a French factory and could provide wood, wax, tortoiseshell, and gum copal, in addition to high quality ivory. The slave trade was important; a Portuguese ship was loading a cargo during Peroune's visit. The trade at Glass was dominated by the English, although French merchants were always welcome. Glass and Denis had achieved prosperity honestly, but Peroune learned that two French vessels had been seized by Quaben and Kringer, who were dangerous and untrustworthy men.[1]

Peroune's visit was followed by an official reconnaissance of the commercial and political situation on the coast between Senegal and Gabon by Edouard Bouët-Willaumez in the *Malouine*. The idea for the Malouine expedition was developed by Bouët-Willaumez and the

[1] 'Report of M. de Peroune', Archives d'Outre-Mer, Sénégal, iv, 37, a, Pts. I and II, 18 Apr. 1838. According to his letter of nomination for the Legion of Honour, Denis's brother had served in Napoleon's Old Guard. Admiral Duperré to the King, 16 Sept. 1839, Archives d'Outre-Mer, Sénégal, iv, 37, a.

merchant Victor Calvé. Bordeaux commercial groups backed the proposal and the Ministry of the Marine gave its approval to the project in 1837. Bouët-Willaumez was accompanied on his mission by Captain Broquant, a veteran Bordeaux trader whose ship had recently been seized by Kringer. The *Malouine* left Gorée in October 1838 with orders to examine commercial possibilities along the coast, punish chiefs at Gabon and Bonny for violence against French shipping, and capture any slavers encountered.[1]

Gabon became a focal point for the expedition for two reasons. Bouët-Willaumez was so impressed by the estuary's potential as a naval base that, without orders, he negotiated a treaty of union with King Denis.[2] Although noting that British traders were active on the north bank, the French officer enthusiastically observed that the south shore was 'occupied by a population eminently French in language, manners, habits, and sentiments'. French traders, including slavers, had been instrumental in raising the people of Denis 'to a degree of civilization astonishing for such a distant part of Africa'. Denis himself was an intelligent and honest ruler who had always gone out of his way to aid shipwrecked French sailors. Bouët-Willaumez strongly urged the opening of a French factory 'among our ancient and faithful allies of the Gabon'.[3]

The Denis treaty, concluded on 9 February 1839, was the first step in the establishment of French rule in Gabon, an event which, in the words of a Gabonese historian, 'allows us to glory in the fact of being French for more than one hundred and twenty years'.[4] In return for presents, Denis ceded a strip of territory near his village on which the French could erect any houses or forts they desired.[5] Denis no doubt expected the French to build a trading post which would be profitable to him and his subjects. He also wanted to use the French against his commercial rivals on the north bank.

---

[1] Bernard Schnapper, *La Politique et le commerce français dans le Golfe de Guinée de 1838 à 1871* (Paris, 1961), pp. 16–18; Hubert Deschamps, *Quinze Ans de Gabon; les débuts de l'établissement français, 1839–1853* (Paris, 1965), pp. 289–91.

[2] Schnapper, *Politique et commerce*, p. 19.

[3] 'Esquisse commerciale de la côte occidentale d'Afrique', by Bouët-Willaumez, 6 May 1839, p. 46. Archives d'Outre-Mer, Sénégal, iii, 5, b.

[4] Abbé André Raponda Walker, *Notes d'histoire du Gabon* (Brazzaville, 1960), p. 25.

[5] Treaty text in Schnapper, *Politique et commerce*, p. 263. The present consisted of 20 pieces of cloth, 250 pounds of gunpowder, 20 guns, 2 sacks of tobacco, a barrel of eau-de-vie, and 10 white hats. Deschamps, *Quinze Ans*, p. 292.

In addition to the fact that it offered the advantages of a naval and commercial base in friendly territory, the attention of French officers was also drawn to the Gabon by attacks on French boats, especially by Quaben's people. In 1837 two ships, including one under the command of Bouët-Willaumez's colleague Broquant, had been pillaged. Kringer, a village chief, seems to have been the chief culprit.[1] The ships were attacked after their crews had been weakened by disease.[2] In January 1839 the brig *Trazus* of Bordeaux was run aground, allegedly on purpose, by a pilot from Quaben's town. The captain and crewmen were beaten and robbed by Quaben and Kringer's men, who stole the ship's cargo of redwood, ebony, ivory, and wax. The battered Frenchmen eventually reached chief Louis, who helped them get safely across the river to Denis.[3]

Admiral Montagniès de la Roque, Bouët-Willaumez's superior, arrived in the river two weeks after the conclusion of the 1839 Denis treaty to punish the Mpongwe for these attacks. Kringer's son Manuel and several others were held as hostages until Kringer and Quaben paid a large indemnity. Collection was slow but a year later, de la Roque agreed to call off a bombardment of Kringer's village and reduce the indemnity. Denis, now a member of the Legion of Honour, had acted as an intermediary. He was able to convince the Admiral that the traders' claims were exaggerated, secured the release of the hostages, and helped collect the ivory, ebony, and wax from the culprits.[4]

French naval and business circles were not enthusiastic about the expansionist programme urged by Bouët-Willaumez, and there was no immediate response to his report. Bouët-Willaumez did visit the river again and on 18 March 1842 signed a treaty with 'King' Louis on the north bank. Louis made his mark on a document conveying 'full and entire' sovereignty over his domains to France and allocating a piece of land for a fort.[5] Although no further action was taken at the time, the Louis treaty provided France with a base for future expansion.

1 'Report of de Peroune', Pt. II.

2 'Esquisse commerciale', Bouët-Willaumez, p. 45.

3 'Report of Montagniès de la Roque', 24 Apr. 1840, annexes 1 and 2, Archives d'Outre-Mer, Sénégal, iv, 37, a.

4 Treaty of 6 Mar. 1840, Archives d'Outre-Mer, Sénégal, iv, 37, a, and 'Report of de la Roque', loc. cit. Denis was nominated to the Legion of Honour after the 1839 treaty (Adm. Duperré to the King, 16 Sept. 1839). In the same year Denis received a gold medal from Queen Victoria for rescuing four British sailors (Abbé Walker, *Notes*, p. 27).   5 Treaty text in Deschamps, *Quinze Ans*, p. 295.

The first whites to form a permanent settlement in Mpongwe territory were American missionaries. On 22 June 1842 the Reverends John Leighton Wilson and Benjamin Griswold landed at Glass and almost immediately decided to establish a mission there. The missionaries represented the American Board of Commissioners for Foreign Missions, a Congregationalist body based in Boston which also supported 'New School' Presbyterian missionaries.[1] Wilson had founded the first African station of the A.B.C.F.M. at Cape Palmas in 1834. The mission had not been notably successful and several missionaries had died of disease. Prospects were further darkened by the conflicts between the indigenous Grebo population and the Afro-American colony of Maryland, which generally found the mission in the middle distrusted by both groups. The mission staff was eager to seek a new location.[2] Captain Richard Lawlin, a veteran American trader and a good friend of the missionaries, suggested that Cape Lahou (in modern Ivory Coast) and the Gabon would be promising sites. Lawlin was well known in both places and offered to take Wilson and Griswold with him on a trading voyage down the coast.[3] The evangelists agreed and landed with Lawlin at Glass, the centre of English trade, on 22 June. Within a few days they decided that Gabon would be an excellent field and had selected a station site near Glass called Baraka, after an old Portuguese slave barracoon which formerly stood there.[4]

Gabon was attractive for several reasons. Other than two British Baptists on Fernando Po, there were no other missionaries in the entire region and the population, while certainly heathen, seemed unusually promising. After three days on the scene, Wilson enthusiastically reported that the Mpongwe were 'a good deal more advanced in civilization than any natives I have before seen or expected to see on the western coast of Africa'.[5] 'Wherever a person

---

[1] Arthur Judson Brown, *One Hundred Years: A History of the Foreign Missionary Work of the Presbyterian Church in the U.S.A.* (New York, 1936), p. 40. The Presbyterians had split into two wings in 1838; the relatively liberal 'New School' group collaborated with the A.B.C.F.M., which had already supported a few individual Presbyterian missionaries.

[2] Rufus Anderson to John Latrobe, 3 Nov. 1841, American Board of Commissioners for Foreign Missions Letterbooks, 15.1, vol. ii, No. 18; J. L. Wilson and five others to Prudential Committee, 1 Jan. 1842, A.B.C. 15.1, vol. ii, No. 22.

[3] J. L. Wilson, 'Letter of March 31, 1842', *The Missionary Herald*, xxxviii (1842), p. 381. This journal will henceforth be cited as *M.H.*

[4] J. L. Wilson, 'Letter of June 25 1842', *M.H.*, xxxviii (1842), pp. 497–8; Benjamin Griswold to Rufus Anderson, 4 July 1842, A.B.C. 15.1, vol. ii, No. 153.

[5] Wilson, 'Letter of June 25, 1842', p. 498.

goes there', wrote Griswold, 'he is impressed with the superiority of the Gaboon natives over others upon the coast of Africa.' Furthermore, he continued, 'the Gaboon people desire instruction. Within the past year a request has been forwarded by them to the Wesleyan missionaries at Cape Coast, for a missionary teacher.'[1] The Gabon River, a potential highway to the interior, provided an excellent harbour and was frequented by merchant ships which could bring supplies to the station. And, according to Captain Lawlin, the Gabon was one of the healthiest places on the coast. Griswold returned to Cape Palmas to arrange the transfer of staff and furnishings, while his colleague remained to preach, erect buildings, and learn the Mpongwe language. The people were eager to start schools and large crowds assembled to hear Wilson's sermons.[2]

Wilson was joined in December by the Reverend William Walker; Griswold returned in January 1843 and B. V. R. James, the American Negro printer at the Cape Palmas mission, reached Gabon a year later. In early 1844 the mission received further reinforcements.[3] The evangelists were assisted by several African Christian teachers from Cape Palmas. By May 1843, preaching was being conducted at four locations before large congregations. Fifty or sixty students were attending school. The headmen at Glass refused to load wood onto a British steamer on the Sabbath; King George requested a school and a mission.[4] The brother of King Glass, a regular at all services, had denounced idolatry and delighted the missionaries by casting a bundle of fetishes into the river.[5] Religious materials had been printed in Mpongwe in 1843 at Cape Palmas[6] and, after the transfer of James and the printing press, small books were printed in Gabon in early 1844.[7]

However, not all of the omens were favourable. The staff, although enjoying 'very good African health', suffered from sickness. 'Every day', reported Walker, 'we are reminded that this is not a New

[1] Griswold, 'Letter of July 18, 1842', *M.H.*, xxxviii (1842), p. 498.
[2] Wilson, 'Letter of July 28, 1842', *M.H.*, xxxix (1843), pp. 156-7.
[3] Personnel changes in the mission up to 1863 are detailed in William Ireland, *Historical Sketch of the Zulu Mission, in South Africa, as also of the Gaboon Mission, in Western Africa* (Boston, 1863), p. 30.
[4] 'Letters of Griswold and Wilson', *M.H.*, xxxix (1843), p. 404.
[5] Wilson to Anderson, 10 Mar. 1843, A.B.C. 15.1, vol. ii, No. 102.
[6] William Walker to Prudential Committee, 28 Dec. 1843, A.B.C. 15.2, vol. ii, No. 28.
[7] Wilson, 'Letter of July 20, 1844', *M.H.*, xli (1845), p. 28.

England clime.'[1] Preaching was carried on in Glass, the neighbouring Mpongwe and Shekiani villages, and at George's and Tom Larsen's towns on the south bank, but there were still no potential converts. Five schools were taught by African converts from Cape
Palmas,[2] but Griswold complained that the Mpongwe opposed
training for girls and were only interested in literacy for their sons
because it would 'make them more successful traders'.[3] Even more
menacing for the mission's future were the encroachments of the
French. Quaben's town was already under the 'deplorable' influence
of the French naval base; Catholic priests were expected to follow.[4]

France gained its first permanent foothold in Gabon in 1843, a
year after the arrival of the Americans. Bouët-Willaumez had continued to lobby for the erection of fortified trading points along the
coast and late in 1842 the French government, fearful of British
expansion, suddenly decided to adopt this policy.[5] Work was begun
on blockhouses at Grand Bassam and Assini in the modern Ivory
Coast and on 18 June 1843 Commandant Félix de Monléon arrived
in the Zèbre to begin construction of a fort at Louis.[6] The site at
Denis was not used because the higher north bank was believed to be
healthier. The work was completed in a few months; meanwhile the
French had strengthened their legal position by signing a treaty with
Quaben, Louis's nominal superior.[7] France could now claim
sovereignty over all of Quaben's territories and had a treaty arrange-
ment with Denis on the south bank.

The Mpongwe were surprised and confused by these events.
Monléon reported that Kings Glass and Quaben were asking to send
people to the blockhouse to learn French, get presents, and spy on the
small garrison.[8] Denis was suspicious enough of French designs on
his own territories to rebuff overtures for establishment of a fort on

1 Wm. Walker to Prudential Committee, 28 Dec. 1843.
2 Ibid.
3 Griswold to Anderson, 26 Dec. 1843, A.B.C. 15.1, vol. ii, No. 167.
4 W. Walker, 'Letter of August 15, 1843', M.H., xl (1844), p. 62.
5 Schnapper, Politique et commerce, p. 29.
6 Schnapper (p. 31) gives this name as Monléon, which agrees with the signature on the documents cited below. Deschamps (Quinze Ans, p. 298), Abbé
Walker (Notes, p. 35) and Père Gautier (Étude historique sur les Mpongués et
tribus avoisinantes, Brazzaville, 1950, p. 58) give the name Mauléon.
7 Excerpts from this treaty, signed on 27 April (not August), are given in
Deschamps, Quinze Ans, pp. 299-300.
8 Monléon to Governor of Senegal, 14 July 1843, Archives d'Outre-Mer,
Sénégal, iv, 38, a.

the south bank in November 1842 and in February 1843,[1] but by then Louis had already signed a treaty. The new blockhouse alarmed both the Mpongwe and the Protestants. A letter seeking British aid was composed by the missionaries on behalf of the chiefs and sent to the anti-slave trade leader Thomas Fowell Buxton only days after Monléon's arrival. The chiefs were angry at Quaben for allowing the French to continue construction, but, beyond hoping for aid from their English trading partners, they did not know what to do about it.[2] Wilson asked the A.B.C.F.M. directors to inquire about the attitudes of the American and British governments to further French encroachments.[3]

The diplomatic struggle continued as the French put increasing pressure on other Mpongwe rulers for treaties. One target was Denis, who they considered the most influential of the Mpongwe kings. Repeated attempts were also made to get a treaty with King Glass, whose domains bordered the new French post and were seen as a centre of alien activity, frequented as they were by English traders and American missionaries. Denis was able to resist a new treaty, despite a naval demonstration near his village.[4] He managed to rebuff the French, but, by giving them information and advice on local affairs, was able both to keep their confidence and direct their attention to the north side of the river. Denis convinced Lieutenant Fance that the British were going to build a fort at Glass, despite the objections of the leading men and the ambivalent attitude of King Glass.[5] This unfounded rumour caused the French to shift their attention from Denis back to their own neighbours on the north shore.

Glass thus became the focal point of the Franco–Mpongwe struggle. Events there were followed closely by all of the people in the river, for if the people of Glass with their powerful English and American allies succumbed to French pressure, resistance by the others was surely hopeless. King Glass himself, an elderly man over-fond of strong drink, had little influence,[6] but Toko, a village chief

---

[1] Wilson to Anderson, 10 Nov. 1842, A.B.C. 15.1, vol. ii, No. 100; Griswold to Anderson, 8 May 1843, ibid., No. 163.

[2] Chiefs of Gabon to Thomas Fowell Buxton, 30 June 1843; copy in Wm. Walker to Anderson, 29 Dec. 1843, A.B.C. 15.2, vol. ii, No. 29.

[3] Wilson to Anderson, 15 July 1843, A.B.C. 15.1, vol. ii, No. 106.

[4] William Walker Diary, iii, 7 Nov. 1843. William Walker Papers, State Historical Society of Wisconsin.

[5] Lt. Fance to Ministère de la Marine, 21 Oct. 1843, Archives d'Outre-Mer, Sénégal, iv, 38, d.

[6] Gabon Mission Report for 1843, M.H., xl (1844), p. 186.

and wealthy merchant, provided strong leadership against the French. Toko, 'as honorable, intelligent, and influential as any man in the river', was highly regarded by both the traders and the missionaries.[1] The Mpongwe were well aware from naval visits that both the English and Americans came from countries powerful enough to check the French fleet.

The French authorities began to apply pressure on Glass late in 1843. On 1 November overtures were made both to King Glass and to Toko, whose great influence was recognized by the French. The king dismissed the French officer with a curse; Toko refused an offer of ten pieces of cloth, five guns and a quantity of gunpowder for his signature.[2] A few days later Lieutenant Fance proposed a revised treaty to King Glass which, while ceding rights of sovereignty to France, would have guaranteed Mpongwe political and religious autonomy and allowed free trade with all nations. This draft was also rejected.[3] Several new advances were made over the next few months. One treaty was rejected on 14 March 1844,[4] just two weeks before the disputed events of 27–8 March, when a treaty was finally obtained by Captain Darricau.

According to Darricau, the proceedings went very smoothly. He was on his ship, at anchor off the new fort on 28 March 1844, when 'at six o'clock in the morning, having been informed of the favourable attitude of King Glass', Darricau and the French merchant J-B. Amouroux landed on the beach in front of Glass-town. A large crowd gathered to greet him, including the English merchant Samuel Dyer and James, the mission printer. The party went to Glass's house where the captain read the draft treaty phrase by phrase in French. Petit Denis, the son of King Denis, translated the document into Mpongwe. Darricau, Glass, and all the chiefs present signed the treaty, a twenty-one gun salute was fired by Darricau's ship, the *Eperlan*, and the assembled dignitaries went aboard for a celebration 'during which the greatest gaiety prevailed'. Shortly before noon the Mpongwe guests departed and the French sailors were given leave to continue the festivities on shore.[5]

---

[1] Wm. Walker to Anderson, 29 Dec. 1843.

[2] Wm. Walker Diary, iii, 1 Nov. 1843.

[3] Fance to Min. Marine and encl., proposed treaty dated 5 Nov.

[4] Wm. Walker Diary, iii, 14 Mar. 1844.

[5] 'Process-verbal constatant la signature du traité passé au village du Roi Glass . . .', 28 Mar. 1844, Archives d'Outre-Mer, Sénégal, iv, 38, b. Also printed in Parliamentary Papers, Commons, 1845, l, Class C, No. 153, encl. 1.

The Mpongwe had a different version of the affair. On the night of 27 March King Glass was visited by a friend, the French merchant Amouroux, who brought along a jug of brandy. Petit Denis, Governor (Goaven), Tim Glass, and the King's son Dowe completed the party. After much drinking, Amouroux produced what he claimed was a letter of friendship to the King of France and asked King Glass to sign it so that French vessels could anchor at his town as well as at Quaben. The document was signed by all present. The next morning, Darricau showed up and, with Petit Denis again acting as interpreter, read the paper to Glass and asked him if he had signed it. The interpreter gave the same incomplete translation as the night before, so Glass acknowledged his signature. Darricau proclaimed the treaty to be in effect and walked over to the missionary buildings, where he informed Mrs. Wilson that she was on French territory and was 'so frank as to state that Amouroux procured the King's mark in the night, and called him out of his berth at two o'clock in the morning, to come up and ratify the treaty'.[1] Once the Mpongwe became aware of the nature of the 'treaty', and heard Petit Denis's confession that only part of the document had been read in Mpongwe, they vigorously protested its validity.

Deschamps has concluded that the Mpongwe had no case and were simply trying to evade a legitimate agreement. In his view, the Mpongwe probably invented a story of French deception to fool the missionaries into acting as their defenders. He thought that since the Glass treaty was somewhat less restrictive than earlier agreements, it must have been the result of genuine bargaining.[2] However, since King Glass had been offered a fairly generous treaty in November 1843 and had rejected a similar proposal as recently as 14 March, this argument is not convincing. The king's alleged change of mind was indeed sudden and inexplicable.

Many of the circumstances surrounding the signing are also highly suspicious. Darricau never said who woke him up at six in the morning with the news that King Glass urgently desired to sign a treaty, but it was almost certainly Amouroux. But where would Amouroux have learned this and why would he have rushed out to the *Eperlan* at such an hour? The claim of a late drinking party seems quite

---

[1] Wm. Walker to Rev. Green, 4–5 Apr. 1844, A.B.C. 15.4, vol. iii, No. 41. Details of the Mpongwe version are given in this document; in 'Protest of Glass and Headmen to Governor Bouët', 31 Mar. 1844, A.B.C. 15.4, vol. iii, No. 41; Glass to Darricau, 22 May, 1844, A.B.C. 15.4, vol. iii, No. 39; and Wm. Walker Diary, iii, 30 Mar. 1844.   [2] Deschamps, *Quinze Ans*, pp. 301–2.

plausible. Another discrepancy is in the timing of the actual signing. In the Mpongwe version, Amouroux, Glass, and two of his subjects signed that night, along with Petit Denis as a witness. Darricau added his signature the next morning. The French officer, on the other hand, stated that the treaty was actually signed in the morning, by all the chiefs present, presumably a fairly large number. He specified that Glass, Dowe, Goaven, and Tim went out to the party on the boat, along with several other prominent men. However, only the four named citizens of Glass did in fact sign, exactly as the Mpongwe claimed.

The roles of the unofficial participants in the affair, Amouroux and Petit Denis, are quite questionable. The Glass people were by this time naturally suspicious of uniformed naval officers who wanted their signatures; Amouroux, a private trader well known in the river, would have aroused less apprehension. Petit Denis, the interpreter, was a son of King Denis. He freely admitted that the treaty had not been correctly translated and claimed that during the nocturnal proceedings Amouroux had given him only one paragraph to translate.[1] Several months later he told a British officer sent to investigate the affair that neither Amouroux nor Darricau had said anything about cession of sovereignty. Being illiterate, he could only translate what the French said was on the paper.[2]

The treaty was concluded while Wilson and Walker were visiting across the river and hence unavailable for consultation.[3] Toko, 'our virtual minister of foreign affairs', was in town, but was not summoned and, like the other elders, had no knowledge of the proceedings until Darricau's surprise arrival on the morning of the twenty-eighth. Old King Glass and the three others, none of them men of influence, were the only Mpongwe consulted. They were tricked into signing a document of cession, an act which in fact they had no legal power to do. Such an important treaty could only be ratified by a general public assembly.[4]

[1] 'Protest of Glass and Headmen'. Amouroux was also involved in an abortive cotton concession scheme at Denis. A. Le Cour, 'Projet d'un établissement à créer du Gabon', (Nantes, 1844) and 'Rapport sur la colonization du Gabon et de l'Afrique centrale', (Nantes, 1848), pamphlets in the Archives du Cong. St. Esp., 148, ii.

[2] Captain of H.M.S. *Éclair* to Commodore Jones, 13 Jan. 1845, Archives d'Outre-Mer, Afrique, vi, 3, b. Petit Denis's testimony essentially confirmed the Glass version of the treaty signing.

[3] Wm. Walker Diary, iii, 30 Mar. 1844.

[4] 'Protest of Glass and Headmen'.

The timing of Darricau's initiative is also suspicious. He had recently arrived from Gorée to take command in Gabon, with instructions to get all of the chiefs under the French flag.[1] His superior, Admiral Bouët-Willaumez, arrived in the river on the twenty-eighth, the very day Darricau secured the treaty from the stubborn people of Glass. A desire to please the admiral, whose ship was expected daily, could explain Darricau's haste to conclude an agreement, even if it perhaps had to be done by somewhat devious means. Darricau, like other ambitious and dedicated men on the frontiers of empire, was beyond the immediate supervision of his superiors. He, the 'man on the spot', acted and reported on his actions as he believed necessary. His tactics in the Glass affair were unsavoury, but no more so than those of dozens of other agents of imperialism in nineteenth-century Africa.

King Glass and his people were convinced that the treaty had been obtained fraudulently and that it was at any rate not binding because it had not been ratified by the general community. When Wilson and Walker returned to Glass on the night of 30 March, they found the village in an uproar, but a strategy of peaceful protest was soon agreed upon. A petition and letter writing campaign began. On 1 April Walker noted in his diary that 'Mr. Wilson and I spent the evening in preparing papers at the earnest solicitation of the people.' Captain Samuel Dyer, an English trader who had himself unsuccessfully sought a concession in Glass in June 1843, spent the next day gathering signatures for petitions of protest. The Mpongwe insisted on sending petitions to Queen Victoria and King Louis Phillipe; one hundred and ten made their marks.[2]

Besides appealing to Europe, the Mpongwe protested to the local French authorities. Admiral Bouët-Willaumez arrived in the river just after Darricau's triumph. Angered by the refusal of the people of Glass to attend his friendship banquet, the Admiral tore up the protest addressed to him without reading it, and sailed away on 5 April. Darricau was left in charge and threatened to blockade the village if defiance continued.[3] However, he assured Wilson that he was not a violent man and, although French prestige was involved, he would

[1] Darricau to Min. Marine, 16 Apr. 1844, Archives d'Outre-Mer, Sénégal, iv, 38, b; also in P.P., Commons, 1845, l, Class C, No. 153, encl. 2.

[2] Wm. Walker Diary, iii, 30 Mar.–4 Apr. 1844. The petition to Queen Victoria is printed in P.P., Commons, 1845, l, Class C, No. 142, encl.; both petitions are copied in A.B.C. 15.4, vol. iii, No. 41. Dyer's attempt to acquire land was noted in Wm. Walker's Diary, iii, 26 June 1843.

[3] Wm. Walker to Green, 4–5 Apr. 1844.

exhaust all remedies before blockading Glass.[1] Wilson was relieved by this, as he warned Darricau that the Mpongwe would resist forcibly since they were determined to maintain their independence. He suggested that the return of the old treaty and the negotiation of a new one would be the most honourable course for France, but this drew no response.[2]

Darricau was determined to have the treaty acknowledged. The French seized some Mpongwe boats, allegedly in retaliation for the destruction of two survey beacons, and offered to return them if all the people would add their signatures to the treaty.[3] When this offer was rejected, Darricau responded with fair words and threats. He assured King Glass that France had no intention of interfering with local politics or trade, or taking any land, but accused the Mpongwe ruler of bad faith. 'You have willingly accepted and after abiding the counsels of some interested people you have refused.' He warned King Glass that breaking a treaty was equivalent to a declaration of war and that this was the last chance to avoid war.[4] Glass replied that since he could not read or write, he had indeed the necessity of the 'assistance of another' in his correspondence, but that his people were determined to maintain their independence. He repeated the Mpongwe version of the events of 27-8 March, and denied that any treaty was in effect. Although he offered to sign a friendship treaty with France if the old one were returned, he threatened to meet force with force.[5] Darricau responded by denying the validity of the petitions to France and England and by a unilateral declaration that the treaty was in effect.[6] The situation remained stalemated for some months as the disputants awaited word from Europe.

The Mpongwe protests aroused some interest in the British government and there was considerable correspondence on the subject between London and Paris.[7] British merchants active in the Gabon were also concerned with the Glass controversy and, upon the prompting of Wilson and of Captain Dyer,[8] several Liverpool and

[1] Darricau to Wilson, 6 Apr. 1844, A.B.C. 15.4, vol. iii, No. 36.
[2] Wilson to Darricau, 8 Apr. 1844, A.B.C. 15.4, vol. iii, No. 37.
[3] Wilson to Green, 8 May 1844, A.B.C. 15.4, vol. iii, No. 98.
[4] Darricau to King Glass and His Headmen, 19 May 1844, A.B.C. 15.4, vol. iii, No. 38.
[5] Glass to Darricau, 22 May 1844, ibid., No. 39.
[6] Darricau to Glass, 24 May 1844, ibid., No. 41.
[7] P.P., Commons, 1845, l, Class C, *passim.*
[8] Wilson to Messrs. King, 5 Apr. 1844 and Samuel Dyer to Messrs. King, 5 Apr. 1844, P.P., Commons, 1845, l, Class C, No. 145, sub-encl. 1 and 2 in encl. 3.

Bristol trading houses urged the British government to investigate the situation[1]. The Bristol firm of Richard and William King feared that French control would mean the end of their thirty-year-old business in the Gabon.[2] An investigation was eventually ordered.

The French authorities were of course suspicious of the role of the foreign establishment at Glass, especially since Kings Denis, Quaben, and George, and various minor chiefs agreed to a similar treaty on 1 April.[3] At first Darricau apparently thought that Dyer was the culprit instigating the Mpongwe to go back on their agreement, as his initial report made no mention of the missionaries.[4] Admiral Bouët-Willaumez promised that the new regime would not in any way imperil the missionaries, but that he would certainly complain to the British government about Dyer's conduct.[5] Later, when the Admiral expressed some doubts about the activities of Wilson and Walker during the crisis, he stressed that there was no proof against them, and that they would not be expelled. Captain Dyer was still considered the chief agitator.[6]

Although Wilson and Walker had in the past maintained good relations with the French, they were clearly opposed both to a take-over of Glass and the possibility of favouritism to the Roman Catholic missionaries whose arrival they believed imminent. They also disliked Darricau intensely.[7] The missionaries enthusiastically aided their Mpongwe friends by drawing up petitions, and attempted to rally the support of British business interests; Wilson acted as secretary for the exchange of notes with the local French authorities. While they no doubt influenced Mpongwe tactics by urging a pacific policy[8] and perhaps by suggesting the idea of appeals to Europe, they did not have to persuade the people to protest. The opposition of the population of Glass to the treaty was spontaneous; no outside agitators were needed to whip up anti-French feeling.

Captain Dyer's role was also that of a channel for rather than a creator of African protest. He gathered signatures for the petitions, but, although over one hundred people signed, Darricau was un-

[1] Earl of Aberdeen to Lord Cowley, 6 Sept. 1844, ibid., No. 143.
[2] Richard and William King to Earl of Aberdeen, 29 July 1844, ibid., encl. 1.
[3] Deschamps, *Quinze Ans*, p. 302.
[4] Darricau to Min. Marine, 16 Apr. 1844.
[5] Wm. Walker Diary, iii, 2 Apr. 1844.
[6] Bouët-Willaumez to Min. Marine, Aug. 1844, Archives d'Outre-Mer, Sénégal, iv, 38, b.
[7] Wm. Walker to Green, 5 June 1844, A.B.C. 15.4, vol. iii, No. 69.
[8] Wilson to Green, 8 May 1844, ibid., No. 98.

impressed. 'Signatures are easily obtained in an assembly of Africans', wrote Darricau, in words that might be applied to his own treaty as well as to Dyer's petitions. 'All readily make their marks, whether or not they understand the matter.'[1] Dyer, after being involved in a trade dispute at Louis, wrote an extremely insulting letter to Darricau and their personal relations degenerated to the level of a feud. Dyer attempted to stir up unrest by warning King Denis and other chiefs on the south shore that they were no longer free, but the slaves of the French.[2] He may well have erected the 'Lewis Phillip, wood and ivory merchant' sign at Glass that Darricau personally tore down as an insult to the French monarch.[3]

During the lull while the protagonists awaited news of official French ratification or possible British intervention, the first Catholic missionaries arrived. The Congrégation du Saint-Esprit was dispatching missionaries to various points along the West African coast in the early 1840s and Gabon was chosen as one of the sites because of its new position as a French *comptoir*. Father Bessieux and Brother Grégoire arrived in September 1844 and founded the mission of Sainte-Marie du Gabon just north of the French fort.[4] The worst fears of the Protestants were realized. The home board reminded its Gabon staff that papal missionaries, 'the emissaries of darkness', had long been expected and should not give cause for alarm. The best way to ward off the onslaught of those who 'are wrongly called by the name of Christians', was to continue the good work already begun.[5]

A British warship reached Gabon in January 1845 to investigate the Glass situation. Surprisingly, Darricau's successor suggested that the ship's officers use Wilson as an interpreter. The Glass people were all anti-French and, through their spokesman Toko, repeated their version of the treaty affair. After interviewing Petit Denis and others, the investigators concluded that the Mpongwe had not understood the treaty properly and would not have signed it if they had.

[1] Darricau to Min. Marine, 16 Apr. 1844.

[2] Dyer to Darricau, May 1844, and 'Déposition des chefs de la rive gauche', 29 May 1844, Archives d'Outre-Mer, iv, 38, b; encls. 1 and 2 in Darricau to Governor of Senegal, 29 May 1844.

[3] Wm. Walker Diary, iii, 4 Aug. 1844.

[4] Père J-B. Piolet, *Les Missions catholiques françaises au XIXe siècle*, v, *Missions d'Afrique* (Paris, 1902), pp. 220–1. The Catholic mission will be discussed in the next chapter.

[5] Rufus Anderson to Gaboon Mission, 19 Nov. 1844, A.B.C. 15.1, vol. ii.

They also condemned Dyer's provocative conduct toward Darricau.[1] But the British officers were only able to promise the good offices of their government with France, and this proved insufficient to prevent formal ratification of the treaty.[2]

However, the British naval visit greatly encouraged the Mpongwe. Quaben, Denis, and the other chiefs now regretted ever having signed treaties and were following developments in the Glass affair closely, knowing it was the test case for all of the Mpongwe. The French realized that their position in Gabon was weak; not even their 'ancient ally' Denis recognized the authority of the *comptoir* commander.[3] The authorities were determined to force acknowledgement of the treaty; the people of Glass remained defiant. Wilson predicted that while nominal French rule might not be opposed, any attempt at real control would be met with force.[4] The stalemate continued during the first half of 1845.

The people of Glass continued their old custom of raising the national flag of whatever ship, generally English, was anchored off their town; but the sight of the Union Jack flying over the town symbolized defiance to the French in the blockhouse and on the *stationnaire*. Finally, on 5 May Commandant Fournier arrived in the river with orders to execute the treaty. The French insisted that their flag be flown daily as a symbol of sovereignty, but were willing to permit the flags of other nations to be raised in addition when a ship of that nation was at anchor. Brisset, the officer in command of the fort, believed that the Mpongwe would agree, as they were too cowardly to resist. The only complicating factor was, in his view, the presence of the American missionaries, whom he thought were promising British and American aid.[5]

Mpongwe defiance became evident on 27 June when they raised the English and American flags to salute a visiting British ship. A detachment from the French warship was landed to lower the flags, but had to retreat in the face of an armed and menacing crowd. The French responded by declaring a blockade and seizing boats and boatmen from Glass and from the mission. A compromise was arranged and the prisoners were released. The truce collapsed on

[1] Captain of H.M.S. *Éclair* to Commodore Jones, 13 Jan. 1845.

[2] Wilson to Anderson, 30 Jan. 1845, A.B.C. 15.4, vol. iii, No. 103.

[3] Governor of Senegal to Min. Marine, 9 May 1845, Archives d'Outre-Mer, Sénégal, iv, 38, c.

[4] Wilson, 'Letter of December 9, 1844', *M.H.*, xli (1845), p. 157.

[5] Brisset to Min. Marine, 11 May 1845, Archives d'Outre-Mer, Sénégal, iv, 38, c.

12 July when a new commandant, La Hardrouyère, anchored the
Tactique off Glass. The people responded by raising both French
and British flags, even though there was no British ship in the river.
Despite a mediation attempt by Louis, the blockade resumed.
When the French began to fire on people walking on the beach or
attempting to fish, the Mpongwe moved their families and goods into
the bush. The French tried unsuccessfully to prevent the other
Mpongwe towns from sending food supplies to beleaguered Glass.

Another temporary truce was concluded on 25 July. The Mpongwe
were led to believe that if they hoisted the French banner to salute
the *Tactique*, the French would be satisfied and leave. The salute
was given on the morning of 26 July, but, according to the French,
on the wrong flagpost. The weeks of verbal quarrels and threats
abruptly ended when the *Tactique* began firing on the town. Senegalese
troops had been marched to Glass beforehand; they immediately
attacked from the north while a landing party from the warship
moved in from the beach. Wilson raised the American flag over the
mission, ostensibly to proclaim neutrality. The French took this for
an act of defiance and shells began falling closer to the mission until
the banner was hauled down. The Mpongwe retired into the bush
without resistance, allowing the attackers to pillage the town at their
ease. No casualties had been suffered by either side. The French flag
flew alone over Glass on the morning of 27 July.[1]

The people of Glass remained on their farms in the bush for several
months after the attack. They threatened to move north on the coast
to Batanga, but finally returned to their old town at the end of October.[2] There was no further defiance of the French, but King Glass
refused to accept the annual French present to subject chiefs until
1847. Even then, Toko refused to acknowledge alien rule and declined
his *cadeau*.[3]

---

[1] This account is from Deschamps, *Quinze Ans*, pp. 306–7; Wilson to Anderson,
27 July 1845, A.B.C. 15.4, vol. iii, No. 108; and La Hardrouyère to Min. Marine,
15 Aug. 1845, Archives d'Outre-Mer, Sénégal, iv, 38 c. The American version of
the controversy is sketched in Clarence C. Clendenen and Peter Duignan,
Americans in Black Africa up to 1865 (Stanford, 1964), pp. 72–5; and described
much more extensively in Henry H. Bucher, Jr., 'The Village of Glass and
Western Intrusion: An Mpongwe Response to the American and French Presence
in the Gabon Estuary: 1842–1845', *The International Journal of African Historical
Studies*, vi (1973), pp. 363–400.

[2] Wilson to Anderson, 9 Nov. 1845, A.B.C. 15.4, vol. iii, No. 112.

[3] Wm. Walker to Anderson, 31 Dec.–7 Feb. 1846–7, A.B.C. 15.4, vol. iii, No.
363.

French attitudes towards the missionaries had hardened during the crisis. La Hardrouyère was convinced that opposition came 'solely from the support of the missionaries', who, he was told by King Denis, had great influence on Toko and the younger Mpongwe. He had in fact taken Wilson's use of the American flag as an act of defiance and had fired a few shots near his house until it was lowered.[1] Brisset shared these views and expressed the hope that he would be able to report the departure of the 'Methodistes' [sic] in his next letter.[2] The missionaries were well aware of their precarious position, but were determined to try to stay.[3] The arrival in August of an American warship, the *Truxton* of Commander Henry Bruce, gave them some hope. Wilson complained about the bombardment of Glass and the mission, and Bruce took up the matter with the French.[4]

While the American officer did not condone Wilson's use of the American flag,[5] he did not share the view of an anonymous American officer who accused Wilson of leading the opposition to France,[6] and the naval visit may have reminded the French that the missionaries could be protected. Meanwhile, fearing the worst, Wilson sold most of the mission's property[7] and suggested that Cape Lopez or Cape St. Catherine be occupied if Gabon became untenable.[8] Baudin, the new French commander, was a little sorry that the Americans seemed about to leave, because they in fact had done much good work. The people of Glass were the most civilized in the river, 'malgré les idées un peu anglais'.[9]

But the missionaries were never expelled and they soon decided to remain. In late February 1846 Captain Darricau, who even in the

---

[1] La Hardrouyère to Min. Marine, 15 Aug. 1845.

[2] Brisset to Min. Marine, 20 Aug. 1845, Archives d'Outre-Mer, Sénégal, iv, 38, c. Brisset commanded the fort at Louis; La Hardrouyère was in charge of naval affairs.

[3] Wilson to Anderson, 6 Aug. 1845, A.B.C. 15.4, vol. iii, No. 109.

[4] La Hardrouyère to Min. Marine, 15 Aug. 1845, and encls.; Letters Received by the Secretary of the Navy from Commanding Officers of Squadrons, African Squadron, National Archives Microfilm, No. 89, Reel 102, No. 81, Bruce to Commodore Skinner, 18 Oct. 1845, and encls.

[5] Wilson to Anderson, 24 Jan. 1845, A.B.C. 15.4, vol. iii, No. 115.

[6] Letter by an officer of the Truxton in the *New York Mirror*, 6 Dec. 1845, A.B.C. 15.4, vol. iii, No. 42.

[7] Wilson to Anderson, 9 Nov. 1845.

[8] Wilson to Anderson, 29 Jan. 1846, A.B.C. 15.4, vol. iii, No. 115.

[9] Baudin to Min. Marine, 15 Dec. 1845, Archives d'Outre-Mer, Sénégal, iv, 38, c.

midst of the 1844 crisis had expressed his admiration for the mission's work and for Wilson personally,[1] returned to Gabon. He wrote to Wilson, expressing official regrets that the mission had been endangered and gave assurances of the Admiral's friendly attitude.[2] Another visit by American warships helped cement the reconciliation. Commodore Reade left a letter for the Admiral, which apparently convinced the French that there was official interest in the fate of Wilson and his colleagues.[3] Within a few years, relations between the two parties had become quite amicable.

Between 1842 and 1845 the Mpongwe had seen the sudden appearance and settlement of three groups of aliens. Mpongwe commercial success had put the Gabon on the map. The American Protestants had learned of Gabon from traders and had established themselves in Glass, the centre of English and American commerce. French naval interest in the region was both commercial and strategic. Originally attracted to the area as a possible trading zone and by the desire to punish Kringer for his attacks on French shipping, the navy quickly came to appreciate Gabon's fine harbour. The Catholic missionaries had simply followed the navy.

The newcomers had not yet had much impact on Mpongwe life. The Catholics were not very active and their mission was still very small. Protestant religious and educational activity had been much more intensive, but no converts had been made. The people of Glass had attempted to use the pastors in their struggle to ward off the French, but the failure of this strategy resulted in a great loss of influence for the missionaries. Treaties had been obtained from all four major Mpongwe rulers by gifts, trickery, or the threat and use of naval gunfire, but French power was still not felt in most areas of Mpongwe life. Although no attempt had yet been made to control local politics, alter the old trading system, or even to end the export of slaves, the Mpongwe were teetering on the brink of colonial rule.

[1] Lieutenant Darricau, 'Rapport de M. Darricau', *Revue coloniale*, iii (1844), pp. 598–602. For similar praise of the American mission see Bouët-Willaumez's 'Rapport sur les comptoirs fortifées de la côte d'Afrique, 1 May 1844', Archives d'Outre-Mer, Sénégal, iv, 30, a.

[2] Wilson to Anderson, 27 Feb. 1846, A.B.C. 15.4, vol. iii, No. 118.

[3] Wilson to Anderson, 21 Sept. 1846, A.B.C. 15.4, vol. iii, No. 121.

CHAPTER VI

The Mpongwe and The Europeans:
1845–1875

THE bombardment of Glass clearly established French hegemony in the Gabon; the Mpongwe never again challenged the fact of alien rule. In addition to the loss of their political independence, the Mpongwe were threatened culturally by the Christian missions and economically by the rise of the factory system. The Mpongwe continued to enjoy much internal autonomy during the early years of colonial rule, but, as will be discussed below, they suffered an almost complete eclipse by the end of the period.

In 1845 the Gabon base seemed essential to the French Navy. France had just negotiated a new anti-slavery treaty with the British which abolished the mutual rights of visit to suspected slavers. In return for this concession, which meant in practice that English warships could no longer search (and allegedly harass) French vessels suspected of slaving, France had to agree to maintain a large African squadron to police slavers operating under the French flag. Gabon became the southern base for the anti-slavery squadron and for a few years the *comptoir* was of real use. However, most of the squadron was withdrawn during the domestic crisis of 1848, and Gabon lost its strategic importance. The reduced African squadron continued to use the river as a base from time to time during its rather feeble campaign against the slave trade south of the equator, but the *comptoir* was more of a burden than an aid to the navy after 1848.[1]

The *comptoir* lingered on after that date. A small garrison of Senegalese troops was maintained in the fort near Louis and an armed hulk was anchored offshore. The French establishment at the 'Plateau' in Quaben's old domains suffered severely from the climate and tropical diseases. Gabon was an unpopular post; most officers assigned there were primarily interested in serving their tour and getting out as soon as possible. 'All Frenchmen seem to dislike the

[1] Bernard Schnapper, *La Politique et le commerce français dans le Golfe du Guinée de 1838 à 1871* (Paris, 1961), pp. 76–86.

coast of Africa,' wrote one of the American missionaries, 'and the Gaboon in particular.'[1] Richard F. Burton, who visited the Gabon in 1862, found the French officials there quite unhappy with their lot. Although they had neat houses and gardens at the post, the officers slept on board the *stationnaire* rather than expose themselves to the malignant 'climate'. 'Besides fear of fever, they are victims to *ennui* and nostalgia and, expecting the Comptoir to pay large profits, they are quite disappointed by the reverse being the case.' The French spent much of their time in the 'Hôtel Fischer', run by an enterprising Swiss widow, where they whiled away the time, eating, drinking, and playing dominoes.[2] A few exceptional men did exert themselves enough to police the river or undertake short exploring trips, but most were content to live quietly in the fort or on the ship, counting the days until they were replaced.[3]

The French force varied in strength from year to year. Fifty-six men were based in Gabon in 1845; this number rose to 195 two years later at the height of naval activity in the region. After 1848 the garrison was sharply reduced; only fifty-seven officers and men were present in 1852. This small force was sufficient to overawe the local population, but was hardly adequate to control it. The administration of the *comptoir* was further weakened by the rapid turnover in personnel; fourteen commanders served in the first fifteen years of the post's existence. The Gabon *comptoir* was a dependency of Senegal from 1843 to 1854 and then of Gorée until 1859, when the Ministry of the Navy made it the administrative centre for all of the Gulf of Guinea *comptoirs*.[4]

The commanders' duties included maintaining French sovereignty and public order, developing legitimate commerce with France, suppressing the slave trade, and, after 1849, administering Libreville,

[1] William Walker to Anderson, 20 Apr. 1865, American Board of Commissioners for Foreign Missions Letterbooks, 15.1, vol. iv, No. 316.
[2] Richard F. Burton, *Two Trips to Gorillaland and the Cataracts of the Congo* (London, 1876, reprinted 1967), i, pp. 4–14. The quotation is from p. 5.
[3] Hubert Deschamps, *Quinze Ans de Gabon; les débuts de l'établissement français 1839–1853* (Paris, 1965). The vicissitudes of the French post are described on pp. 92–100 and 308–23. Captain Vignon, a former commander, gives a brief description in 'Le Comptoir français du Gabon sur la côte occidentale d'Afrique', *Nouvelles Annales de voyages*, iv (1856), pp. 282–4.
[4] 'Les Colonies françaises: établissements de la Côte d'Or et du Gabon', *Revue maritime et coloniale*, ix (1863), p. 45. A partial list of commanders is given on pp. 45–6. See also Guy Lasserre, *Libreville, la ville et sa région* (Paris, 1958), pp. 112–13.

the tiny settlement for recaptured slaves. The original inhabitants of Libreville were about fifty survivors of a slaver taken near Loango in 1846. The recaptives were first taken to Senegal and in 1849 some were moved to Gabon where they were given houses and gardens near the government post. The settlement was occasionally reinforced by handfuls of later recaptives, but it always remained small and unimportant. Most of the men drifted into the employ of the French post or the traders.[1]

Commanders had two major ways of carrying out these functions; the military strength of the garrison and visiting warships, and the control of presents for the chiefs. The Mpongwe were well aware of the strength of European arms and, except for an episode in 1848 when a warship shelled Quaben's town to force the surrender of a criminal, they made no further attempt to challenge the French presence militarily. However, the French were not strong enough to interfere in local affairs nor, as will be discussed below, to put a stop to the export of slaves. By the terms of the treaties of cession, Mpongwe leaders were entitled to annual presents. These *cadeaux* were supposed to be compensation for ending the slave trade and were used as a 'carrot' to ensure good behaviour on the part of the chiefs.[2] In 1852 the presents totalled 10,000 francs in cash and goods; Denis got 1,015 francs, Quaben 700, Glass and George 600 each. Chief Louis's present was raised to 700 francs in appreciation for recent services. Forty-two other Mpongwe and several Shekiani and Fang chiefs shared the remainder. Recalcitrant individuals found their *cadeau* reduced or eliminated.[3] French political demands were not particularly stringent in the '40s and '50s. The Mpongwe were allowed to regulate their own affairs as long as order prevailed and there was no attempt to repudiate French overlordship. The authorities did intervene in capital cases, disputes involving Europeans, and to prevent sacrifices of slaves at the funerals of Mpongwe notables. 'But', observed an American evangelist, 'they do not interfere very much with native customs.'[4] Abolition of the traffic in slaves was the most threatening demand made

---

[1] Lasserre, *Libreville*, pp. 66–8; Deschamps, *Quinze Ans*, pp. 311-13, and 316-18.

[2] 'Rapport du 9 avril, 1847', Archives d'Outre-Mer, Sénégal, iv, 39, a.

[3] 'Arrêt sur le présent état de répartition montant à la somme de dix-mille francs', 1852, Archives d'Outre-Mer, Sénégal, iv, 40, b; 'Compte des dépenses effectuées en 1855 pour présents et coutumes aux chefs de la côte', Archives d'Outre-Mer, Gorée, iv, 1, a.

[4] Wm. Walker to Anderson, 20 Apr. 1865, A.B.C. 15.1, vol. iv, No. 316.

by the commandants and this was not consistently enforced for many years.

The French first began to move against the Mpongwe slave trade in 1845. However, despite the vociferous complaints of the American missionaries and frustrated British navy men, their measures were intermittent and ineffectual for many years. Until after the resolution of the Glass crisis, the authorities were too unsure of their own position to risk arousing further Mpongwe hostility by attacking the lucrative trade in slaves.[1] The French, while admitting their own inability to control the traffic, refused to allow the British to make captures in the river.[2] However, after the subjugation of Glass, France took measures to close the barracoons at Denis and put an end to the small boat traffic. La Hardrouyère's proposal for a base on the south bank to cut the overland trade from Denis to Cape Lopez was not acted upon, but on 15 October Baudin and Brisset, the commanders of the fleet and the blockhouse respectively, issued a proclamation banning the slave trade in the Gabon River. The Brazilian factors at Denis were given three months to wind up their affairs and leave. Orders were given to capture the small boats which were plying the river, bringing slaves from as far as Corisco Island. Recaptured slaves were to be sent to Gorée.[3]

These stern measures seemed successful. With the departure of the Brazilian factors, the barracoons at Denis were closed down. A Brazilian brig was searched in the river and one chained slave was rescued from a captured canoe.[4] But the very base of the French squadron charged with suppressing the slave trade soon became a hotbed of slaving activity.

Large vessels were no longer loaded in the Gabon, but slaves were still sent from the river in small batches to the Orungu barracoons. In 1847 William Walker observed that Spanish agents from Cape Lopez were buying slaves in Glass;[5] a year later Spaniards visited

[1] Governor of Senegal to Min. of Marine, 9 May 1845, Archives d'Outre-Mer, Sénégal, iv, 38, c.

[2] Captain of H.M.S. *Éclair* to Commodore Jones, 13 Jan. 1845, Archives d'Outre-Mer, Afrique, vi, 3, b.

[3] La Hardrouyère to Min. of Marine, 15 Aug. 1845, Archives d'Outre-Mer, Sénégal, iv, 38, c; 'Instructions pour le bâtiment stationnaire dans le Gabon', 4 Nov. 1845, and encl. 'Proclamation of 15 Oct. 1845', Archives d'Outre-Mer, Sénégal, xiv, 4.

[4] Brisset to Min. of Marine, Jan. 1846, Archives d'Outre-Mer, Sénégal, xiv, 4.

[5] William Walker Diary, v, 11 Sept. 1847. William Walker Papers, Box II, Wisconsin State Historical Society.

Glass two or three times weekly to buy slaves at forty dollars apiece. Slaves were also purchased at Quaben and Louis, under the very guns of the blockhouse. There again were two barracoons at Denis; from them fifteen or twenty slaves a week were sent to Sangatanga. Chief Duka also maintained a barracoon. Walker apparently did not report this information to the authorities, who he concluded either did not care about enforcing the law or were such utter fools that they were incapable of doing so.[1] Spanish purchases on the north bank continued into 1849.[2]

Two British naval vessels visited the river in 1849 and submitted reports to their superiors which were very critical of the French regime's anti-slaving efforts.[3] These complaints led to diplomatic exchanges between London and Paris which forced the French Foreign Minister to seek information from the Navy about British charges of official laxity in the Gabon.[4] The local authorities maintained that reports of slaving were greatly exaggerated and that naval surveillance was quite vigilant.[5] While they admitted that there was perhaps some smuggling, the French officials argued that the situation was impossible to control completely because hundreds of canoes were active in the estuary and surrounding creeks day and night. As the British had learned for themselves in the Sierra Leone Rivers, such small-scale slaving was impossible to stop, even with a large fleet.[6]

Despite their embarrassed denials and evasions, the naval authorities had not been able to make any headway against the trade, which, as they were well aware, flourished all around them.[7] In the words of one officer,

nos relations et notre influence dans le pays etaient si peu etabli, malgré les

---

1 Wm. Walker Diary, vi, 10 Aug. 1848; and Wm. Walker to Anderson, 11 Aug. 1848, A.B.C. 15.1, vol. 3, No. 370.

2 Wm. Walker Diary, vi, 28 Jan. and 6 Feb. 1849.

3 Commander Chamberlain to Commodore Fanshawe, 30 June 1849, Parliamentary Papers, Commons, 1850, lv, Class A, No. 182, encl. 2 for the visit of the *Britomart*; and Min. of Foreign Affairs to Min. of Marine, 9 Apr. 1849, Archives d'Outre-Mer, Sénégal, xiv, 4 for the visit of H.M.S. *Alert*.

4 Min. of Foreign Affairs to Min. of Marine, 9 Nov. 1849, Archives d'Outre-Mer, Sénégal, xiv, 4.

5 Ibid., Baudin to Min. of Marine, 16 Mar. 1850.

6 Ibid., Bouët-Willaumez to Min. of Marine, 26 Jan. 1850. This letter and the one cited in n. 4 above are printed in P.P., Commons, 1851, lvi, Part II, Class B, No. 279, encls. 2 and 3.

7 Deschamps, *Quinze Ans*, pp. 114-15.

cadeaux annuels assez considerables, que la traite des esclaves se faisait encore dans les villages plus proches voisins.

Even inhabitants of Libreville had been sold.[1] The controversy did stimulate the French into more vigorous patrolling of the estuary, which temporarily cut down the traffic.[2]

Within a few months the trade had revived. Slaves were once again sold at Glass, transported across the estuary in canoes, and marched overland from Denis to Sangatanga. During a brief feud between Kings Glass and Denis, King Passol sent boats directly to Glass to pick up slaves.[3] The French managed to catch one of these canoes at Glass. Six slaves were liberated and a Spanish factor named Fontan and his three Orungu colleagues were arrested. J. L. Wilson interceded on behalf of the Mpongwe dealer, who received a short term in jail, but Fontan and his crew were sent to Senegal for trial.[4]

By the mid-fifties the Mpongwe slave trade had almost ceased. The reduced demand following the closure of the Brazilian markets could be met by shipments down the Ogowe; there was no need to run even the modest risk of capture by the French in the Gabon. The revival of the slave trade to São Tomé and Principe in the 1860s led to a few slaving incidents involving the Mpongwe, but the bulk of this traffic was directed to the less carefully patrolled coasts of Cape Lopez and Fernan Vaz.[5]

The last large-scale Mpongwe involvement in the slave trade was that sponsored by the French government. In 1855 the commander of Gabon was instructed to pay up to 200 francs each for thirty *captifs* to be used in Gorée as soldiers. He was ordered to hurry, because

[1] 'Rapport sur le Gabon, Grand Bassam, Assini', 1 Mar. 1855, p. 7, 'État en 1850', by Auguste Bouët. Archives d'Outre-Mer, Gorée, iv, 1, a.

[2] Martin to Naval Commander, West Africa, 20 May 1850, Archives d'Outre-Mer, Sénégal, xiv, 4.

[3] 'Inspection de 1851, Comptoir du Gabon', by Charles Penard, 12 Dec. 1851, Archives d'Outre-Mer, Sénégal, iv, 40, a.

[4] Charles Penard to Min. of Marine, 20 Nov. 1851, Archives d'Outre-Mer, Sénégal, xiv, 4. Fontan was a crewman on a slave ship who had been abandoned at Cape Lopez by his captain. He had been employed as a trading agent by King Passol for the ten months preceding his arrest in August 1851. The four slavers were tried in Senegal and acquitted on a technicality. 'Rapport du magistrat sur Fontan', 26 July 1853, Archives d'Outre-Mer, Sénégal, xiv, 4.

[5] Ira Preston to Secretary of State Seward, 12 Aug. 1865, United States Consular Reports, Gabon, National Archives microfilm; and Wm. Walker Diary, x, 22 Aug. 1865 and 5 Mar. 1867. Several attempts to kidnap residents of Libreville, the settlement for slaves recaptured by the French, were foiled by the authorities. 'Rapport sur le Gabon', 21 Dec. 1866, Archives d'Outre-Mer, Gabon, i, 6, d.

troops were needed quickly.[1] Some unscrupulous Mpongwe offered their slaves as 'volunteers'; the slave became a soldier and the master pocketed the enlistment bonus.[2] The major French demand for slaves began in 1857 when the firm of Régis Frères got a government contract to supply fourteen thousand voluntary emigrant labourers to Martinique and Guadeloupe.[3] Slaves brought to the coast were purchased under the supervision of French naval officers, 'ransomed', loaded onto a boat, and sent off as sort of indentured servants to the West Indies. Most of the chained 'emigrants' were acquired in the Congo River, but a few ships bought their human cargoes in the Gabon.[4]

Whatever the legalities of the status of the 'emigrants' in the West Indies, the effect of their procurement in Africa was to stimulate the slave trade. As an American missionary wrote,

The French have opened the slave trade in this river. It may be called elsewhere by another name. Here it is known only by the above title. The natives know of no distinction between this and the Spanish and Portuguese slave trade.[5]

At least eight hundred slaves were taken from the Gabon before intensive British diplomatic pressure forced France to abandon the labour scheme in 1862.[6] This episode was, except for some minor smuggling to the Portuguese islands in the 1860s, the last gasp of the slave trade in the estuary.[7]

[1] 'Instructions au Commandant du Gabon', 29 Sept. 1855, Archives d'Outre-Mer, Gorée, iv, 3, b.

[2] R. P. Neu, 'Travail du R. P. Neu sur le Gabon', unpublished MS. (c. 1885), Archives of the Cong. St. Esprit, Boîte 148, I.

[3] Schnapper, *Politique et commerce*, p. 160. The original agreement was for twenty thousand labourers, but this was reduced in 1859 in response to heavy British pressure.

[4] A. Bosse to Min. of Marine, 24 June 1859, Archives d'Outre-Mer, Gabon, i, 2, a; ibid., Min. of Marine to Captain Didelot, 10 Oct. 1861. L. Protet, the commander of Gorée, defended the emigrant scheme against English press 'diatribes' in his report of 2 Sept. 1858, ibid. Protet, like past generations of defenders of the slave trade, claimed that the trade was saving Africans from ignorance and human sacrifice and giving them a chance to live in a civilized, Christian environment.

[5] Jacob Best to Anderson, 9 June 1858, A.B.C. 15.1, vol. iii, No. 45.

[6] Bushnell to Anderson, 2 Feb. 1849, A.B.C. 15.1, vol. iii, No. 190; Bushnell, 'Letter of June 1, 1859', *The Missionary Herald*, lv (1859), p. 290.

[7] In 1866 the French broke up attempts to seize residents of Libreville and send them as slaves to Cape Lopez. Commandant du Gabon to Admiral de Langle, 29 Dec. 1866, Archives d'Outre-Mer, Gabon, i, 6, d.

Missionaries, both Protestant and Catholic, had little more success converting the Mpongwe to their respective forms of Christianity than the navy did in forcing them to end the slave trade. The centre of Protestant activity continued to be at Glass; the Catholics established themselves a few miles north in the territory of Quaben, near the government post. Relations between the two missions were far from cordial. Missionaries of the two groups generally regarded each other as unscrupulous rivals spreading 'heretical' or 'papist' falsehoods, and rejoiced in their fellow Christians' lack of success. French priests complained that their 'Méthodiste' competitors enjoyed lavish financial support and were too involved with commerce; the American ministers, being teetotalling Sabbatarians, were horrified by 'Jesuit' religious processions and tolerance of rum. A few missionaries tried to bridge the cultural and theological chasm by exchanging visits and linguistic data, but usually the two bodies did their best to ignore each other.

The Protestants conducted energetic prosyletizing campaigns at their base at Baraka in Glass town, at a few outstations, and by preaching tours to other villages. In 1848, when it became apparent that the French were not going to expel the mission, eight new evangelists were sent to the Gabon. Six Mpongwe were baptized; others were 'inquiring' and the field 'never was more encouraging'.[1] The missionaries extended their operations to George's town, Nengue-Nengue Island on the Como, the Bakalai villages near the Moondah and, briefly, to Fernan Vaz on the coast south of Cape Lopez. Despite the opposition of 'fanatical movements', especially among the women, and the disastrous influx of American rum which did the Mpongwe 'ten thousand times more injury than French guns', the mission's prospects appeared bright.[2]

But evangelical optimism proved premature. In 1852 the missionaries reported that their ranks had been thinned by disease, school attendance was down, and outstations had been abandoned.[3] Educated 'native assistants' were drawn away by the lure of trade profits, as were the schoolboys.[4] Reinforcements were sent again in 1853 and 1857, but most of the recruits soon died or returned to

[1] 'Report of the West Africa Mission for 1848', A.B.C. 15.1, vol. iii, No. 3.
[2] 'Report for 1849', A.B.C. 15.1, vol. iii, No. 5, and Wilson to Anderson, 13 Sept. 1849, A.B.C. 15.1, vol. iii, No. 501.
[3] 'Report of the Gaboon Mission for the Year 1852', A.B.C. 15.1, vol. iii, No. 10.
[4] Wm. Walker to Anderson, 1 Apr. 1850, A.B.C. 15.1, vol. iii, No. 390.

America.[1] By 1859 the Board was becoming discouraged with the Gabon station, as converts were few and fickle, while the missionary death rate was high.[2] And, although the Board was not yet fully aware of it, the staff in the field was torn by dissension. The frustrated and disease-racked missionaries quarrelled over doctrine, the use of ale as medicine, the propriety of one of their number acting as the United States Commercial Agent, educational policy, and social relations with European traders; personal vanities and feuds became as important as policy decisions.[3] Younger missionaries criticized the conservative 'preach and hope' tactics of their elders, which failed to attract or hold converts and had not produced an indigenous clergy. Most of the dissidents eventually either quit or joined the Presbyterian mission on Corisco.[4] William Walker and Albert Bushnell, despite their very strained personal relations, doggedly stayed on at Baraka for another decade, but by 1860 it was evident that the A.B.C.F.M. venture in Gabon had failed.

The Gabon mission was taken from the feeble hands of the American Board by the Presbyterian Church in the U.S.A. in 1870. The Presbyterians had begun work on Corisco in 1850 and had expanded their activities to several points along the Rio Muni coast by 1870. Unlike the A.B.C.F.M., they had had considerable success in getting converts and creating an African clergy. After the ending of an internal schism, those 'New School' Presbyterians who had been affiliated with the Congregationalists of the A.B.C.F.M. returned to the fold. A number of mission stations, including Gabon, were transferred at the same time. Bushnell, a Presbyterian, remained at Baraka.[5]

---

[1] William Ireland, *Historical Sketch of the Zulu Mission, in South Africa, as also of the Gaboon Mission, in Western Africa* (Boston, 1863), p. 30.

[2] *M.H.*, lv (1859), p. 331.

[3] See, for example, Bushnell to Anderson, 24 June 1867, A.B.C. 15.1, vol. iv, No. 139, and Wm. Walker to Clark, 4 May 1869, ibid., No. 342.

[4] Clark to Anderson, 13 Sept. 1860 and 29 Dec. 1860 (two letters), A.B.C. 15.1, vol. iv, Nos. 195, 196, 197.

[5] For a general account of Presbyterian activities in the area and the transfer of missions, see Arthur Judson Brown, *One Hundred Years: A History of the Foreign Missionary Work of the Presbyterian Church in the U.S.A.* (New York, 1936), especially pp. 196–251; and Robert H. Nassau, *Corisco Days: The First Thirty Years of the West Africa Mission* (Philadelphia, 1910). A union of the Gabon and Corisco missions had been discussed by the missionaries in the field as early as 1867. Robert H. Nassau to Walter Lowrie, Mar. 1867, Presbyterian Church in the U.S.A., Board of Foreign Missions, Correspondence and Report Files, Africa, vol. ix, No. 1, microfilm reel 70.

The new missionaries were pleased with the initial Mpongwe response to their teachings. Fourteen members were admitted in 1871 and others were seeking instruction.[1] The schools were well attended, congregations were large, Mr. Truman, a Benga 'native helper' was busy at Nengue-Nengue, and the French officials were friendly. Optimism reigned at Baraka; the only obstacles seemed to be rum and the jealousy of the less successful Roman Catholics, with whom relations continued to be far from cordial.[2] 'How much better', asked Bushnell, 'are papal than pagan superstitions?'[3] As we shall see in the next chapter, the Protestants extended their work into the Ogowe in 1874, thus stealing a march on their Catholic rivals.

Roman Catholic activity in Gabon had its origins in the efforts of two American clergymen, Monsignor (later Bishop) Edward Barron and Father John Kelly, to establish a mission in Liberia. Work began in 1842 at Cape Palmas, the site of the A.B.C.F.M.'s first African venture. Barron then went to France to seek aid and reinforcements.[4] His appeal came at an opportune moment, as French governmental and ecclesiastical interest in Africa was then very high. On 14 November 1843 Père Libermann of the Order of the Sacred Heart of Mary signed an agreement with the Naval Ministry governing mission activity in the new *comptoirs*. The government was to provide transport, buildings, and an annual subsidy of 1,500 francs for each priest and 400 francs for each brother; in return the clergy were to submit annual reports to the local commander and would not preach in the interior without official permission.[5] Seven priests had already embarked on a French warship for Cape Palmas, where they arrived in January 1844.

Fever struck within a few days. In March the survivors abandoned Cape Palmas and moved to the Assinie and Grand Bassam *comptoirs*; two continued on to Gabon. Père Bessieux and Frère Grégoire landed on 28 September 1844 and were given food and lodging by the naval

---

[1] J. C. Kops to Lowrie, 2 Oct. 1871, Presbyterian microfilms, vol. ix, No. 280, reel 71.

[2] Bushnell to Lowrie, 27 Jan. 1872, ibid., vol. ix, No. 311, reel 71, and 29 Sept. 1873, ibid., vol. ix, No. 477, reel 71.

[3] Bushnell to Lowrie, 13 Nov. 1871, ibid., vol. ix, No. 292, reel 71.

[4] Clarence C. Clendenen and Peter Duignan, *Americans in Black Africa up to 1865* (Stanford, 1964), pp. 79–80.

[5] 'La Première Expédition des missionnaires du Saint-Coeur de Marie en Guinée (1843–1845)', pamphlet c. 1930 in the Archives of the Congrégation des Pères du Saint-Esprit, published in the *Bulletin général de la congrégation du Saint-Esprit*, xxxiv (1929–30), pp. 540–88.

authorities. Bessieux and his colleague built their own quarters, began to learn Mpongwe, and within four months had opened a school. For over a year the two laboured on alone, without a word from their superiors, who believed them dead. Indeed, the whole African mission seemed to have been a disaster. Disease had carried off all the priests in the Ivory Coast *comptoirs*, Barron and Kelly had gone home in despair, and for a year there had been no letters from Gabon. When one of Bessieux's letters finally reached France, his overjoyed superiors sent out reinforcements. Priests from the newly-formed Congrégation du Saint-Esprit and sisters of the order of the Imma-culée-Conception des Castres reached Gabon in 1848 to work under Bessieux's direction.[1]

Like their American counterparts, the French Catholics found the Gabon a difficult field. The climate was unpleasant and unhealthy; disease struck down many missionaries. Relations with the secular authorities were often tenuous. Quarrels over the state subsidy were frequent and the officials resented clerical criticism of their personal behaviour and failure to attend church. Indeed, Protestant fears of a state–church alliance against them proved completely unfounded. The local Africans were thinly scattered over a wide area and spoke several difficult languages. Worst of all they were polygamists, steeped in sin and too obsessed with trade and quick profits to seek salvation. Many of the priests and brothers became discouraged by the lack of response to their teachings; frustration and sickness led to internal bickering. Some resented Bessieux's imperious leadership and his insistence on agricultural labour for all; student, convert, and missionary.[2]

The first thirty years of evangelical work seemed to have had little impact on the Mpongwe. Neither mission made much headway in terms of conversions and, despite Bishop Bessieux's constant efforts to retain 'latinistes' in his school and the Protestants' search for young men strong enough in the faith to resist the lure of trade, no progress was made toward the creation of an indigenous clergy. In

[1] 'La Première Expédition', pp. 19–45; Père J. B. Piolet, *Les Missions catholiques françaises au XIXe siècle*, v, *Missions d'Afrique* (Paris, 1902), pp. 221–4. Bessieux became a bishop in 1864 and served in Gabon until his death in 1876.

[2] 'Notes sur les difficultés de la Mission d'Afrique', by R. P. Briot (1853?), Cong. St. Esp., Boîte 148, III; 'Rapport du Frère Antoine (Roussel) sur les divers postes de la Mission du Gabon', 17 July 1853, Cong. St. Esp., 148, III; 'Mission du Gabon—rapport du R. P. Le Berre', (1857), Cong. St. Esp., 167, V.

1860 the Catholics claimed 493 baptized members;[1] this figure included over 100 school children, plus infants, adults baptized *in
extremis*, and foreigners. Most of the 'converts' were far from active.
School enrolment had grown to about 150–200 during the 1860s.
Boys, educated by the priests, were easier to attract than the girls in
the Sisters' school. The Protestants had very rigid standards for
converts and subjected church members to strict discipline; they
rarely claimed more than forty or fifty adherents. Their schools were
also smaller, but were sometimes considered superior to the Catholic
institutions.[2] By the 1860s Protestant fortunes were clearly on the
wane; for example in 1864, a good year, there were only 22 boys
and 23 girls in school and many of the 47 church members were on
the verge of expulsion.[3]

Mpongwe attitudes toward the missions ranged from courteous
curiosity to indifference. Missionaries hopefully noted short periods
of 'greater interest' from time to time, but encountered little real
hostility. Attendance at boarding schools was irregular and many
students soon dropped out;[4] adult church attendance was as in-
constant. 'The fact is', wrote one discouraged Protestant, 'our
converts need to be converted over again pretty often.'[5] Those
attracted to the missions were usually persons of low status. Mpongwe
kings and merchants sometimes went to services, sent some of their
children to school, and maintained friendly relations with the
priests and pastors, but almost never became adherents of the new
religions.[6] The son of Toko, the Glass merchant, did become a
Protestant, but he was a leper.[7] Women seemed especially resistant to
Christian teachings; the Protestants did not claim their first female
convert until after twenty years of work.[8] Most Protestant members
and 'inquirers' were Bakalai or other non-Mpongwe people; many
were of slave status.[9] The Catholics attracted persons of similar background; in addition slaves recaptured by the authorities were placed

[1] 'État Semestriel, 1860, janvier-juin', Cong. St. Esp., Boîte 167, VI.
[2] 'Comptoir du Gabon, Inspection de 1852', Archives d'Outre-Mer, Sénégal,
iv, 40, b.
[3] 'Twenty-Third Annual Report—1864', A.B.C. 15.1, vol. iv, No. 9.
[4] 'Rapport du Frère Antoine', 1853.
[5] Wm. Walker to Anderson, 23 Feb. 1864, A.B.C. 15.1, vol. iv, No. 304.
[6] *Bulletin général*, iii, No. 23 (1862), p. 115; Bushnell to Anderson, 22 July
1865, A.B.C. 15.1, vol. iv, No. 110.
[7] Wm. Walker to Anderson, 4 July 1864, A.B.C. 15.1, vol. iv, No. 307.
[8] Bushnell to Anderson, 13 July 1864, A.B.C. 15.1, vol. iv, No. 94.
[9] Wm. Walker to Anderson, 27 June 1865, A.B.C. 15.1, vol. iv, No. 318.

in their care as well as fugitives from the Portuguese islands.[1] Indeed, a French traveller in the early 1870s wrote that most of the few sincere Catholics in the Gabon were 'Black Portuguese' escapees from São Tomé and Principe.[2]

Several factors help explain the missions' failure to attract significant local support in this period. Disease weakened the effort considerably; the missionaries were few in number and often in poor health. Tactics of evangelization seem to have been rigid and not adapted to local conditions. Catholics and Protestants alike placed great stress on boarding schools, but education had little attraction for most Mpongwe. Boys could acquire knowledge useful in trade, but most parents saw no reason to send their daughters to school.[3] The Mpongwe were 'addicted' to commerce; even those interested in religion were exposed to temptation during trading trips and, to the dismay of the Protestants, had to deal in rum.[4] The behaviour of secular Europeans in the Gabon hardly reinforced missionary teachings on honesty, charity, temperance, and monogamy. But most important, few Mpongwe saw any reason to abandon their old religion and adopt one of those preached by the whites. Despite considerable stress, Mpongwe society continued to maintain much of its internal vitality.

However, despite the apparent meagreness of the harvest from more than thirty years of intensive missionary activity, the foundation for a Christian community in the Gabon had been laid by 1875. Converts were still few and often weak in the faith, students were still more interested in learning skills useful in commerce than in religious subjects, but the missions, both Catholic and Protestant, were physically and financially well established and after years of frustration had finally begun to attract a nucleus of followers.

Just as foreign political and religious influences failed to overwhelm the Mpongwe after 1845, the economic consequences of the commencement of colonial rule were not immediately apparent. Except for the slave trade, commerce went on as before for a number of years. The Mpongwe continued to act as middlemen between the

---

[1] *Bulletin général*, v, No. 40 (1867), p. 759; ibid., ix, No. 85 (1873), p. 472.
[2] Marquis de Compiègne, *L'Afrique équatoriale: Gabonais, Pahouins, Gallois* (Paris, 1875), pp. 349–50.
[3] 'Mission du Gabon—rapport du R. P. Le Berre'.
[4] Bushnell to Anderson, 23 Feb. 1866, A.B.C. 15.1, vol. iv., No. 117.

Europeans and the interior peoples. French merchants failed to displace the established American and especially British traders. Indeed, Anglo-American commerce grew and, although the spread of the factory system was beginning to threaten the Mpongwe middleman role, Glass remained prosperous as the commercial centre of the estuary.[1] During the first eight months of 1850, twenty-one British, three American, and four French ships visited the river; only two of the latter were merchantmen. French goods were unable to compete on the Gabonese market, partly because the prices were so high that even the officers of the *comptoir* bought their supplies at the factories in Glass.[2] In addition, French merchants did not set up factories, nor would they extend the twelve or eighteen months credit advanced by the British.[3] For decades, to the chagrin of the authorities, the people of Glass ignored the French language in favour of English and used English weights and measures; the 'French' villages demanded in vain that French vessels come to trade with them.[4]

American trade with Gabon fell off after 1860; no more than two or three ships entered the river annually even after the end of the Civil War. German traders replaced the Americans during the 1860s and established factories at Glass. In 1868 Britain still dominated the Gabon trade; together with the Germans they reportedly accounted for four-fifths of all commerce. American ships called on occasion for barwood; French trade was insignificant.[5] This situation remained unchanged for many years; the French were unable to profit commercially from their political control of the region.

By 1860 the Mpongwe middleman position was beginning to break down under the impact of the factory system. The early development of permanently manned European trading posts is obscure. A post

---

[1] 'Comptoir du Gabon, Inspection de 1852', Archives d'Outre-Mer, Sénégal, iv, 40, b.

[2] Charles Penard to Min. of Marine, 17 Dec. 1850, Archives d'Outre-Mer, Afrique, i, 8, b.

[3] 'Rapport sur le Gabon', 1 Sept. 1854, Archives d'Outre-Mer, Sénégal, iv, 40, d.

[4] 'Extrait d'une lettre de M. Auguste Bouët au Directeur des Colonies', 1 Sept. 1851, Archives d'Outre-Mer, Sénégal, iv, 40, a; Capt. Manon to Minister, Apr. 1884, Archives d'Outre-Mer, Gabon, i, 21, b.

[5] Henry May to Seward, 16 June 1863, U.S. Consular Reports, Gabon; Wm. Walker to Seward, 22 Dec. 1868, ibid. The United States maintained a 'Commercial Agency' in the Gabon between 1856 and 1888. The position, a sinecure, was usually held by one of the missionaries.

existed when the American missionaries first arrived; in 1845 there was an English factory at Glass and Régis Frères maintained an agent near the French fort. These factories were abandoned in 1846, but revived in the following year. English factories were active at Glass in 1850 and seem to have been in continuous operation since that date. In 1862 Burton found four English factories at Glass, including representatives of Hatton and Cookson of Liverpool. Resident German agents represented one or two Hamburg firms.[1]

The growth of the factory system during the early years of French rule was closely connected with major social and demographic changes, as well as a commercial revolution. The village of Glass doubled in population to about 1,400 between the 1840s and 1862; during the same period Quaben had fallen from 1,500 to 400. On the south bank, Denis still had 600 subjects, only a modest decrease, but only 80 people still remained with King George. The Mpongwe were evidently tending to congregate at the busiest trade centre, Glass.[2] But Mpongwe were not the only people attracted to the villages of the north bank. Protected by the French and encouraged by the missionaries and traders, Bakalai, Shekiani, and Fang came to the coast as visitors, casual labourers, or settlers.[3] Africans from further afield also came to the estuary. Besides the freed slaves at Libreville and the Senegalese troops in the French garrison, trading agents and labourers from Senegal, Sierra Leone, Liberia, the Gold Coast, and Fernando Po had found their way to the Gabon by the 1860s.[4] In 1867 between fifty and a hundred Kru from the Liberian coast were employed in the factories at Glass; twice as many worked for the French at the Plateau.[5]

Glass and the Plateau area rapidly took on the more unsavory aspects of the bustling, cosmopolitan seaports they were becoming. Missionary priests and pastors were horrified at the drunkenness and vice prevalent in the towns and at the conduct of most members of the European commercial and governmental communities. The French priests, although not opposed to the moderate use of alcohol,

---

[1] Deschamps, *Quinze Ans*, p. 121; Twenty-Seventh Annual Report, for 1868, 6 Jan. 1869, A.B.C. 15.1, vol. iv, No. 9½; Burton, *Two Trips*, i, p. 17.

[2] 'Les Colonies françaises: établissements de la Côte d'Or et du Gabon', *Revue maritime et coloniale*, ix (1863), p. 52. The 1862 figures may not include Louis. For earlier estimates, see ch. III.

[3] Bushnell to Anderson, 23 June 1866, A.B.C. 15.1, vol. iv, No. 122.

[4] 'Twenty-Seventh Annual Report—1868'.

[5] Bushnell to Clark, 22 Nov. 1867, A.B.C. 15.1, vol. iv, No. 149.

were as concerned as the Protestants about the heavy consumption of rum and other beverages sold at the factories.[1] Virtually all of the resident European traders and officials lived with African concubines whom they 'rented' from their husbands for fees of 15–25 francs a month.[2] Women were also provided by Mpongwe merchants to gain the trust and goodwill of visiting captains. Casual clients, Africans as well as common sailors, were of course much more numerous. According to one American seaman, customers bargained with the lady's husband, who collected the fee and later rewarded the woman.[3] Slave women were often hired out as prostitutes or concubines by their husbands and/or masters; so lucrative was this practice that young female slaves sold for fifty per cent more than males.[4] And, as might be expected, theft and other crimes were fairly common in the towns.[5]

The Mpongwe, active in coastal trade since the late sixteenth century, had long been accustomed to their profitable role as coastal middlemen. Trade freed the Mpongwe from subsistence agriculture and provided highly valued consumer goods. Moreover, successful commerce with Europeans distinguished the Mpongwe from their neighbours, the despised 'bush' people of the interior. The trade boom of the 1850s and '60s seemed to present opportunities for quick wealth to a population already committed to merchant values. The ambition of young Mpongwe men was to become '*grand monde*'; to become rich through trade and thus gain respect and esteem. Wealth was measured in wives, slaves, and European goods and status was further displayed in conspicuous idleness, except of course when there was trading to be done. The successful man possessed an array of imported goods ranging from clocks, sofas, and clothes to pictures in gilt frames and fine wines. European manners were admired and copied; Mpongwe were eager to show off their knowledge of European languages. Only the white man's religions seemed unworthy of attention; but, as the Mpongwe readily observed, French lieutenants

[1] 'Rapport du Frère Antoine'.
[2] Ibid.
[3] John R. Congdon, 'Private Journal kept on the Bark *Montgomery* of Providence, R.I., 28 August 1846–9 June 1847', entry for 3 Jan. 1847, p. 132. MS., Rhode Island Historical Society.
[4] R. P. Le Berre, 'De l'esclavage au Gabon', *Bulletin général*, No. 92 (1873), p. 759. Females aged 15 to 20 sold for 150 francs, males of similar age for 100 francs.
[5] Bushnell to Clark, 17 Oct. 1868, A.B.C. 15.1, vol. iv, No. 164.

and British factors could be *'grand monde'* without paying heed to their priests and preachers.[1]

Although some Mpongwe profited during the early years of French rule, the rise of the factory system swung the balance of commercial power strongly toward the Europeans. Mpongwe traders no longer dealt with relatively inexperienced captains anxious to complete their cargoes and leave the river as quickly as possible, but with men thoroughly familiar with local economic conditions; men who knew who could be 'trusted' with goods, and who could afford to wait until high price demands were lowered. The European traders could seize the relatives of defaulting debtors and hold them as security for trusted merchandise, much as captains used to hold 'pawns' on board ship in the late eighteenth century. Physical protection and a *Conseil Commercial* to settle trade disputes were provided by the colonial administration.[2]

Most ominous from the Mpongwe point of view were the successful efforts of the Europeans to get into direct commercial contact with the interior peoples. Eager to dispense with the African middleman, the white factors encouraged Fang and Bakalai to visit Glass under their protection and began to send their own trading canoes up the creeks. Mpongwe tales of the ferocity of the interior tribes were no longer a deterrent to the now better-informed whites, who in turn were discovered by the 'bush' people to be fabulously wealthy as well as reasonably peaceful. The use of force by the Mpongwe was precluded by the fear of French retaliation against their coastal villages, whose vulnerability had been demonstrated by the bombardment of Glass. Thus, the coastmen could only watch helplessly as the Europeans began to establish small trading posts in the interior, and thereby end centuries of Mpongwe commercial domination.[3]

The Mpongwe continued to play a role in the region's commerce, but as agents for European firms rather than as independent merchants.

[1] These impressions were common to virtually all contemporary observers. See, for example, 'Rapport du Frère Antoine'; Bessieux to T. R. P., 17 May 1855, Cong. St. Esp., Boîte 172, VI; Derano to his brother, 21 Feb. 1850, Cong. St. Esp., 172, II; John Leighton Wilson, *Western Africa: Its History, Condition, and Prospects* (New York, 1856), pp. 261–2.

[2] Deschamps, *Quinze Ans*, pp. 120–1.

[3] Burton, *Two Trips*, i, pp. 195–6. Burton visited a factory located up the Como River among the Fang. The factory was managed by a Mr. Tippet, 'an intelligent coloured man from the States'.

Today [1872] the profession of free merchant (*courtier*) no longer exists, the whites having, to their great advantage, penetrated far into the interior and established direct relations with its people. The ex-merchants have become agents (*traitants*); they are usually attached to one or another factory from which they buy goods and carry them away to sell at a higher price; sometimes also they operate small factories which are not important enough to justify the presence of a white agent.[1]

In less than three decades the Mpongwe had been transformed from powerful middlemen dominating the trade of the estuary into a group of wandering peddlers, hawking beads and rum in the villages of the hinterland.

While the Mpongwe were losing their dominance on the coast, important changes were occurring among the peoples of the hinterland. The Shekiani and Bakalai were rapidly being displaced by the Fang, a large Bantu-speaking group, who appear to have begun migrating south from their homeland in east-central Cameroun during the eighteenth century.[2] Hardly known on the coast in the 1830s, the Fang were important suppliers of forest products twenty years later.[3] In 1845 the Americans reported that the 'Pangwe people, respecting whom you have heard some favorable reports, are migrating in large numbers towards the coast'.[4] Eight years later Fang villages were established on the lower Como and Bokwe Rivers; the Fang were now the major ivory hunters of the area.[5] Some Fang clans continued to move south; they were well established in the bush south of the estuary and on the mid-Ogowe by the early 1870s.[6] The Mpongwe were terrified by the encroachment of the reputedly cannibalistic Fang,[7] but needed them as suppliers of ivory. By the late 1850s Mpongwe merchants on the Como were seeking marriage alliances with Fang groups and bringing Fang friends to the coast for visits.[8] Later, the Mpongwe were engulfed by the newcomers, but during the period under consideration, population changes in the

[1] Compiègne, *Gabonais*, pp. 189–90.

[2] Pierre Alexandre, Proto-histoire du groupe beti-bulu-fang: essai de synthèse provisoire', *Cahiers d'études africaines*, (1965), pp. 546–8. The Fang were called 'Pangwe' by the Mpongwe and 'Pahouin' by the French.

[3] John Leighton Wilson, *Western Africa*, p. 302.

[4] *M.H.*, xli (1845), pp. 267–8. The evangelists were eager to work among these promising people, still uncontaminated by the vices of the coast, but were never able to do much beyond a few preaching tours because of lack of staff.

[5] 'Mr. Preston's Journal', *M.H.*, il (1853), pp. 13–18.

[6] See, for example, Compiègne, *Gabonais*, end map.   [7] Ibid., pp. 152, 155.

[8] Ira M. Preston to Anderson, 25 Dec. 1860, A.B.C. 15.1, vol. iv, No. 239.

interior seem to have had little effect on the Mpongwe other than temporary trade dislocations caused by skirmishes among the Fang or between them and other groups.

The Mpongwe, besides suffering political and economic eclipse, did not fare well demographically in the early years of the colonial presence. One French officer reported in 1865 that their numbers had dropped by two-thirds since 1843, and his observation was by no means isolated.[1] Early American missionaries had estimated the Mpongwe population to be five or six thousand; two decades later French sources listed only three thousand.[2] Even allowing for exaggeration, the effects of a recent smallpox epidemic, and the fact that Europeans at this time confidently expected the 'effete' coastal tribes to die out and be replaced by supposedly superior peoples from the interior,[3] it is probable that the Mpongwe suffered a real population decline in this period.

Contemporary observers blamed this phenomenon on debauchery, alcoholism, and disease.[4] Prostitution had been widely practised since the early seventeenth century, when Dutch sailors disgusted their officers by flagrantly enjoying the charms of the Mpongwe ladies. The greater number of ships calling in the nineteenth century, to say nothing of the permanent presence of French officers and their Senegalese troops after 1843, provided enhanced opportunities for the spread of venereal diseases. Syphilis was very common, despite the use of local medicinal plants which were said to be infallible cures.[5] The disease caused both adult and natal mortality. Another factor reducing the birth rate was abortion, which was

[1] 'Rapport annuel—établissements de la Côte d'Or et du Gabon', by Laffon de Ladebat, 17 Feb. 1865, Archives d'Outre-Mer, Gabon, i, 3, b. According to Griffon du Bellay, ('Le Gabon', Le Tour du monde, xii (1865), p. 288) the general reaction of officers returning to Gabon after a long absence was shock at the population decline.

[2] Wilson, Western Africa, p. 292; 'Les Colonies françaises: établissements de a Côte d'Or et du Gabon', Revue maritime et coloniale, ix (1863), p. 52; 'État semestriel, janvier-juin 1860', Cong. St. Esprit, Boîte 167, vi, 1860.

[3] In the case of Gabon, the Mpongwe were believed to be approaching extinction and would soon be replaced by the Fang who were migrating to the coast. See, for example, Burton, Two Trips, i, pp. 77, 225; and Rollin Porter to Anderson, 1 Oct. 1851, A.B.C. 15.1, vol. iii, No. 325.

[4] Bellay, 'Le Gabon', p. 288; Lt. R. Avelot, 'Recherches sur l'histoire des migrations dans le bassin de l'Ogooué et la région du littoral adjacente', Bulletin de géographie historique et descriptive, xx (1905), p. 396.

[5] Lestrille, 'Note sur le comptoir du Gabon', Revue coloniale, xvi (Oct. 1856), p. 425. T. E. Bowdich also mentioned an 'anti-venereal' plant in Mission from Cape Coast Castle to Ashantee (London, 1819, reprinted 1966), p. 444.

widely practised, allegedly because pregnant women could not make money for themselves and their masters or husbands by prostitution, and because women tended to lose their figures after pregnancy and thus lost earning power.[1] Lieutenant Boteler was surprised not to see any mulattoes in the Gabon during his 1826 visit; he concluded that abortion or infanticide must have been widely practised to explain the absence of persons of mixed ancestry.[2]

The Mpongwe sexual response to the European presence was not the only factor adversely affecting their numbers. Alcoholism may have been a serious problem in the mid-nineteenth century, although the teetotalist American missionaries probably exaggerated the evil effects of imported liquor. Closer contact with Europe also helped spread other diseases. For example, a French steamer brought in smallpox from Senegal in 1864 and the Gabon region suffered severely in the resulting epidemic.[3] It is clear that, although the tribe did not become extinct as some observers predicted, European contact with the Mpongwe had a significant demographic effect.

Although the Mpongwe enjoyed considerable political autonomy during this period, their monarchs lost most of their wealth and prestige during the thirty years following the suppression of Glass. King Denis, located across the river from the French and hence relatively immune from interference in his day by day affairs, suffered greatly from the curtailment of the slave trade. None the less, as will be described in the next chapter, his prestige remained high enough in 1862 for him to mediate between the French and the Orungu. Already described in 1852 as being 'weakened by age', he was a pitiful figure twenty years later. 'Today he vegetates, ill and without strength, his authority gone, his house fallen into ruin, his sons wretched drunkards.'[4] King Denis died in 1876.[5]

[1] Lestrille, 'Note', pp. 438-9. Lestrille, a surgeon, was unable to discover the abortive technique employed.

[2] Thomas Boteler, *Narrative of a Voyage of Discovery to Africa and Arabia, Performed in His Majesty's Ships, Leven and Barracouta, from 1821 to 1826, Under the Command of F. W. Owen, R.N.* (London, 1835), ii, p. 285. Burton did see a few mulattoes in 1862 (*Two Trips*, i, p. 72).

[3] Wm. Walker to Anderson, 22 Sept. 1864, A.B.C. 15.1, vol. iv, No. 311; Laffon de Ladebat to Min. of Marine, 23 July 1865, Archives d'Outre-Mer, Gabon, i, 5, a.

[4] 'Arrêt. Le Présent état de répartition montant à la somme de dix-mille francs, 1852', Archives d'Outre-Mer, Sénégal, iv, 40, b; Compiègne, *Gabonais*, p. 196.

[5] Abbé André Raponda Walker, *Notes d'histoire de Gabon* (Brazzaville, 1960), p. 29.

King George, who had greeted Bowdich in 1818, was deeply in debt to the Bakalai as early as the 1840's.[1] Described by the French as being poor and with but little influence, in 1852,[2] George lingered on in dwindling circumstances until his death about 1860. Several other 'Georges' reigned until the early 1880's when the village was abandoned and the region taken over by Fang settlers.[3] Quaben and Louis were simply smothered by the French presence and are rarely mentioned in contemporary documents. In 1845 they were reportedly unable to pay trust debts because the luxury goods they had bought were unacceptable to the interior ivory suppliers.[4] Louis died in 1867;[5] Quaben's date of death is uncertain.

In Glass, the site of most of the European factories, the monarchy also suffered a severe decline. The king who had signed the treaty with France died early in 1848; the French were happy that no human sacrifices were conducted at his funeral.[6] King Glass had accepted a *cadeau* just before his death;[7] Toko the arch-enemy of the French, did not accept one until 1852.[8] Three weak and aged monarchs enjoyed brief reigns as 'King Glass' between 1848 and 1865. The prestige of the office of king had so declined by that time that it was very difficult to attract a suitable candidate. 'Those who are wanted do not want the throne. Those who are not wanted are anxious to get it.'[9] The man finally installed in 1865 was 'a mere farce as far as power and influence are concerned'.[1]

The decline of the Mpongwe kings, who as has been shown in chapter three were never very powerful figures, is poorly documented. Mpongwe rulers were clearly unable to solve the problems created by the colonial presence and the extension of European trading

1 Wm. Walker Diary, iv, 2 Feb. 1847 and vii, 23 June 1849.

2 'Le Présent État de répartition'.

3 Bushnell to Clark, 12 Dec. 1866, A.B.C. 15.1, vol. iv, No. 129; Abbé Walker, *Notes*, p. 41. Abbé Walker incorrectly ascribes George's death to the period 1879–82.

4 H. Baudin to Min. of Marine, 3 Apr. 1845, Archives d'Outre-Mer, Sénégal, iv, 30, a.   5 Abbé Walker, *Notes*, p. 36.

6 Commandant Gorée to Min. of Marine, Archives d'Outre-Mer, Sénégal, iv, 39, b.

7 'Cadeaux pour chefs du Gabon', 28 Dec. 1847, Archives d'Outre-Mer, Sénégal, iv, 32, b.

8 'Le Présent État de répartition'; Toko died six years later. Wm. Walker Diary, ix, 3 Dec. 1858.

9 Bushnell to Anderson, 22 July 1865, A.B.C. 15.1, vol. iv, No. 110; Wm. Walker Diary, x, 8 Aug. 1865.

1 Bushnell to Anderson, 25 Sept. 1865, A.B.C. 15.1, vol. iv, No. 113.

contacts into the interior. As the factory system developed, the kings could no longer extract the duties and presents they had received from ships. Younger men, products of the mission schools who had acquired basic literacy and the ability to keep simple accounts, proved more valuable to the resident traders.[1] Such men were able to get jobs with the Europeans as clerks and trading agents as Mpongwe economic independence slipped away. Suffering economic decline along with their subjects, the aged kings slipped into senescence and obscurity. For all practical purposes, the monarchical institution died along with the venerable incumbents in office when the French first arrived.

The Mpongwe were subjected to severe pressure from several outside forces during the 1845–75 period; the French colonial regime, Christian missionaries, and European traders, with the advancing Fang clans a constant background threat. Against any one of these groups the Mpongwe might have been able to maintain their autonomy, but the combination of factors was overwhelming.

French rule, except for the eventual abolition of the slave trade, was relatively light. Mpongwe political action was limited by the colonial authorities but no attempt was made to tax them, nor did the French meddle in routine internal affairs. However, the French did play a vital role by providing physical protection for missionaries and factory-based traders.

Likewise, by 1875 the missionaries had not yet made a profound impact on Mpongwe society. They found the coastmen to be a sophisticated, worldly group, more interested in the lure of commerce and profit than in Christian teachings. Both Catholic and Protestant proselytizers were anxious to reach the supposedly simple and virtuous agricultural peoples of the interior, who were still unspoiled by the vices of the seaport. However, the missionaries were persistent and by 1875 were beginning to attract the first of what later became a wave of converts. Like the Fang, the missions were soon to become a major factor in Mpongwe life.

European traders based in permanent factories posed the most immediate and profound threat to the Mpongwe way of life. The factory system destroyed the Mpongwe middleman role and the resulting economic collapse contributed to political and cultural decline. The existence of the colonial regime was crucial to the break-

[1] Bushnell to Anderson, 21 June 1861, A.B.C. 15.1, vol. iv, No. 47.

ing of the traditional trade network. The Mpongwe would certainly have forbidden the erection of factories, or at least have closely regulated the activities of the factors, were it not for the fear of French military reprisals.

The situation in the Gabon in 1845 and for several years thereafter could best be described as protocolonial. The Mpongwe had lost 'external' sovereignty, but still retained control over internal affairs. Over the next two decades, however, thanks in large measure to the actions of British traders, the existing autonomy was whittled away. By 1875, years before the 'Scramble', the Mpongwe had already lost their political and economic independence.

CHAPTER VII

The Demise of the Orungu State: 1860–1875

THE decline of the slave trade and the opening of the Ogowe to European traffic were the two major causes for the disintegration of the Orungu kingdom during the decade and a half after the death of King Ombango Passol. Orungu attempts to counter these threats were unsuccessful and to some extent self-defeating. Although, in contrast to the situation in the Gabon estuary, there was no colonial occupation of Orungu lands until the 1880s, they had, like the Mpongwe, suffered disastrous blows to their once powerful economic and political position by 1875.

Although the declining slave trade had already created an economic crisis during the latter years of King Ombango Passol's reign, the death of that formidable ruler may be taken as the end of the era of Orungu strength. Avaro dates Ombango's death to 1862,[1] but it is clear from Burton's evidence that he died some time earlier, perhaps in 1860. There apparently was a succession struggle between two brothers of the deceased monarch; Ndebulia, the elder, emerged victorious with the support of King Denis.[2] The 'King of Cape Lopez' spent two or three weeks 'visiting' in the Gabon in August 1860;[3] in view of Ombango's paralysis, this king was almost certainly Ndebulia, who was probably either seeking the support of Denis or thanking him for aid in securing the throne. When Burton visited Sangatanga in March 1862, Ndebulia was already well established at Mpembe, near the mouth of the Nazareth. Sangatanga itself had been abandoned and burned after Ombango's death. Many of the people had moved to coastal villages north of the old capital; others had gone south with the new ruler.[4]

[1] J. Ambouroué Avaro, 'Le Bas-Ogowé au dix-neuvième siècle', doctoral thesis (University of Paris, Sorbonne, 1969), p. 264.

[2] Abbé André Raponda Walker, *Notes d'histoire du Gabon* (Brazzaville, 1960), p. 74.

[3] William Walker Diary, ix, 29 Aug. 1860. William Walker Papers, State Historical Society of Wisconsin.

[4] Richard F. Burton, *Two Trips to Gorillaland and the Cataracts of the Congo*

The Orungu economy was in a state of virtual collapse at this time. The drastic decline in slave exports produced a great shortage of the European goods upon which the Orungu had become dependent. In Avaro's words, they had become accustomed to prosperity coming from the sea, and were unwilling to return to farming and collecting forest products on the land. The new king especially felt the squeeze; he was unable to support his wives, slaves, and followers and maintain the tradition of generosity established by his predecessor.[1] Ndebulia tried to meet this challenge by continuing in the old ways; at his new capital in the delta he hosted two white factors who supervised a clandestine flow of slaves to the Portuguese islands.[2]

The Orungu were temporarily rescued from commercial oblivion by the agricultural revival of São Tomé and Principe. The islands, an economic backwater since about 1600 when the sugar industry collapsed, began to experience a boom in coffee and cocoa about 1860. Slaves, thinly disguised as voluntary contract labourers, were sent from Angola to meet the labour demand.[3] In addition, a regular small boat traffic sprang up between the Orungu and the islands which the British and French were unable to stop. Slaves worth twenty dollars on the coast were sold for five times that on São Tomé.[4] A few years previously slaves had been worth only twenty-five dollars on the islands;[5] but now, for the first time in decades, there was a significant demand for slaves for local use rather than for re-export, and the servile population began to rise.[6] The demand for

(London, 1876, reprinted 1967), i, pp. 142–3. According to Burton, a son of Ombango had succeeded him, but had soon died, leaving the throne to Ndebulia.

[1] Avaro, 'Bas-Ogowé', pp. 267–70; Burton, *Two Trips*, i, pp. 135–6, 141–3.

[2] Burton, *Two Trips*, i, pp. 142–3; Baron Didelot to Min. of Marine, June 1862, Archives d'Outre-Mer, Gabon, iv, 9.

[3] James Duffy, *A Question of Slavery: Labour Policies in Portuguese Africa and British Protest, 1850–1920* (Cambridge, Mass., 1967), pp. 26–7.

[4] Commodore Edmonstone to Admiral Walker, 7 Nov. 1861, Parliamentary Papers, Commons, 1863, lxxi, Class A, No. 81, encl. 1.

[5] J. L. Wilson to Rufus Anderson, Feb. 1843, American Board of Commissioners for Foreign Missions Letterbooks, 15.1, vol. ii, No. 103.

[6] There were about 5,000 slaves on the islands in the mid-'40s, only a slight increase in the numbers present thirty years previously (José Joaquim Lopes de Lima, *Ensaios sobre a Statistica das Possessões Portuguezas na Africa Occidental e Oriental; na Asia Occidental; na China, e na Oceania* (Lisbon, 1844), Book ii, Pt. I, p. 2a; and Archivo Histórico Ultramarino, São Tomé, caixa 18, 1810, 'List of Slaves', Nos. 1–4, compiled by Governor Lisboa). In 1859 the number of 'Africans', i.e. slaves exceeded 10,000. The slave population reached

labour spurted in 1864 when smallpox decimated the islands' slave population.[1]

Although voyages to the islands took only a few days, the trip often involved great hardships for the slaves, especially if the small and often decrepit ships were becalmed. The *Apta*, a Principe schooner taken in 1833, was only thirty feet long and eleven feet at the beam, but she carried fifty-four slaves, a crew of ten, and one 'passenger'. So unseaworthy was the ship that the British prize crew only dared sail it as far as Fernando Po.[2] In 1854 the American merchantman *Cortez* met a São Tomé vessel which had been becalmed after loading fourteen slaves at Cape Lopez. The slavers were out of water and eventually gave the Americans two girls aged four and seven in return for a supply. The children were brought to Gabon and placed in the care of the American missionaries.[3] Other incidents could be cited, but the mortality figures in Table V (p. 80 above) should suffice to illustrate the point.

The demand for slave labourers grew as the agricultural boom continued and was fed by the high slave mortality rate on the islands.[4] Slaves ran away from the plantations whenever they could, which was often enough to constitute a real drain on the labour supply. Many joined the Maroon colonies which flourished in the hills.[5] Others seized boats and tried to escape to the mainland. Some succeeded, and those who reached Gabon were cared for by the missionaries,[6]

16,000 by 1867 and 25,000 in 1874. Manuel Ferreira Ribeiro, *A Provincia de S. Thomé e Principe e suas Dependencias* (Lisbon, 1877), pp. 526–7.

[1] Report of W. Vrendenburg, 25 Oct. 1864, P.P., Commons, 1865, lvi, Class A, No. 90, encl. 1.

[2] H.M. Commissioners to Lord Palmerston, 27 June 1834, P.P., Commons, 1835, li, Class A, No. 36.

[3] 'Rapport sur Gabon', 5 Apr. 1854, Archives d'Outre-Mer, Sénégal, iv, 40, d.

[4] Wilson to Anderson, Feb. 1843. In 1874 and 1875 deaths exceeded births by several hundred (Ribeiro, *Provincia de S. Thomé*, p. 534). Duffy (*Question of Slavery*, p. 96) estimated slave mortality at 20 per cent annually.

[5] Marquis de Compiègne, *L'Afrique équatoriale: Okanda, Bangouens, Osyeba* (Paris, 1875), pp. 258, 261.

[6] Ibid., p. 262. Compiègne met a Principe planter in 1874 who had brought a boatload of thirty slaves from the Gabon coast five weeks previously. Fifteen had already died and eleven others had stolen his boat and fled. The missionaries reported their activities in Rev. Ira Preston to Secretary of State Seward, 12 Aug. 1865, U.S. Consular Reports, Gabon, National Archives Microfilm. Escapees from the Portuguese islands also established Maroon colonies on the southern part of Fernando Po. See Vice-Admiral A. Fleuriot de Langle, 'Croisières à la côte d'Afrique', *Le Tour du monde*, xxxi (1876), p. 256. Paul Du Chaillu also met Gabonese fugitives from São Tomé on Fernando Po, as described in *My Apingi*

but the French navy sometimes found overturned canoes or boats with dead or dying fugitives.[1] The governor of São Tomé once had the audacity to request the return of some escapees who he thought had fled to Gabon; the French naturally refused.[2]

By the mid-1860s seven hundred to a thousand slaves a year were being sent to the islands from the Cape Lopez area, despite more determined French measures to halt the traffic.[3] French and British warships made some captures and in 1868 and 1870 the French burned offending villages, but mulatto traders from the islands remained active and by 1871 they had even revived Sangatanga as a slaving centre.[4] The American consul in Gabon estimated in 1874 that, despite the best efforts of the French, from 1,000 to 2,000 slaves a year were exported from Cape Lopez and Fernan Vaz.[5] In the same year an American missionary on the Ogowe reported a legitimate merchant's estimate that about 1,500 people were sold down the river annually. About 500 of these were kept as domestic slaves by the Omyene peoples, and the remainder exported. French naval authorities estimated exports at 250 to 300 a month in 1875.[6] A year later, canoes full of slaves were said to be coming at night to Denis from Cape Lopez. Most of them were young children who had been scared into silence by a fetish ceremony.[7]

As long as the demand for slave labour remained strong on São Tomé and Principe, the French were unable to do more than harass the traffic. Only one or two steam gunboats were available to patrol the Gabon, the Cape Lopez area, and the Ogowe, a force

Kingdom: With Life in the Great Sahara and Sketches of the Chase of the Ostrich, Hyena, etc. (New York, 1870), pp. 235–42.

[1] Hyacinthe Hecquard, *Voyage sur la côte et dans l'intérieur de l'Afrique occidentale* (Paris, 1853), p. 35.

[2] Admiral Dariac to Min. of Marine, 22 July 1868, Archives d'Outre-Mer, Gabon, i, 7, c.

[3] Rev. Albert Bushnell, 'Letter of 25 June 1867', *The Missionary Herald*, lxiii (1867), p. 367; Preston to Seward, 12 Aug. 1865; Commander Aube to Admiral de Langle, 21 Dec. 1866, Archives d'Outre-Mer, Gabon i, 6, d.

[4] Commodore Wilmot to Secretary of the Admiralty, 1 Dec. 1864, P.P., Commons, 1865, lvi, Class A, No. 151; Captain of the Bellone to Admiral Commanding, West Africa, 10 Apr. 1871 and 25 July 1871, Archives d'Outre-Mer, Gabon, i, 9, b.

[5] Bushnell to Secretary of State Fish, 25 Mar. 1874 and 21 May, 1874, U.S. Consular Reports, Gabon.

[6] Robert Nassau to Bushnell, 14 Dec. 1874, U.S. Consular Reports, Gabon; 'Cahiers de Le Troquer', Archives du Cong. St. Esprit, Boîte 173, C, I, Cruise 7.

[7] Clement to Min. of Marine, 9 Sept. 1876, Archives d'Outre-Mer, Gabon, i, 12, b.

completely insufficient to halt the small boat traffic in the maze of creeks and channels which made up the Ogowe delta. The reports of one officer, Captain Yves-Marie Le Trocquer, vividly illustrate the difficulties confronting the authorities. The delta population rarely supplied information to the French voluntarily, but word of the gun-boat's movements spread so rapidly that it was almost impossible to surprise slavers. Suspicious canoes hailed by the French showed great speed and often tried to escape up creeks too narrow for the gunboat to follow. Le Trocquer had to fire on fleeing craft rather than allow them to escape, although this risked killing the innocent slaves as well as their captors.[1]

Sporadic captures and punitive attacks on depots and villages failed to halt the determined and resourceful slave merchants. Exports from the river were reported in 1878 and 1882[2] and a few people were sold to the islanders even after that date. In the late '70s a Portuguese named José Elias ran a small trading post in an Orungu village appropriately called 'Lisboa'. This factory, located in the delta near the royal village of Mpembe, was merely a cover for a barracoon hidden in the nearby forest. Aided by a Brazilian mulatto, José Elias collected slaves brought from up river by canoe and smuggled them out to São Tomé. This activity continued, at least intermittently, until 1887 when Elias was denounced to the French by a disgruntled Mpongwe employee.[3] According to traditions collected by Deschamps, a few slaves were sold to the Portuguese as late as 1900.[4] However, the trade in *libertos* or technically free labourers from Angola grew in the mid-1870s[5] and gradually replaced the riskier source of supply in Gabon.

This last gasp of the Atlantic slave trade merely postponed the final economic and political collapse of the Orungu kingdom. Indeed, the monarchy gained little from the clandestine revival of the trade. Harassment by British and French warships had forced the slavers to

1 Le Trocquer, 'Cahiers', i, Cruises 6, 7, 8, 16; iii, Report of 24 Feb. 1879.

2 Bushnell to Secretary of State Evarts, 12 Feb. 1878, U.S. Consular Reports, Gabon; and 'Voyage dans l'Ogowe', Capt. Minier, 8 Dec. 1882, Archives d'Outre-Mer, Gabon, iii, 4, p. 13.

3 Avaro, 'Bas-Ogowé', pp. 277-8.

4 Hubert Deschamps, *Traditions orales et archives au Gabon* (Paris, 1962), p. 117.

5 Duffy, *Question of Slavery*, pp. 96-8. The existence of bona-fide, old-fashioned slaving on the Gabon coast attracted much less humanitarian attention than the *liberto* trade. It is clear, however, that Gabonese as well as Angolan slaves played a major role in the rise of the cocoa islands.

decentralize their operations. Instead of loading cargoes from barracoons at the royal village, the schooners picked up slaves at scattered
and shifting locations in the maze of creeks which made up the
Ogowe delta.[1] Under these conditions the king was unable to monopolize the slave trade and, with the loss of this monopoly, the monarchy lost its most important source of revenue. Local clan chiefs and
others were now able to compete economically with the king; the
monarchy soon lost its political hold as well.

While the Orungu were struggling to continue their role as slave
dealers, their control of the Ogowe mouth was being threatened and
finally broken by European explorers and merchants. Eager to get
some return for the expenses of maintaining the Gabon *comptoir*, the
French became increasingly interested in tapping the supposedly
rich trade of the Ogowe valley. The French expedition of 1862 was
the first step toward opening the river to European traders, but it
was not, as is generally believed, the first reconnaissance of the Ogowe
by white men. The Spanish slaver Antonio and the missionaries
William Walker and Ira Preston had ascended the Ogowe in 1843
and 1854 respectively.[2] However, Lieutenant Serval and Dr. Griffon
du Bellay were apparently unaware of their predecessors when in
July 1862, during the dry season, they entered the Nazareth mouth of
the river in the steamer *Pioneer* with a pilot reluctantly supplied by
Ndebulia. The steamer was forced to halt at Ndambo because of low
water; the explorers continued upstream as far as Lake Onangue by
canoe.[3] Two years later d'Albigot and Touchard reached the
Ngounie confluence; Lieutenant Aymes pushed a few miles further in
1867, but failed to reach his goal, the rapids at Lope.[4]

Meanwhile, attempts were being made to open a land route
between the Gabon and the mid-Ogowe. In December 1862, after

[1] Le Trocquer, 'Cahiers', i, Cruise 7.

[2] See ch. IV, above. These voyages, unlike those undertaken in the 1860s and
'70s, had the approval of the Orungu king.

[3] Griffon du Bellay, 'Exploration du fleuve Ogo-Wai, côte occidentale d'Afrique', *Revue maritime et coloniale*, ix (1863), pp. 66–89, 296–309. David Living-
stone had used the *Pioneer* on the Zambezi.

[4] Henri Brunschwig, *Brazza Explorateur: l'Ogooué 1875–1879* (Paris, 1966),
p. 94, n. 1; Lt. A. Aymes, 'Exploration de l'Ogoway: recherches géographiques
et ethnographiques sur le bassin du Gabon', *Revue maritime et coloniale*, xxvii
(1870), pp. 525–61; xxix (1870), pp. 54–73.

their return from the *Pioneer* expedition, Serval and Griffon du Bellay set out from the upper Remboue toward the Ogowe-Ngounie confluence. The objective of this exploration was to determine the feasibility of channelling the Ogowe trade overland to the Gabon, thus by-passing the Orungu. Serval was forced to leave his ailing companion in a friendly village, but succeeded in reaching the Ogowe.[1] Lieutenant Genoyer reached the confluence area in 1864 by marching south-south-east from the mid-Bokwe.[2] The British trader R. B. N. Walker, anxious to win the commerce of the Ogowe for his firm, Hatton and Cookson, reached the Ogowe–Ngounie confluence from the Remboue in 1865. Although detained for several months by the Enenga, Walker was able to visit the Lope rapids and ascend the Ngounie for several miles.[3]

The future, however, lay with the river route. The overland routes, already mostly abandoned by African traders, were used from time to time by Europeans in the early '70s when the Orungu tried to block the river, but were almost totally abandoned in later years. Even Mary Kingsley's inimitable account of her 1895 journey from Lamberene to Libreville failed to revive interest in the forest paths; the Ogowe was too convenient a highway.[4]

European traders, led by R. B. N. Walker, began to enter the river in the early '70s and established factories at Adolinanongo, near the modern town of Lambarene. Walker had opened a small factory at Yombe, in Orungu territory at the mouth of the river in 1867,[5] but he was eager to trade directly with the interior tribes. Already, Portuguese boats were able to go upstream as far as the Ngounie to procure slaves; their voyages continued at least until 1874.[6] Walker had accompanied the Aymes expedition in 1867; in 1872 he ascended the river in the *Pioneer* and established the first European

[1] Lt. P. Serval, 'Reconnaissance d'une des routes qui mènent du Rhamboe à l'Ogo-Wai', *Revue maritime et coloniale*, ix (1863), pp. 309–15.

[2] Aymes, 'Explorations', p. 530 and endmap after p. 561.

[3] R. B. N. Walker, 'Relation d'une tentative d'exploration en 1866 de la rivière de l'Ogowé et de la recherche d'un grand lac devant se trouver dans l'Afrique centrale', *Annales des voyages*, i (1870), pp. 58–80, 120–44.

[4] Mary Kingsley, *Travels in West Africa; Congo Français, Corisco and Cameroons* (3rd ed., London, 1965; 1st ed. 1897), pp. 231–352.

[5] Aymes, 'Exploration', p. 534; Avaro, 'Bas-Ogowé', p. 276.

[6] R. B. N. Walker, 'Relation', pp. 70, 72; Aube to de Langle, 21 Dec. 1866, Archives d'Outre-Mer, Gabon, i, 6, d; Robert Hamill Nassau, *My Ogowe; Being a Narrative of Daily Incidents During Sixteen Years in Equatorial West Africa* (New York, 1914), p. 14.

factory in the interior.[1] Agents for the John Holt Company and the German firm of Woermann quickly followed Walker's lead and began trading for rubber, ivory, and other forest products.

The Presbyterian missionaries at Gabon had long looked for a way to reach the unconverted peoples of the hinterland. The opening of the Ogowe filled them with enthusiasm. Albert Bushnell reported in 1873 that the Baraka station had been visited by 'a native king from the Ogobi', who had perhaps taken advantage of the end of the Orungu blockade to visit Gabon. The king and his followers asked that a 'Baraka' be built in their country.[2] The Reverend Robert H. Nassau began to work near Adolinanongo a little more than a year later.[3] Nassau opened the way for the other missionaries, both Protestant and Catholic, who followed him several years later.

Meanwhile the French, temporarily distracted by the disasters of 1870–1, had not forgotten the Ogowe. Alfred Marche and the Marquis de Compiègne explored the middle and upper Ogowe between 1872 and 1874; Savorgnan de Brazza followed their route during the first part of his 1875–9 expedition, when he explored the Ogowe and used it as a route to the basin of the Congo. The mouth of the Ogowe was no longer controlled by the Orungu; the river was rapidly becoming a highway for Europeans.

Increasingly weakened economically and fragmented politically, the Orungu watched the loss of their ancient monopoly of the Ogowe traffic with helpless bitterness. The successors of Ombango Passol struggled in vain to maintain their power by clinging to the increasingly hazardous slave trade. Belatedly, the Orungu made desperate attempts to reassert control over the Ogowe delta, but these efforts failed completely.

King Ndebulia tried, as described above, to solve the Orungu

[1] Nassau, *My Ogowe*, p. 15; Albert Bushnell to Walter Lowrie, 10 Feb. 1873, Presbyterian Church in the U.S.A., Board of Foreign Missions, Correspondence and Report Files, Africa, vol. ix, No. 425, microfilm reel 71. Walker may have sent Mpongwe employees up river even before 1872. See Bushnell to Lowrie, 22 Jan. 1873, ibid., No. 422. See also R. B. N. Walker, 'Letter on a Journey up the Ogowe River, West Africa', *Proceedings of the Royal Geographical Society*, xvii (1873), pp. 354–5.

[2] Bushnell to Lowrie, 21 July 1873, Presb. Church U.S.A., Africa, vol. ix, No. 464.

[3] Nassau, *My Ogowe*, pp. 40–58.

economic crisis by continuing the export of slaves by whatever means possible. However, by 1862 the king had to contend not only with cruising warships, but also with the expansionist designs of the French. The Orungu were recognized by the colonial authorities as the key to the Ogowe. The French also feared British ambitions in this area, mistaking an active interest in suppressing the Cape Lopez slave trade for a desire to annexe the region. Consequently, Ndebulia was pressured in early 1862 to sign a treaty granting sovereignty over his domains to France. Several overtures were rebuffed, but a treaty was finally obtained on 1 June 1862.[1]

The Orungu, while probably unaware of the exact significance of the document, had reason to fear French intentions. However, despite their suspicions, several factors induced the Orungu to sign the treaty. One was a healthy respect for French power. Individual Orungu often visited the Gabon for trade in slaves or foodstuffs,[2] or to visit Mpongwe friends.[3] These trips to the estuary, as well as encounters with warships, had acquainted them with French military strength. Another factor was the intervention of King Denis, who played an important role in the affair.[4] The Mpongwe ruler enjoyed great influence at Cape Lopez; his aid to Ndebulia during the succession struggle undoubtedly increased the weight of his advice. The French probably enlisted the aid of their 'ancient ally' after the rejection of their initial overtures to Ndebulia. According to a contemporary French observer, Denis's help was essential. 'C'est lui qui s'est chargé de la négociation du traité';[5] he also witnessed the actual signing ceremony. Why Denis helped the French is unclear. Probably he believed that nominal French sovereignty and an end to the slave trade were inevitable and that his Orungu friends should follow his own policy of ostensible compliance with French demands while maintaining as much autonomy as possible. Denis, who dwelt safely across the river from the *comptoir*, could give such advice; presumably his colleague Quaben would have had different views on the subject.

Avaro raises a third possible motive for Ndebulia's adherence to the treaty; the desire to receive the accompanying presents and to

[1] Baron Didelot to Min. of Marine, June 1862, Archives d'Outre-Mer, Gabon, iv, 9.
[2] Abbé Walker, *Notes*, p. 78.
[3] Wm. Walker Diary, iv, 18 Apr. 1847 and ix, 29 Aug. 1860.
[4] Didelot to Min. of Marine, June 1862; Avaro, 'Bas-Ogowé', p. 272.
[5] Griffon du Bellay, 'Le Gabon', *Le Tour du monde*, xii (1865), p. 287.

open trade with France.[1] Thirty dignitaries signed along with the king; all were rewarded. A clause in article 1 of the treaty gave the French the right to establish any buildings or posts they deemed necessary; the Orungu may well have been led to believe that a French factory would follow the treaty. Significantly, the pact made no mention of ending the slave trade.[2]

The treaty had little immediate effect on Orungu life. French sovereignty and 'protection' remained purely nominal and no post or factory was set up. However, the French did gain a legal claim to the Ogowe delta and a few weeks after the conclusion of the treaty the *Pioneer* was sent up the river. Six years later France obtained an almost identical treaty from the Nkomi of Fernan Vaz, thus gaining complete control, at least on paper, of the mouths of the Ogowe.[3]

Ndebulia died in 1865, leaving the throne to his brother Ntchegue (or Nschege), an opponent of the 1862 treaty.[4] Ntchegue, the last independent Orungu ruler, was unable to control the slave trade or the entrance to the Ogowe. The clans, after almost a century of subordination to the royal power, were re-emerging as political units as the monarchy continued to decline. Many of the chiefs along the Ogowe had been angered by the signing of the 1862 treaty; King Amale of the frontier village of Orovy refused to recognize Ndebulia's authority.[5] By 1870 the French recognized that the king had no authority over Ningue Nona, the chief of Mandji Island, who did not consider himself bound by the treaty of 1862. The colonial officials in Gabon wanted to force him to sign a treaty, despite orders against new annexations, as this would be a useful 'border rectification'.[6] Yombe Island, the site of a Hatton and Cookson factory, was ruled by a chief Nshango in 1873. Compiègne described him as a *roi*; his

[1] Avaro, 'Bas-Ogowé', p. 268.

[2] Treaty text in De Clercq, *Recueil des traités de la France* (Paris), viii, pp. 413–14.

[3] Text ibid., x, pp. 21–3.

[4] Aube to de Langle, 21 Dec. 1866. Ndebulia reportedly had been dead for more than a year. Ntchegue probably was the brother who challenged Ombango's rule in 1854. Three years later Du Chaillu met this man, who he called Nchouga, in Fernan Vaz where he had sought refuge after being defeated. See Paul B. Du Chaillu, *Explorations and Adventures in Equatorial Africa* (New York, 1861), pp. 225–6. According to Abbé Walker (*Notes*, p. 74), Ndebulia's rival for the throne after Ombango's death had been Ntchuga-Rogombe, who may well have been the same individual.

[5] Griffon du Bellay, 'Exploration du fleuve Ogo-Wai', pp. 297–8.

[6] Captain of the *Olorinde* to Admiral de Langle, 20 Mar. 1870, Archives d'-Outre-Mer, Gabon, i, 8, b.

brothers were even more powerful and had their own domains else-
where in the delta.[1] By 1873 four Orungu chiefs had obtained separate
treaties with the French; one of them, Songue of the village of
'Angola', had made several trips to Brazil on board slavers.[2]
Ntchegue managed to maintain a semblance of power in face of what
Avaro calls *anarchie clanique*, but his authority was mainly moral.[3]

Neither the king nor the local chiefs were able to halt European
penetration of the Ogowe. Although traders did not ascend the river
until the early '70s, the early French explorations thoroughly alarmed
the coastmen. An elderly Orungu trader was shocked to discover
Aymes in Enenga country in 1867. 'What are you doing here?' he
demanded. 'Why don't you go back home and let us live in peace and
trade as we wish?' The old man knew that Aymes would eventually
be followed by European merchants.[4]

The trading steamers which began entering the river in 1872 were
armed against possible Orungu attack. Although these vessels were
too swift to be seriously threatened by the angry Orungu, the traders
feared that a grounded vessel would be vulnerable to attack by war
canoes.[5] French gunboats made occasional cruises on the river to
overawe any African attempt to interfere with the destruction of
the ancient *courtier* system of river trade.

Despite the heavy odds against them, the Orungu, or rather individual Orungu chiefs and their followers, did make two attempts to
close the river by force. At the end of December 1873, word reached
the factories at Adolinanango that the Hatton and Cookson steamer
Delta had been captured at Cape Lopez.[6] Furthermore, an Orungu
force was reportedly moving up river to attack the factories and force
their relocation in the delta, and to kill their arch-enemy, R. B. N.
Walker.[7] Three white factors and the explorers Marche and Com-

[1] Marquis de Compiègne, *L'Afrique équatoriale: Gabonais, Pahouins, Gallois*
(Paris, 1875), p. 297.

[2] 'Voyage dans l'Ogoway', Admiral Du Quilo, 20 July–6 Aug. 1873, Archives
d'Outre-Mer, Gabon, iii, 2, pp. 2, 3, 35.

[3] Avaro, 'Bas-Ogowé', pp. 284–5.

[4] Aymes, 'Explorations', p. 59.

[5] Nassau, *My Ogowe*, pp. 18–19.

[6] The 1873–4 troubles are described in Albert Marche, *Trois Voyages en
Afrique occidentale: Sénégal, Gambie, Casamance, Gabon, Ogowé* (Paris, 1879),
pp. 182–7.

[7] Besides their wrath at Walker for opening the river to European traders, the
Orungu were enraged by his recent downgrading of the factory at Yombe.
Compiègne, *Gabonais*, p. 296.

piègne were at Adolinanango at the time; they and their employees prepared to defend themselves. The local Galoa people, equally anxious to cut out the Orungu middlemen, pledged their aid. However, the attack never materialized. A few days later the defenders learned that the *Delta* had been attacked but not taken; a French gunboat punished the culprits.

Two years later the Orungu made their last attempts to regain control of the river mouth. This time they struck in the dry season when the movements of the gunboat would be hindered by low water. In August 1876 the American missionary Nassau and a colleague were robbed by a delta chief, Azizi-N'Gile. Nassau, believing that the Orungu had reconciled themselves to the loss of their trade monopoly, decided to go up to his station in a canoe rather than wait for a steamer. The missionary party was forced to land and stood surrounded by Azizi's 'forty armed, war-painted, angry, shouting' men. After a tense two-hour bargaining session, the missionaries were allowed to pass with the payment of a 'present' of forty dollars in trade goods.[1] A few days later a German schooner was robbed and consternation spread among the trading community. Azizi-N'Gile then led a sixty-man force up the Ogowe to attempt to capture the factors and force them to relocate on the coast. However, a French punitive expedition was dispatched; several Orungu were killed, a fine was levied, and a number of canoes captured. Forty Orungu visitors had been seized at Gabon and were held until the fine was paid.[2] The commander of Gabon made the overland crossing from the Como to Adolinanango during the dry season of 1877 specifically to show the Orungu that the factories could be protected even if the river were too low to permit gunboats to go that far upstream.[3] The Orungu made no further efforts to disrupt river traffic.

The Orungu, unable to deal in slaves or control the flow of goods to and from the Ogowe valley, rapidly sank into economic obscurity. A few people found work as boatmen or agents with the inland factories; most turned to farming and fishing. The Ogowe delta was no longer a commercial centre, but an economic backwater. Steamers

[1] Nassau, *My Ogowe*, pp. 149–52.
[2] Ibid., pp. 152, 169; Avaro, 'Bas-Ogowé', pp. 281–3; Henri Brunschwig, 'Expéditions punitives au Gabon', *Cahiers d'études africaines*, vii (1962), pp. 357–9.
[3] Marche, *Trois Voyages*, pp. 352–3.

passed through Orungu territory on their way to and from the up-river factories, but they almost never stopped to trade. Politically, the trend toward decentralization continued. When Ntchegue was visited in 1882 by a French officer, he was still recognized as monarch, but he could not deal with the French until four other powerful chiefs had arrived. 'He lives almost alone in a poor village composed of four or five ruined houses', wrote Captain Minier. 'He is an old man whose authority is, I am sure, more nominal than real, and it is sad and disturbing to see him abandoned in his old age.'[1] Two other men held the title of king after his death; the institution finally expired in 1927.[2] France did not bother to formally occupy the Orungu lands for some time. A temporary post was erected on Mandji Island in 1883;[3] a permanent customs post was established there in 1894 and the city of Port-Gentil began to form around it.[4]

Long before the effective occupation of their country by the French, the Orungu had suffered complete political and economic collapse with the loss of their almost two-hundred-year monopoly of the Ogowe traffic. The Orungu, though a small group, had prospered because their geographical position gave them control over the Ogowe trade, especially the export of slaves. Wealth from the slave trade had been the main support of a powerful monarchy; an almost unique institution among the peoples of the coast of the Bight of Biafra. But the Orungu state was utterly unable to deal creatively with the challenges of the post-1850 era. Clinging to a dwindling and dangerous commerce in human beings and lacking the military and commercial strength to defend their erstwhile dominance of the river mouth, the Orungu quickly faded into insignificance in the 1870s.

[1] 'Voyage dans l'Ogowé', Minier, 1882, p. 2, pp. 15–16.
[2] Abbé Walker, *Notes*, p. 75.
[3] Avaro, 'Bas-Ogowé', p. 303.
[4] Abbé Walker, *Notes*, p. 76.

CHAPTER VIII

Summary and Conclusions

COMMERCIAL and political developments on the northern Gabon coast paralleled those elsewhere on the West African littoral. The slave trade and the factory system began somewhat later on the Gabon coast than in areas of more extensive commerce, but here, as elsewhere, relations with Europeans had a profound impact on the evolution of African societies. Although the region was relatively poor and sparsely populated, the Mpongwe and Orungu were able to take advantage of water transport to draw slaves and forest products from an extensive hinterland. The major factor in the pre-colonial history of the Mpongwe and Orungu peoples which distinguished them from other groups in the area was their role as coastal middlemen. Indeed, few African peoples devoted themselves so wholeheartedly to commerce.

Specialization in trade influenced both economic and political development. The coastmen tended to neglect traditional crafts in favour of imported goods; agriculture was largely relegated to women and slaves. New skills had to be developed for success in commerce. The traders had to be able to bargain, to judge the quality of goods and the market conditions for them, to deal with foreigners and speak their languages. Diplomatic skills and the ability to keep complicated accounts without the aid of writing were essential assets. Men who possessed these qualities, whether kings or commoners, were able to achieve wealth and status. The most respected men in nineteenth-century coastal society were the successful merchants, not the chiefs, warriors, hunters, or spiritual leaders.

The mechanics of European–African trade on the Gabon coast were similar to commercial patterns elsewhere in western Africa. Dashes had to be given to African chiefs and merchants, 'trust' was extensively used, and the captains had to present well-assorted bundles of goods. Bargaining was long and arduous, with both parties seeking greater profits by artifice and occasionally by force. Successive tiers of middlemen controlled the flow of goods to and from the coast.

European traders in the nineteenth century were eager to maximize their profits by breaking through the middlemen who separated them from the interior producers, and they found increasing support from their governments. Mpongwe and Orungu traders felt this pressure earlier and more strongly than most other coastal Africans. Although the permanently manned factory was a relatively late development in Gabon, the French military presence in this sparsely populated region gave the whites a great advantage. The Africans were too feeble militarily and divided politically to regulate or destroy the factories and steamboats which were undercutting their economic position. By the 1870s the Mpongwe had lost their commercial importance and the Ogowe had been opened to white traders. European commercial encroachment had begun elsewhere by the 1870s, especially in Senegambia and in the Niger Delta where navigable waterways facilitated the European advance, but Gabon was one of the first places on the western coast where the indigenous trading system was challenged and smashed.

External commerce strongly influenced political development in northern Gabon. The Orungu state was an anomaly in a region characterized by acephalous or weakly centralized political systems. Orungu rulers were able to gain and retain control over the slave trade which developed in the late eighteenth century and were able to use the resulting wealth to strengthen the monarchy. The Mpongwe, on the other hand, never developed the strong, unitary state which characterized the Orungu, but remained divided into small, weak political units. Mpongwe kings had the trappings, but not the powers of Orungu monarchs; the position of the king more closely resembled that of a prestigious businessman whose success was recognized by election to the chairmanship of the board than a real ruler.

These striking differences in political organization resulted from the interaction of several factors. As was suggested in chapter one, the original Mpongwe inhabitants of Cape Lopez probably had a more centralized political system than their northern neighbours as early as the seventeenth century. The Orungu took over these institutions about 1700, and the process of conquering the coast may well have further strengthened the monarchy. Geography also played a role. Cape Lopez, a prominent navigational landmark, was often visited by ships. The Orungu king controlled the only two trading places in his domains; the royal village and the tip of Cape Lopez, which was uninhabited except when people came from the capital to fish or to trade with ships anchored there. Conversely, the placid waters of the Gabon estuary had many excellent trading sites, each of which was controlled by an independent political community. If one king extracted too many 'presents' or attempted to raise prices, the Europeans could always move to another village. Competition for commerce among the various kingdoms prevented any one of them from gaining control of enough trade wealth to achieve dominance over the others. Rulers were unable to secure personal power in their own communities and were in no position to extend their territories. Kings and kingdoms waxed and waned in wealth and influence, but not enough to create a powerful monarchy or to unify the Mpongwe into a single state.

It is probable that the nature of the commodities traded helps explain, at least in part, the differences in political organization. Gray and Birmingham have suggested that there is a positive correlation between a slave-trading economy and political centralization, while trade in forest products usually does not stimulate state formation.[1] Since the Orungu specialized in slaving and much of the Mpongwe trade was in ivory and wood, the commodity thesis deserves examination, even though the model is not exact because both groups were essentially middlemen rather than producers. Although the Orungu were buying most of their slaves rather than obtaining them in wars conducted by the king or as tribute payments from subject peoples, it is reasonable to suppose that slave dealing required more organization than commerce in forest products. Slaves had to be guarded and fed in transit and while awaiting shipment, whereas an individual could haul a tusk or bundle of dyewood around in his canoe and store the produce in his own house or shed without worrying about the maintenance or escape. Rulers would find it easier to regulate or monopolize trade in a conspicuous commodity like slaves. Hence, the slave trade would be more likely to add to the king's wealth and power than other branches of commerce.

The slave trade did not, of course, always lead to the development of strong centralized states, as the case of the Kongo amply demonstrates. Benin flourished for centuries with a very low level of slave exports and indeed relatively little commerce of any kind with

[1] Richard Gray and David Birmingham, eds., *Pre-Colonial African Trade: Essays on Trade in Central and Eastern Africa before 1900* (London, 1970), pp. 16–18.

Europeans. The city-states of the Niger Delta exported huge numbers of human beings without becoming large in territory or necessarily despotic in government. While slaves may have been an easier commodity to regulate than, say, dyewood, the crucial problem for a ruler was to extract profits from whatever trade went on, and to use the revenue effectively to increase royal power.[1]

All African coastal states came under increasing European commercial and political pressure in the nineteenth century, but rulers dependent on revenues from the slave trade became especially vulnerable when Great Britain and other powers took measures to halt the traffic. Dahomey, a strong, highly centralized kingdom located far enough inland to be safe from European fleets and landing parties, had some success in switching from slave to palm oil exports, as did the Niger Delta states. The Orungu kingdom, a weak state exposed to naval attack, was much less flexible in the face of European pressure. Unlike the Delta states, the Orungu made no attempt to develop 'legitimate commerce'. They clung to the slave trade until the last possible moment and suffered ignominious collapse as a result. In striking contrast to the Mpongwe, the Orungu political and economic system fell apart long before physical occupation of their territory by the colonial regime. The Orungu were of course in a difficult dilemma, but in retrospect it seems probable that a policy of accommodation with the anti-slavery forces coupled with attempts to develop trade in other commodities would have bought time for the Orungu state and perhaps cushioned its fall.

Because their commercial prominence attracted foreign attention to the fact that they lived on one of western Africa's best natural harbours, the Mpongwe were subjected to colonial rule and missionary propaganda decades before other peoples of the region. Unable to oppose French encroachment, the Mpongwe none the less managed to maintain considerable political and economic autonomy during the early years of colonial rule, and stoutly resisted missionary blandishments. Their eclipse was gradual and less traumatic than that of their southern neighbours.

Gabon, selected as a *comptoir* in 1839, was one of France's oldest colonies in Africa. The *comptoir* proved to be of little military or commercial value, but it was held and provided the nucleus for later French expansion. Roman Catholic missionaries were sent to Gabon

[1] Patrick Manning, 'Slaves, Palm Oil, and Political Power on the West African Coast', *African Historical Studies*, ii, 2 (1969), p. 286.

only because it was a French base. Missionary activity has been continuous and extensive since 1844; today Gabonese Catholics number over 230,000, roughly fifty per cent of the total population.[1] The American Board of Commissioners for Foreign Missions was hardly attracted to the Gabon by the French presence, but the pioneering American missionaries persevered and, even in failure, laid the foundation for further Protestant efforts. American Presbyterians took over the Gabon station in 1870 and began work on the Ogowe in 1874. In 1892, after it had become apparent that the colonial regime would no longer tolerate foreign, especially non-francophone missionaries, the Protestant stations were handed over to the Paris Evangelical Society. By 1968 the French Protestants were able to claim about 80,000 adherents.[2]

The establishment and retention of the *comptoir* ensured that Gabon would eventually become a French colony. If Gabon had remained unclaimed by any European power at the time of the scramble, it is reasonable to assume that it eventually would have fallen to Britain, the leading trading nation in the area. Or, since German trade in the Gabon and on the Ogowe also exceeded that of France in the 1870s,[3] it is possible that, as they did in the Camerouns, the Germans might have annexed an area in which their trade was second to that of the English.

France, however, for reason of pride and inertia, maintained the Gabon post, despite the fact that only foreign merchants profited from its trade. The Ivory Coast *comptoirs* (Assini, Grand Bassam, and Dabou), were abandoned as useless financial burdens in 1871, although France retained its rights of sovereignty.[4] In the same year, Admiral Bourgois complained that Gabon, rather than supporting the fleet, was supported by it. Steps were taken to reduce expenses and plans for abandoning Gabon were advanced. Protests by the Catholic missionaries, who feared the loss of their subsidy and military protection, and opposition to the abandonment scheme by some commercial and naval circles helped save Gabon from the fate of the other *comptoirs*. A more decisive reason for the retention of

[1] H. Wakelin Coxhill and Sir Kenneth Grubb, eds., *World Christian Handbook* (New York, 1968), p. 27.

[2] *World Christian Handbook*, p. 69.

[3] Marquis de Compiègne, *L'Afrique équatoriale: Okanda, Bangouens, Osyeba* (Paris, 1875), p. 226.

[4] Bernard Schnapper, *La Politique et le commerce français dans le Golfe de Guinée de 1838 à 1871* (Paris, 1961), p. 253.

Gabon was the stimulus to trade given by the British in 1871, when a fortnightly steamer service was inaugurated. It began to appear that Gabon might show a profit at last.[1]

Gabon had in fact been considered expendable for many years and, along with the posts on the Ivory Coast, was repeatedly offered to Great Britain in exchange for the Gambia. Negotiations were conducted during the 1860s and early 1870s, but the parties never agreed on terms and the last exchange scheme was dropped in 1876.[2] By this time the Ogowe had been opened to trade, customs revenues had risen, and France never again considered leaving Gabon. Brazza's first Ogowe expedition (1875-9) was the opening act in a new role for the old *comptoir*; Libreville became France's initial base for the exploration of the territories which were to comprise Afrique Équatoriale Française.

The leaders of post-1960 Gabon, committed as they are to extremely close ties with France, view the early years of colonial rule in a romantic perspective rather unusual in modern Africa. President Albert Bongo, speaking on the occasion of President Pompidou's visit in February 1971, claimed that there was no 'spirit of domination' in the old French treaties with the Mpongwe. Praising France's peaceful assumption of responsibility over 'unhappy and backward isolated communities', President Bongo asserted that since 1839 Franco–Gabonese relations had been characterized by 'entente and harmony which has never known a discordant note'.[3] These words are more than ceremonial rhetoric; similar conceptions of the past are widespread among the Gabonese and are part of the national myth. The slavers and ivory merchants, the Orungu state and the Mpongwe kings encountered in 1839 by the agents of France have long passed from the scene. The Orungu and Mpongwe peoples are now only tiny minorities in their ancient homelands, but France, despite the formalities of 1960, is still very much in Gabon.

[1] Ibid., pp. 254-5.
[2] Details of these complex negotiations are given in John D. Hargreaves, *Prelude to the Partition of West Africa* (London, 1963), pp. 136-95; and Schnapper, *Politique et commerce*, pp. 240-5.
[3] 'Pompidou Tour Diary', *West Africa*, 20-6 Feb. 1971 (No. 2,802), p. 211.

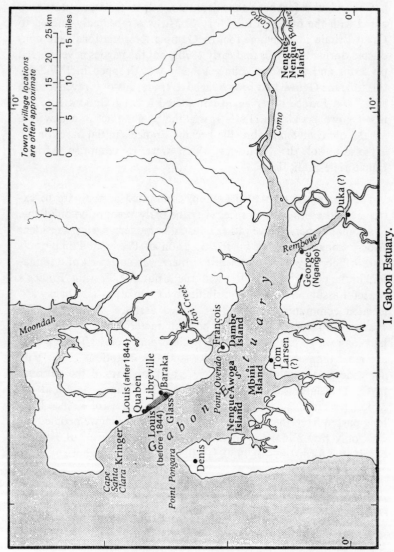

I. Gabon Estuary.

II. Cape Lopez and the Lower Ogowe.

Bibliography

A. UNPUBLISHED SOURCES

Archival materials for this study were consulted in France, Portugal, and the United States. French sources for the pre-1839 period are housed in the Archives Nationales; the relevant documents are mostly commercial surveys or proposals. Abundant documentation for the *comptoir* is held in the Archives d'Outre-Mer, but much consists of administrative minutiae of little interest to the Africanist. The Bibliothèque Nationale has a rich collection of maps of Africa, but few cover the Gabon area. Portuguese authorities on São Tomé and Principe supplied some information about the adjacent coast in reports to Lisbon, but much data is buried in petitions, wills, and other legal documents. As might be expected, only a very small fraction of the São Tomé records were relevant to this study. American sources for Gabonese history are surprisingly rich, due to the early arrival of American missionaries. Their writings are an invaluable complement to the administrative reports of the French officers. The dispatches of the United States Commercial Agent, who was usually a resident missionary, provide data on trade and slaving. Finally, the papers of a few American mariners provide information on nineteenth-century Gabon.

France (Paris)

   Archives de la Congrégation des Pères du Saint-Esprit. Boîtes 148, 167, 168, 172, 173.

   Archives Nationales. Colonies, C⁶.

   Archives Nationales. Section d'Outre-Mer. Ancienne série C; Sénégal, Gorée, Gabon, Afrique.

   Bibliothèque Nationale. Cartes et plans.

Portugal (Lisbon)

   Archivo Histórico Ultramarino. São Tomé, caixas 1–21; maços 1–17.

   Archivo Nacional da Torre do Tombo. Junta do Comercio, maço 20.

United States

   Essex Institute. Salem, Mass. Log of the Bark *Reaper*.

Houghton Library. Harvard University. Cambridge, Mass. American Board of Commissioners for Foreign Missions Letterbooks, Gabon Mission.

Peabody Museum. Salem, Mass. Samuel Swan Letterbook; Journal of the Brig *Neptune*.

Presbyterian Church in the U.S.A., Board of Foreign Missions, African Materials, 1837–1903. Consulted on microfilm at Stanford University.

Rhode Island Historical Society. Providence, Rhode Island. Journals of John R. Congdon.

State Historical Society of Wisconsin. Madison, Wis. William Walker Papers.

United States. Department of the Navy. Letters received from Commanding Officers of Squadrons, African Squadron. National Archives Microfilm.

United States. Department of State. Consular Reports, Gabon. National Archives Microfilm.

B. PUBLISHED DOCUMENTS

BENNETT, Norman R. and George E. BROOKS, Jr., eds. *New England Merchants in Africa: A History Through Documents 1802 to 1865.* Boston, 1965.

BRASIO, Padre Antonio Duarte, ed. *Monumenta Missionaria Africana. Africa Ocidental.* 10 vols. Lisbon, 1952–65.

BRUNSCHWIG, Henri. *Brazza Explorateur: L'Ogooué 1875–1879.* Paris, 1966.

CORTESÃO, Armando and Avelino TEIXEIRA DA MOTA. *Portugaliae Monumenta Cartographica.* 5 vols. Lisbon, 1960.

DE CLERCQ. *Recueil des traités de la France,* vols. viii and x. Paris, 1867, 1872.

DONNAN, Elizabeth. *Documents Illustrative of the History of the Slave Trade to America.* 4 vols. Washington, D.C., 1930–5.

Great Britain. Parliamentary Papers. Slave Trade. Searched for 1787–1870.

C. PRIMARY SOURCES

ADAMS, John. *Remarks on the Country Extending from Cape Palmas to the River Congo, Including Observations on the Manners and Customs of the Inhabitants.* London, 1823. New impression, London, 1966.

ATKINS, John. *A Voyage to Guinea, Bresil and the West Indies, in H.M.S. the Swallow and Weymouth*, London, 1735.

AUBRY, S. 'Note sur le commerce du Gabon et de ses dépendances', *Revue coloniale*, xiii (1854), pp. 468–73.

AYMES, Lieutenant A. 'Exploration de l'Ogoway: recherches géographiques et ethnographiques sur le bassin du Gabon', *Revue maritime et coloniale*, xxvii (1870), pp. 525–61; xxix (1870), pp. 54–73.

BARBOT, John. *A Description of the Coasts of North and South Guinea and of Ethiopia Inferior, Vulgarly Angola*, vol. v in Awnsham and John Churchill, eds., *Collection of Voyages and Travels*. London, 1732.

BATTELL, Andrew. *The Strange Adventures of Andrew Battell of Leigh, in Angola and the Adjoining Regions*, ed. E. G. Ravenstein. London, 1901.

BOSMAN, Willem. *A New and Accurate Description of the Coast of Guinea*, vol. xvi in John Pinkerton, ed., *A General Collection of the Best and Most Interesting Voyages and Travels in All Parts of the World; Many of Which Are Now First Translated in English. Digested on a New Plan*. London, 1814. The Dutch original appeared in 1705; a fourth English edition was printed in London, 1967.

BOTELER, Captain Thomas. *Narrative of a Voyage of Discovery to Africa and Arabia, Performed in His Majesty's Ships, Leven and Barracouta, from 1821 to 1826, Under the Command of Captain F. W. Owen, R.N.* 2 vols. London, 1835.

BOUËT-WILLAUMEZ, Louis Edouard. *Commerce et traite des noirs aux côtes occidentales d'Afrique*. Paris, 1848.

BOWDICH, T. Edward. *Mission from Cape Coast Castle to Ashantee*. London, 1966. 1st ed. 1819.

BROECKE, Pieter van den. *Reisen naar West Afrika (1605–1614)*, ed. K. Ratelband. The Hague, 1950.

BRUN, Samuel. *Samuel Brun, des Wundartzet und Bergers zu Basel, Schiffarten*, ed. S. P. L'Honoré Naber. The Hague, 1913.

BURTON, Richard F. *Two Trips to Gorillaland and the Cataracts of the Congo*, vol. i. London, 1967. 1st ed. 1876.

COMPIÈGNE, Victor le Marquis de. *L'Afrique équatoriale: Gabonais, Pahouins, Gallois*. Paris, 1875.

——. *L'Afrique équatoriale: Okanda, Bangouens, Osyeba*. Paris, 1875.

'D.R.' 'The Passage from the Gold Coast to the Kingdome of Benni, or Rio de Benni, and Rio Floreado: The Citie, Court, Gentry, Apparell: Also Other Places Adjoyning, Described.' In Samual Purchas, ed., *Hakluytus Posthumus or Purchas His Pilgrimes*, vol. vi, pp. 353–66. Glasgow, 1905–7. Original ed. 1625.

DU CHAILLU, Paul B. *Explorations and Adventures in Equatorial Africa; with Accounts of the Manners and Customs of the People, and of the Chase of the Gorilla, the Crocodile, Leopard, Elephant, Hippopotamus, and Other Animals.* New York, 1861.

——. *My Apingi Kingdom, with Life in the Great Sahara, and Sketches of the Chase of the Ostrich, Hyena, etc.* New York, 1870.

FLEURIOT DE LANGLE, Vice-Admiral A. 'Croisières à la côte d'Afrique', *Le Tour du monde*, xxxi (1876), pp. 241–304.

FORÊT, Auguste. 'Le Fernan-Vaz', *Bulletin de la Société de géographie*, xix (1898), pp. 308–27.

GRIFFON DU BELLAY, M. T. 'Exploration du fleuve Ogo-Wai, côte occidentale d'Afrique', *Revue maritime et coloniale*, ix (1863), pp. 66–89; pp. 296–309.

——. 'Le Gabon', *Le Tour du monde*, xii (1865), pp. 273–320.

HAUG, Ernest. 'Le Bas-Ogooué', *Annales de géographie*, xii (1903), pp. 159–71.

HECQUARD, Hyacinthe. *Voyage sur la côte et dans l'intérieur de l'Afrique occidentale.* Paris, 1853.

ISERT, Paul Erdman. *Voyages en Guinée et dans les Îles Caraïbes en Amerique.* Paris, 1793.

KINGSLEY, Mary H. *Travels in West Africa; Congo Français, Corisco and Cameroons.* 3rd ed. London, 1965. First published 1897.

LABARTHE, P. *Voyage à la côte de Guinée, ou description des côtes d'Afrique depuis le Cap Tagrin jusqu'au Cap de Lopez Gonzalves.* Paris, 1805.

LESTRILLE. 'Note sur le comptoir du Gabon', *Revue coloniale*, xvi (1856), pp. 424–49.

LINSCHOTEN, Jan Huygen van. *Beschryvinghe van de Gantsche Cust van Guinea, Manicongo, etc.*, ed. C. P. Burger and F. Hunger. The Hague, 1934.

MARCHE, Alfred. *Trois Voyages en Afrique occidentale; Sénégal, Gambie, Casamance, Gabon, Ogowé.* Paris, 1879.

MAREES, Pieter de. 'A Description and Historicall Declaration of the Golden Kingdome of Guinea Otherwise Called the Golden Coast of Myna.' Vol. vi in Samuel Purchas, ed., *Hakluytus Posthumus or Purchas His Pilgrimes.* Glasgow, 1905–7. 1st ed. 1625.

MONTAUGAN. *Relation Du Voyage de Sibur de Montauban, Capitaine des Flibustiers, en Guinée, en Année 1695.* Microfiche. ed. Paris, 1972. 1st. ed. 1698.

NASSAU, Robert H. *Corisco Days: The First Thirty Years of the West Africa Mission.* Philadelphia, 1910.

——. *My Ogowe; Being a Narrative of Daily Incidents During Sixteen Years in Equatorial West Africa.* New York, 1914.

PACHECO PEREIRA, Duarte. *Esmeraldo de situ orbis,* ed. G. H. T. Kimble. London, 1937.

PIGAFETTA, Filippo and Duarte LOPES. *Description du royaume de Congo et des contrées environnantes,* ed. Willy Bal. Louvain and Paris, 1965.

PIGEARD, Lieutenant. 'Exploration du Gabon, effectuée en août et septembre 1846', *Revue coloniale,* xi (1847), pp. 263–95.

READE, Winwood W. *Savage Africa; Being the Narrative of a Tour in Equatorial, Southwestern, and Northwestern Africa.* New York, 1864.

RUITERS, Dierick. *Toortse der Zee-Vaert,* ed. S. P. L'Honoré Naber. The Hague, 1913.

SERVAL, Lieutenant P. 'Reconnaissance d'une des routes qui mènent du Rhamboé à l'Ogo-wai', *Revue maritime et coloniale,* ix (1863), pp. 309–15.

SWAN, Samuel. 'Captain Samuel Swan's Memoranda on the African Trade', In George E. Brooks, Jr., *Yankee Traders, Old Coasters and African Middlemen: A History of American Legitimate Trade with West Africa in the Nineteenth Century.* Boston, 1970, pp. 313–343.

TAYLOR, E. G. R., ed. *A Brief Summe of Geographie by Roger Barlow.* London, 1932.

TOUCHARD, F. 'Notice sur le Gabon', *Revue maritime et coloniale* (1861), pp. 1–17.

VIGNON, Capt. 'Le Comptoir français du Gabon sur le côte occidentale d'Afrique', *Nouvelles Annales des voyages,* iv (1856), pp. 281–302.

WALKER, R. B. N. 'Letter on a Journey up the Ogowe River, West Africa', *Proceedings of the Royal Geographical Society,* xvii (1873), pp. 354–5.

——. 'Relation d'une tentative d'exploration en 1866 de la rivière de l'Ogowé et de la recherche d'un grand lac devant se trouver dans l'Afrique centrale', *Annales des voyages*, i (1870), pp. 59–80; 120–44.

WILSON, John Leighton. 'Mr. Wilson's Description of the Gaboon', *The Missionary Herald*, xxxix (1843), pp. 229–240.

——. 'Traite des noirs au Gabon', *Revue coloniale*, iii (1844), pp. 408–11.

——. *Western Africa: Its History, Condition, and Prospects*. New York, 1856.

D. SECONDARY WORKS

ALEXANDRE, Pierre. 'Proto-histoire du groupe beti-bulu-fang: essai de synthèse provisoire', *Cahiers d'études africaines*, No. 20 (1965), pp. 503–60.

ARDENER, Edwin. 'Documentary and Linguistic Evidence for the Rise of the Trading Polities Between Rio del Rey and Cameroons, 1500–1650', in I. M. Lewis, ed., *History and Social Anthropology*. London, 1968.

AVARO, J. Ambouroué. 'Le Bas-Ogowé au dix-neuvième siècle'. Unpublished doctoral dissertation, University of Paris, Sorbonne, 1969.

AVELOT, Lieutenant R. 'Recherches sur l'histoire des migrations dans le bassin de l'Ogooué et la région du littoral adjacente', *Bulletin de géographie historique et descriptive*, xx (1905), pp. 357–412.

BIRMINGHAM, David. 'The African Response to Early Portuguese Activities in Angola', in Ronald H. Chilcote, ed., *Protest and Resistance in Angola and Brazil: Comparative Studies*. Berkeley and Los Angeles, 1972.

——. *Trade and Conflict in Angola: The Mbundu and their Neighbours under the Influence of the Portuguese 1483–1790*. London, 1966.

BOUCHAUD, Père J. *La Côte du Cameroun dans l'histoire et la cartographie, des origines à l'annexion allemande (1884)*. Yaounde, Cameroun, 1952.

BROOKS, George E., Jr. *Yankee Traders, Old Coasters and African Middlemen: A History of American Legitimate Trade with West Africa in the Nineteenth Century*. Boston, 1970.

BROWN, Arthur Judson. *One Hundred Years: A History of the Foreign Missionary Work of the Presbyterian Church in the U.S.A.* New York, 1936.

BRUNSCHWIG, Henri. 'Expéditions punitives au Gabon', *Cahiers d'études africaines*, No. 7 (1962), pp. 347–61.

BUCHER, Henry H., Jr. 'The Village of Glass and Western Intrusion:

An Mpongwe Response to the American and French Presence in the Gabon Estuary: 1842–1845', *The International Journal of African Historical Studies*, vi (1973), pp. 363–400.

CLENDENEN, Clarence C. and Peter DUIGNAN. *Americans in Black Africa up to 1865*. Stanford, Calif. 1964.

'Les Colonies françaises: établissements de la Côte d'Or et du Gabon', *Revue maritime et coloniale*, ix (1863), pp. 31–65.

COXILL, H. Wakelin and Sir Kenneth GRUBB, eds. *World Christian Handbook*. New York, 1968.

CURTIN, Philip D. *The Atlantic Slave Trade: A Census*. Madison, 1969.

—— and Jan VANSINA. 'Sources of the Nineteenth Century Atlantic Slave Trade', *Journal of African History*, v (1964), pp. 185–208.

CUVELIER, Mgr. J. and ABBÉ L. Jadin. *L'Ancien Congo d'après les archives romaines (1518–1640)*. Brussels, 1954.

DAPPER, Olfert. *Beschreibung von Afrika*. New York, 1967. A reprint of the 1670 German edition.

——. *Description de l'Afrique*. Amsterdam, 1686.

DAVIDSON, Basil. *The African Slave Trade: Pre-Colonial History 1450–1850*. Boston, 1961.

DAVIES, K. G. *The Royal African Company*. London, 1957.

DESCHAMPS, Hubert. *Quinze Ans de Gabon; les débuts de l'établisse-ment français 1839–1853*. Paris, 1965.

——. *Traditions orales et archives au Gabon: contribution à l'ethno-histoire*. Paris, 1962.

DIKE, Kenneth Onwuka. *Trade and Politics in the Niger Delta, 1830–1885*. London, 1956.

DU BOSE, Hampden C. *Memoirs of Rev. John Leighton Wilson, D.D.* Richmond, Va., 1895.

DUFFY, James. *A Question of Slavery: Labour Policies in Portuguese Africa and British Protest, 1850–1920*. Cambridge, Mass., 1967.

DUPRÉ, Georges. 'Le Commerce entre sociétés lignagères: les Nzabi dans la traite à la fin du XIXe siècle (Gabon-Congo)', *Cahiers d'études africaines*, No. 4 (1972), pp. 616–58.

GASTON-MARTIN. *Nantes au XVIIIe siècle; l'ère des négriers (1714–1774)*. Paris, 1931.

GAUTIER, Père. *Étude historique sur les Mpongoués et tribus avoisinan-tes*. Brazzaville, 1950.

GRAY, Richard and David BIRMINGHAM. *Pre-Colonial African Trade: Essays on Trade in Central and Eastern Africa Before 1900*. London, 1970.

GUTHRIE, Malcolm. 'Some Developments in the Prehistory of the Bantu Languages', *Journal of African History*, iii (1962), pp. 273–82.

HAIR, P. E. H. 'The Earliest Vocabularies of Cameroons Bantu', *African Studies*, xxviii (1969), pp. 49–54.

HARGREAVES, John D. *Prelude to the Partition of West Africa.* London, 1963.

HAUSER, André. 'Notes sur les Omyene du Bas-Gabon', *Bulletin de l'Institut français d'Afrique noire*, B, xvi (1954), pp. 402–15.

IRELAND, Rev. William. *Historical Sketch of the Zulu Mission, in South Africa, as also of the Gaboon Mission, in Western Africa.* Boston, 1863.

JONES, D. H. 'Problems of African Chronology', *Journal of African History*, xi (1970), pp. 161–76.

KOELLE, Sigismund Wilhelm. *Polyglotta Africana.* Graz, Austria, 1963. Original ed. London, 1854.

LASSERRE, Guy. *Libreville: la ville et sa région.* Paris, 1958.

LLOYD, Christopher. *The Navy and the Slave Trade: The Suppression of the African Slave Trade in the Nineteenth Century.* London, 1949.

LOPES DE LIMA, José Joaquim. *Ensaios sobre a Statistica das Possessões Portuguezas na Africa Occidental e Oriental; na Asia Occidental; na China, e na Oceania.* Lisbon, 1844.

MCCALL, Daniel F. Review of *Ships and Seamanship in the Ancient World* by Lionel Casson, *International Journal of African Historical Studies*, v (1972), pp. 668–70.

MANNING, Patrick. 'Slaves, Palm Oil, and Political Power on the West African Coast', *African Historical Studies*, ii (1969), pp. 279–88.

MARTIN, Phyllis. *The External Trade of the Loango Coast 1576–1870: The Effects of Changing Commercial Relations on the Vili Kingdom of Loango.* Oxford, 1972.

——. 'The Trade of Loango in the Seventeenth and Eighteenth Centuries', in Richard Gray and David Birmingham, eds., *Pre-Colonial African Trade: Essays on Trade in Central and Eastern Africa Before 1900.* London, 1970, pp. 139–61.

NASSAU, Robert H. *Fetishism in West Africa: Forty Years' Observation of Native Customs and Superstitions.* New York, 1904.

NØRREGÅRD, Georg. *Danish Settlements in West Africa, 1658–1850.* Boston, 1966.

OGILBY, John. *Africa, Being an Accurate Description of the Regions of Aegypt, Barbary, Lybia, and Billedulgerid, the Land of the Negroes, Guinea, Aethiopia, and the Abyssines.* London, 1670.

OWEN, Captain W. F. W. *Narrative of Voyages to Explore the Shores of Africa, Arabia, and Madagascar.* 2 vols. London, 1968. A reprint of the 1833 edition.

PATTERSON, K. David. 'Early Knowledge of the Ogowe River and the American Exploration of 1854', *The International Journal of African Historical Studies*, v, 1 (1972), pp. 75–90.

———. 'Paul B. DuChaillu and the Exploration of Gabon, 1855–1865', to appear in *The International Journal of African Historical Studies*, 1974.

———. 'The Mpongwe and the Orungu of the Gabon Coast 1815–1875: The Transition to Colonial Rule'. Unpublished Ph.D. dissertation, Stanford University, 1971.

PIOLET, Père J. B. *Les Missions catholiques françaises au XIXe siècle*, vol. v., *Missions d'Afrique*. Paris, 1902.

Priestly, Margaret. *West African Trade and Coast Society: A Family Study.* London, 1969.

RANDLES, W. G. L. *L'Ancien Royaume du Congo des origines à la fin du XIXe siècle.* Paris and The Hague, 1968.

REYNARD, Robert. 'Note sur l'activité économique des côtes du Gabon au début du XVIIe siècle', *Bulletin de l'Institut d'études centrafricaines*, N.S., Nos. 13–14 (1957), pp. 49–54.

———. 'Recherches sur la présence des Portugais au Gabon (XV -XIXe siècles)', *Bulletin de l'Institut d'études centrafricaines*, N.S., No. 9 (1955), pp. 15–66.

RIBEIRO, Manuel Ferreira. *A Provincia de S. Thomé e Principe e suas Dependencias.* Lisbon, 1877.

RODNEY, Walter. *A History of the Upper Guinea Coast, 1545–1800.* Oxford, 1970.

RYDER, Alan F. C. *Benin and the Europeans, 1485–1897.* London, 1969.

SALMON, Thomas. *Hedendaagsche Historie of Tegenwoordige Staat van Afrika.* Amsterdam, 1763.

SAUTTER, Gilles. *De l'Atlantique au fleuve Congo: une géographie du sous-population.* 2 vols., Paris and The Hague, 1966.

SCHNAPPER, Bernard. *La Politique et le commerce français dans le Golfe de Guinée de 1838 à 1871.* Paris, 1961.

SMITH, Robert. 'The Canoe in West African History', *Journal of African History*, xi (1970), pp. 515–33.

TEIXEIRA DA MOTA, Avelino. *Topónimos de Origem Portuguesa na Costa Ocidental de Africa desde o Cabo Bojador ao Cabo de Santa Caterina.* Bissau, Port. Guinea, 1950.

THILMANS, G. and J. P. ROSSIE. 'Le "Flambeau de la Navigation" de Dierick Ruiters', *Bulletin de l'Institut fondamental d'Afrique noire,* B, xxxi (1969), pp. 106–19.

VANSINA, Jan. *Kingdoms of the Savanna.* Madison, 1966.

VERGER, Pierre. *Flux et reflux de la traite des nègres entre le Golfe de Bénin et Bahia de Todos os Santos du XVIIe au XIXe siècle.* Paris and The Hague, 1968.

WALKER, Abbé André Raponda. *Notes d'histoire du Gabon.* Brazzaville, 1960.

——. 'Les Tribus du Gabon', *Bulletin de la Société des recherches congolaises,* No. 4 (1924), pp. 55–101.

—— and Robert Reynard. 'Anglais, Espagnols et Nord-Américains au Gabon au XIXe siècle', *Bulletin de l'Institut d'études centrafricaines,* N.S., No. 12 (1956), pp. 253–79.

West Africa. 'Pompidou Tour Diary', No. 2,802, 20–6 Feb. 1971, p. 211.

Index